Entering Uncharted Waters?

Entering Uncharted Waters?

ASEAN and the South China Sea

EDITED BY

PAVIN CHACHAVALPONGPUN

LSEAS

INSTITUTE OF SOUTHEAST ASIAN STUDIES

Singapore

First published in Singapore in 2014 by
ISEAS Publishing
Institute of Southeast Asian Studies
30 Heng Mui Keng Terrace
Pasir Panjang
Singapore 119614

E-mail: publish@iseas.edu.sg
Website: <http://bookshop.iseas.edu.sg>

ISEAS Library Cataloguing-in-Publication Data

Entering uncharted waters? : ASEAN and the South China Sea / edited by Pavin Chachavalpongpun.
  1. South China Sea—Claims.
  2. South China Sea—Claims vs. China.
  3. Dispute resolution (Law)—Southeast Asia.
  4. Conflict management—Southeast Asia.
  5. ASEAN.
  I. Pavin Chachavalpongpun.
KZA1692 E61   2014

ISBN 978-981-4380-26-3 (soft cover)
ISBN 978-981-4380-27-0 (e-book, PDF)

Typeset by Superskill Graphics Pte Ltd
Printed in Singapore by Mainland Press Pte Ltd

CONTENTS

PREFACE

The workshop on "Entering Uncharted Waters? ASEAN and the South China Sea Dispute" was organized by the ASEAN Studies Centre (ASC), Institute of Southeast Asian Studies (ISEAS), on 18 February 2011. It was the initiative of then ISEAS Director, Ambassador K. Kesavapany, who first asked this question: What does the Association of Southeast Asian Nations (ASEAN) have to do with the South China Sea?

In an attempt to answer this question, one may find that ASEAN — not just the ASEAN members that have claims to little pieces of land and vast waters of the South China Sea, not just individual ASEAN members, but ASEAN as a whole — has an abiding interest in peace and stability in this region and in freedom of navigation in and overflight above the South China Sea. Much of ASEAN's commerce, including its members' traded food and energy resources, passes through or over the South China Sea. The stakes of ASEAN and its members in the South China Sea are very high. It is very important for our security and our economies.

Indeed, the ASEAN Political-Security Community Blueprint is quite specific. It calls on ASEAN to continue its "current practice of close consultation among Member States to achieve full implementation of the DOC" — The DOC is the Declaration on the Conduct of Parties in the South China Sea, which China and the ten ASEAN states signed in Phnom Penh in November 2002. The DOC commits ASEAN members and China to the peaceful settlement of their disputes, freedom of navigation and overflight, self-restraint, no new occupations, confidence-building measures, and cooperative activities in the South China Sea. As we all know, the multiple claims to land features and their waters in the South China Sea are one of the critical flashpoints for potential conflict in our part of the world. It is, therefore, valuable for us at least to understand the nature and extent of each party's claims.

ISEAS was, therefore, fortunate to have so many scholars participating in this conference who are experts in South China Sea issues. Even if they did not speak for their respective governments, they at least well understood the positions of those governments. Their discussions offered us hope that this knowledge would lead all claimants to bring their claims as close as possible to the provisions of the 1982 UN Convention on the Law of the Sea (UNCLOS), to which all of them are parties. After all, ASEAN has also sought to promote the rule of law in the region. It is with these objectives in mind — peace, stability, freedom of navigation and overflight, confidence building, cooperation, and the rule of law — that truly inspired this conference.

I would like to express my thanks, first, to Ambassador Kesavapany for his inspiration. My thanks also go to Ambassador Rodolfo C. Severino, Head of the ASC, for his support for this conference and for sharing his view with other participants. I am indebted to all paper presenters for their active participation and their excellent papers; this book will undoubtedly be useful not only for policymakers but also for observers and students who are interested in the issue of the South China Sea. I would like to thank Triena Ong for making this publication a success, all members of the ASC, ISEAS' administrative members, and two trainees at the ASC who helped me in the preparation of this manuscript: Nicholas Zulkoski and Hong Wee Keat.

None of those thanked here are by any means responsible for the content of the book. Any errors that might remain are all mine.

Pavin Chachavalpongpun
Editor
Singapore, August 2013

CONTRIBUTORS

Aileen San Pablo-Baviera is a Professor and former Dean of the Asian Centre, University of the Philippines. She is editor-in-chief of the international journal *Asian Politics and Policy*. Her research focus is on international relations of the Asia-Pacific. She has published extensively on Philippines-China relations, China-ASEAN relations, East Asian regionalism, and the South China Sea disputes.

Robert C. Beckman is the Director of the Centre for International Law (CIL) at the National University of Singapore (NUS) and the Head of its programme in Ocean Law and Policy. He heads the CIL Research Projects on Submarine Cables and Law of the Sea and on International Marine Crimes. He is also an Associate Professor in the NUS Faculty of Law where he currently teaches Public International Law, Ocean Law and Policy in Asia, and International Regulation of Shipping.

Pavin Chachavalpongpun is an Associate Professor at the Centre for Southeast Asian Studies at Kyoto University, Japan. Receiving his PhD from the School of Oriental and African Studies, Pavin has written extensively on ASEAN issues, including his edited volumes of *ASEAN-US Relations: What are the Talking Points?* (2012) and *The Road to Ratification and Implication of the ASEAN Charter* (2009). He was the Lead Researcher for Political and Strategic Affairs at the ASEAN Studies Centre, Institute of Southeast Asian Studies, from January 2008 to March 2012.

Hasjim Djalal is a member of the National Indonesian Maritime Council and former Vice Chairman of the Indonesian delegation to the Third United Nations Law of the Sea Conference. Receiving his Masters of Law from the University of Virginia where he was the University's first Indonesian student, Djalal is also former Chairman and President of the International Seabed Authority.

Wang Hanling is Professor and Director of the Centre for Ocean Affairs and the Law of the Sea, Institute of International Law, Chinese Academy of Social Sciences (CASS). Receiving the degree of Doctor of Law from CASS, he has published widely and submitted numerous consultancy reports to the Chinese central government. He is an expert of special arbitration under Annex VIII of the UN Convention on the Law of the Sea, and served as a UN consultant. He won the highest research award of CASS for his outstanding policy advice to the Chinese central government in 2007 and 2008.

Fu-Kuo Liu is Research Fellow at the Institute of International Relations (IIR), National Chengchi University, Taiwan and Adjunct Professor at the International Doctorate Program in Asia Pacific Studies (IDAS), College of Social Science, National Chengchi University. He received his PhD from the University of Hull. He has written extensively on Taiwan security and South China Sea policy, U.S.-Taiwan relations and cross-strait cooperation.

Dzirhan Mahadzir is a freelance defence journalist based in Kuala Lumpur. He holds an MA in Defence and Security Analysis from the University of Lancaster, United Kingdom, and has written for various international defence publications including *Janes Defence Weekly*, *Janes Navy International*, *International Defence Review*, *Asia-Pacific Defence Reporter*, *Defence Review Asia* and *Asian Military Review*.

Li Mingjiang is an Assistant Professor at the S. Rajaratnam School of International Studies (RSIS), Nanyang Technological University, Singapore. He is also the coordinator of the China Program and the Coordinator of the MSc in Asian Studies Program at RSIS. He received his PhD in Political Science from Boston University. His main research interests include China's diplomatic history, Sino-U.S. relations, Asia-Pacific security, and domestic sources of China's foreign policy. He is the author (including editor and co-editor) of nine books. His recent books are *Mao's China and the Sino-Soviet Split* (2012) and *Soft Power: China's Emerging Strategy in International Politics* (2009). He has published papers in various peer-reviewed journals including *Global Governance, Cold War History, Journal of Contemporary China, The Chinese Journal of International Politics, China: An International Journal, China Security, Security Challenges,* and *The International Spectator.*

Nguyen Thi Lan Anh is Deputy Director of the Centre for South China Sea Studies and Vice Dean of the International Law Faculty of the Diplomatic Academy of Vietnam. Dr Nguyen received her PhD in International Law from the University of Bristol, United Kingdom and has research interests in ocean law and policy, maritime security, and the South China Sea issues.

Rodolfo C. Severino is the Head of the ASEAN Studies Centre at the Institute of Southeast Asian Studies in Singapore and a frequent speaker at international conferences in Asia and Europe. Having been Secretary-General of ASEAN from 1998 to 2002, he has completed a book, entitled *Southeast Asia in Search of an ASEAN Community* and published by ISEAS, on issues facing ASEAN. He has produced a book on ASEAN in ISEAS' Southeast Asia Background Series, one on the ASEAN Regional Forum, and another on the Philippine national territory. Severino was Undersecretary of Foreign Affairs of the Philippines, the culmination of thirty-two years in the Philippine Foreign Service.

Barry Wain, a career journalist, was the Writer-in-Residence at the Institute of Southeast Asian Studies. A former editor of the Asian edition of the *Wall Street Journal*, he also served as the paper's diplomatic correspondent and as a columnist, specialising in the South China Sea and other regional issues.

Mikael Weissmann is a Research Fellow at the Swedish Institute of International Affairs (UI) in Stockholm, Sweden. He is also an Affiliated Researcher at the East Asian Peace Program at Uppsala University. He received his PhD in Peace and Development Research from the University of Gothenburg, Sweden in 2009. Weissmann's research focuses on peace and security in East Asia, soft power in Sino-ASEAN relations and EU-Asia relations. He is also leading a project on "Collaboration at Sea", focussing on the role and impact of collaboration for maritime security. Among others, he has written the monograph *The East Asia Peace: Conflict Prevention and Informal Peacebuilding* (2012).

Part One
Overview

1

PREVENTING CONFLICT IN THE SOUTH CHINA SEA

Rodolfo C. Severino

The Association of Southeast Asian Nations (ASEAN) and the ASEAN-founded and ASEAN-centred, 27-member ASEAN Regional Forum (ARF) are often derided (or worse) for being unable to "do something" about flashpoints for conflict in their respective areas of coverage — Southeast Asia in the case of ASEAN and the larger Asia-Pacific in the case of the ARF — although what precisely they should do is never clear. One of the leading and most prominent of these flashpoints is the South China Sea — the conflicting multiple claims to the land features and waters of that sea (contrary to the government-declared Chinese view, no such claim is "indisputable").

Yet, there is very little likelihood that the sovereignty or other jurisdictional issues can be definitively resolved anytime soon, or ever. This is because each of the claimants considers and projects its position as its national strategic interest — one of its "core interests", if you will. Criticism of ASEAN or of the ARF for their inability to remove the South China Sea flashpoint by resolving the sovereignty and jurisdictional disputes flies in the face of this reality.

The Chinese government — in Beijing or in Taipei — fears that losing control of the South China Sea would render China vulnerable to other powers' attempts to encircle it, "contain" its rise, and prevent it from taking (or re-taking) its rightful place in the world. China has an understandable aversion to foreign military vessels lurking close to its shores. The Chinese are probably concerned about an attack — from the sea or from the air — or even an invasion, from the surface of, under or above the South China Sea to their southeast. For their part, the authorities on Taiwan cannot be seen as taking a "softer" position on territorial questions than their counterparts on the Chinese mainland. The South China Sea is also a lucrative source of fish for Taiwanese fishing fleets as well as for other fishing vessels ranging over that vast and open sea.

Vietnam would find itself almost completely surrounded by China, which occupied it for a thousand years and bloodied its nose in 1988, if it were to lose its foothold in the South China Sea. Having been invaded from across the South China Sea during the Pacific War, the Philippines considers it in its security interest to push its western frontier as far out as possible. Parts of the South China Sea connect as well as separate West and East Malaysia. Brunei Darussalam needs assured access to the oil reserves and fisheries in its continental shelf and exclusive economic zone, which are in the South China Sea and overlap with some neighbours' claims.

These are all in addition to the time-honoured tendency of states, with some exceptions of course, not to compromise on territorial, sovereignty or jurisdictional questions. Therefore, one may have to stop dreaming of having anyone or anything miraculously "resolve" the South China Sea disputes overnight in one big bang, of what Mark Valencia calls a "grand solution" to this problem.

At the same time, all who depend on the South China Sea for commerce or military presence or both, claimants or non-claimants, have a long-term strategic or immediate national interest in peace and stability in the South China Sea area and in freedom of navigation and overflight there. Conflict or instability in the South China Sea would not be in anyone's interest. The disruption of navigation, on the sea or in the air, would be inimical to the international commerce that heavily traverses and has been surging through the area.

Many countries have high stakes in peace, stability, and freedom in the South China Sea, including the United States, Japan, South Korea, India, the oil exporters of the Middle East, some European countries, the littoral and some other states of Southeast Asia, Taiwan, as well as China itself. Yet, it is not clear how much of its perceived interest a claimant is willing to sacrifice for the sake of regional peace and stability. Freedom of navigation and overflight is subject to different and even conflicting interpretations, depending on the interpreting country's perception of its national interest.

Thus, the most and least that the international community can do about the South China Sea disputes, especially the claimants to land features and waters there, is to ensure that the conflicting claims do not erupt into armed violence, as they have on more than one occasion in the past, and to prevent the use of armed might for the enforcement of claims.

BRINGING CLAIMS CLOSER TO UNCLOS

Part of this effort should be moves by all claimants to ensure that their respective claims are at least consistent with the provisions and requirements of the United Nations Convention on the Law of the Sea (UNCLOS). All the claimants are parties to UNCLOS, having signed and ratified it. It is encouraging to recall that the ASEAN member states that have claims in the South China Sea — that is, the Philippines, Vietnam, Malaysia and Brunei Darussalam — have recently taken steps that seem to bring their respective claims closer to alignment with UNCLOS.

In March 2009, the Philippines enacted a law amending, for the second time, the country's baselines act. Contrary to early media reports, the new law, unlike the unsuccessful bill filed by Cebu Representative Antonio Cuenco and like its two predecessors, does not encompass any of the Spratlys but limits itself to the main Philippine archipelago. Just as significant, the law declares a "regime of islands" for the land features that the Philippines claims in the Spratlys and for Scarborough Shoal (or Bajo de Masinloc, its official and Spanish-language name), west of the archipelago, which it also claims. In declaring a "regime of islands" for these features, the new law explicitly invokes Article 121 of UNCLOS, which says, "An island is a naturally formed area of land, surrounded by water, which is above water at high tide" and "Rocks which cannot sustain human habitation or economic life of their own shall have no exclusive economic zone or continental shelf." The Philippine law, however, stops short of designating which of the land features that it claims are islands and which are mere rocks; the Philippine government apparently seeks, at least for now, to reserve for itself a certain degree of ambiguity. Not coincidentally, it thereby leaves equally ambiguous the nature of its claims to the waters in what it calls the Kalayaan Island Group.

What next for the Philippines? Henry Bensurto, Secretary-General of the Centre for Maritime and Ocean Affairs of the Philippines' Department of Foreign Affairs, circulated in January 2011 a paper entitled "Philippine Archipelagic Agenda for the 21st Century". After stating how the Philippines had passed its new baselines law and submitted to the United Nations its (partial) claim to an extended continental shelf, the paper went on:

> Still to be done, however, in order to completely put the Philippine archipelagic house in order are the legislations [sic] on the following: One, to define by law the maritime jurisdictions of the Philippines under UNCLOS; and two, to designate by law the archipelagic sea lanes in Philippine archipelagic waters to rationalise and prevent arbitrary international passage in the Philippine archipelago.

These are Bensurto's prescriptions, of course. It remains to be seen whether the country's President and Congress will go along with them and thus bring the Philippine position closer to, if not completely aligned with, UNCLOS requirements.

For their part, Vietnam and Malaysia filed a partial "joint submission" on 6 May 2009 to the UN Commission on the Limits of the Continental Shelf. That submission, "in respect of the southern part of the South China Sea", projects the proposed extended continental shelf from the coasts of the mainlands of Malaysia and Vietnam rather than from the land features of the Spratlys that they diversely claim. Robert Beckman, director of the Centre for International Law at the National University of Singapore, pointed out in an August 2010 commentary for the S. Rajaratnam School of International Studies, "By not measuring their continental shelves or exclusive economic zones (EEZs) from any of the islands which they claim in the South China Sea, they have in effect taken the position that no islands in the South China Sea should be entitled to more than a 12nm territorial sea — the maximum permitted by UNCLOS."

On 15–16 March 2009, Malaysia's then Prime Minister Abdullah Ahmad Badawi paid a visit to Brunei Darussalam, at the end of which he and the Brunei ruler, Sultan Hassanal Bolkiah, issued a joint statement. The statement referred to an exchange of letters between their governments. According to the statement, among the "key elements" of that agreement were "the final delimitation of maritime boundaries" between the two countries and "unsuspendable rights of maritime access for nationals and residents of Malaysia across Brunei's maritime zones en route to and from their destination in Sarawak, Malaysia provided that Brunei's laws and regulations are observed." On 30 April 2010, Abdullah, no longer prime minister, confirmed on the Malaysian Foreign Ministry's website, "Regarding the maritime area, Malaysia and Brunei also agreed to establish a final and permanent sea boundary. The agreement serves to settle certain overlapping claims which existed in the past." In May 2010, the Foreign Ministry elaborated a little further, "With regard to the maritime areas, the Exchange of Letters established the final delimitation of territorial sea, continental shelf and exclusive economic zone of both States." The letters themselves, however, have not been made public. Nevertheless, they were apparently drawn up in accordance with one of the methods prescribed by UNCLOS.

Neither Beijing nor Taipei have made any similar moves to align their claims closer to the provisions of UNCLOS. In 1947 the nationalist government of China, before it fled to Taiwan, issued the "Location Map of the South China Sea Islands", in which an "interrupted line", now depicted in nine segments, encompassed all of the South China Sea. The line starts between Luzon and Taiwan, skirts the western coasts of the Philippine archipelago and what is now East Malaysia, and rises northwards along the eastern coast of Vietnam. After its victory in the Chinese civil war in 1949, the People's Republic took this map as its own. Beijing reinforced the map's international status by attaching it to China's note protesting the Malaysia-Vietnam "joint submission". China sent its note to the United Nations Commission on 7 May 2009, the day after Malaysia and Vietnam filed their "joint submission". For the first time, China officially filed the map with an international body. Both Beijing and Taipei have declined to explain what the nine bars signify, whether they are meant to claim sovereignty or some kind of maritime jurisdiction over the entire expanse of water that the lines encompass or only over the land features within the "interrupted line". They have persisted in this position even when pressed by ASEAN countries and others in the international community for clarification. Much less has Beijing or Taipei designated which of those land features are islands in the UNCLOS sense and which are mere rocks.

CLASH OF CHINESE AND US INTERESTS

Another source of tension and danger goes beyond the conflicting claims to sovereignty and jurisdiction in the South China Sea. It is the growing global rivalry between China and the United States, a rivalry the existence of which officials in both countries deny. The Chinese insist that they have "indisputable" sovereignty over the South China Sea. Although what that sovereignty covers is not clear, that insistence could imply the right to close the sea to foreign passage if the Chinese deem it in their interest to do so. On the other hand, the Americans, who have not ratified the 1982 UNCLOS, maintain that freedom of navigation in and overflight over the high seas, of which the EEZ beyond the twelve-mile territorial sea is part, is sanctioned by customary international law, and no country can curtail that right.

At the beginning of April 2001, a U.S. Navy EP-3 maritime reconnaissance aircraft collided with a Chinese fighter plane over China's EEZ, killing the fighter pilot. The damaged U.S. plane landed in a military airport on Hainan Island, and its crew was detained but, after several days, repatriated. The Americans charge that the Chinese took the aeroplane apart and examined it. The aircraft was later airlifted to the U.S., where it was reassembled and repaired. In early March 2009, the United States Department of Defence has charged, five Chinese ships "harassed" (the Pentagon's term) the USNS Impeccable (Impeccable-class ocean surveillance ship acquired by the U.S. Navy in 2001), which the United States classifies as an "unarmed ocean surveillance vessel", 120 kilometres south of Hainan, clearly within China's claimed EEZ.

Part V of UNCLOS lays down rules on many things pertaining to the EEZ, including conflict resolution, artificial islands, installations and structures, the conservation and utilization of "living resources", the rights of landlocked and other "geographically disadvantaged" states, law enforcement by coastal states, and the delimitation of overlapping EEZs between states "with opposite or adjacent coasts".

In the cases of the EP-3 and the Impeccable, the disputes are over what a foreign aircraft or vessel is permitted to do within a coastal state's EEZ. Article 56 of the convention confers on the coastal state the right to explore, exploit, conserve and manage the natural resources in the waters, seabed and subsoil of the EEZ. It gives the coastal state jurisdiction in the EEZ over the establishment and use of artificial islands, installations and structures, marine scientific research, and the preservation and protection of the marine environment. At the same time, Article 56 prescribes that, in doing all this, the coastal state is to have "due regard to the rights and duties of other States". Article 58 specifically provides for the right of other states to freedom of navigation in and overflight above the EEZ and to lay submarine cables and pipelines there, but "with due regard to the rights and duties of the coastal State" and in compliance with its laws and regulations and international law.

Washington points out that a country's EEZ is part of the high seas, and its vessels enjoy freedom of navigation in it. The United States claims that the Impeccable was not conducting marine scientific research at the time of the incident involving it. On the other hand, China charges that the U.S. vessel, as well as the EP-3, violated its rights and laws and international law.

The broader consideration is that, for its own strategic purposes, the U.S. wants to know as much as it can of what the Chinese are up to, particularly in terms of military development. Washington officials have been known to complain about the lack of transparency in what China is doing and invoke this to justify the surveillance operation of United States' aircraft and vessels close to Chinese shores, especially to the submarine base at Sanya on Hainan Island. Nevertheless, every intelligence agency has an insatiable appetite for information about other countries' military and other capabilities and intentions, and it is doubtful whether even a full measure of Chinese transparency, unlikely though that might be, would deter U.S. intelligence from doing whatever they are doing. On the other hand, China is determined to keep foreign prying eyes from learning anything about its military modernization and other information that it considers sensitive.

Both China and the United States should be careful about asserting their respective positions on military activities in the EEZ. When the day comes that China acquires the capability to do so, Beijing will be able to send its surveillance aircraft and vessels close to either coast of the mainland United States, not to mention the coasts of Hawaii, Alaska, Puerto Rico and Guam. Insisting on the right to conduct military surveillance in China's EEZ would prevent Washington from complaining credibly about similar Chinese activities off American territory. At the same time, rejecting the United States' right to conduct surveillance activities in China's EEZ would impair China's own right to do so in the United States' EEZ in the future.

It is, of course, not only the United States whose interests might clash with those of China. There are also, to begin with, India and Japan, both of which have territorial disputes with China and have interests in peace and stability in the South China Sea area, as well as in freedom of navigation and overflight there and elsewhere.

IMPROVING SINO-AMERICAN RELATIONS

From the rejection of all "internationalization" of the South China Sea disputes, the Chinese position seems to have been scaled down to admitting that, although the sovereignty and jurisdictional issues are for the claimants to negotiate by themselves, all others concerned are entitled to engage in "confidence-building measures" pertaining to the area. In any case, as noted above and as some legal scholars suggest, Beijing has already internationalized the legal dimensions of the South China Sea dispute by submitting to a United Nations body its map containing the infamous nine bars.

Tensions could be reduced and hostile confrontations avoided if China and the United States (and, perhaps, others that have the capacity to operate in the Chinese EEZ) were to arrive at an agreed understanding of what each could and could not do in the other's EEZ. This would not be beyond the realm of the possible. I understand that the United States and the former Soviet Union had an understanding of an analogous kind, something that was arrived at long before the 1982 UNCLOS went into effect.

All concerned have an interest in good relations between Beijing and Washington (and other powers). Yet, what happened at the ministerial meeting of the ASEAN Regional Forum in July 2010 added the clashing strategic interests of China and the United States in the South China Sea to the lengthening list of issues bedevilling the complicated relations between them.

I have not seen a transcript of what United States Secretary of State Hillary Rodham Clinton actually said at the ARF ministerial meeting. However, the United States Department of State has published the transcript of a media conference that Clinton conducted after the meeting, in which she is quoted as saying:

> The United States supports a collaborative diplomatic process by all claimants for resolving the various territorial disputes without coercion. We oppose the use or threat of force by any claimant. While the United States does not take sides on the competing territorial disputes over land features in the South China Sea, we believe claimants should pursue their territorial claims ... and rights to maritime space in accordance with the UN

convention on the law of the sea. Consistent with customary international law, legitimate claims to maritime space in the South China Sea should be derived solely from legitimate claims to land features.

The Clinton statement did not reflect a shift in the long-established position of the United States. However, the clarity and force with which she articulated it, together with her personal stature, signalled a new United States assertiveness and deeper interest with respect to the South China Sea. Clinton invoked the 1982 UNCLOS, but the United States has not ratified it. American officials have said that they would take steps to seek the United States Senate's advice on and consent to the convention's ratification.

In an account uploaded on to the website of China's Ministry of Foreign Affairs, Chinese Foreign Minister Yang Jiechi is quoted as having quickly responded to Clinton that the South China Sea was, in fact, peaceful and stable and that all claimants were committed to the peaceful resolution of their disputes through "friendly consultations". As "a big country", Yang is quoted to have said, China had legitimate concerns; there was nothing wrong with that. Freedom and safety of navigation, he is said to have pointed out, had not been impaired; indeed, trade in the region had been growing rapidly. The Declaration on the Conduct of Parties in the South China Sea, which had been concluded among ASEAN members and China in 2002, called for the exercise of self-restraint and was meant to promote mutual trust. Yang is reported to have asserted that the territorial and maritime-rights disputes were not an issue between China and ASEAN as a whole but between China and some individual ASEAN countries, disputes that were to be expected between neighbours. Multilateralizing or internationalizing the issue would "only make matters worse and the resolution more difficult", he is quoted as saying.

Although many must have welcomed a new assertiveness and keener interest on the part of the United States with regard to the South China Sea, a wave of nervousness seems to have coursed through the countries of the Asia-Pacific on account of the impact of the Clinton-Yang exchange on the broader state of Sino-American relations. This nervousness might have been behind the remark of the Secretary of Foreign Affairs of the Philippines, a close ally of the United States and one of the claimants to many of the Spratly features, who said, according to Agence France-Presse, "Negotiations should be strictly between the ASEAN and China, without the United States or any other party."

THE INFORMAL WORKSHOPS

The annual informal workshops on managing potential conflict in the South China Sea, which are spearheaded and hosted by Indonesia, help substantially in forming networks, instilling the habit of cooperation in an area of dispute, and building confidence. Led and organized by Hasjim Djalal, one of the world's authorities on maritime issues, the workshops gather experts on the South China Sea, including government officials who participate ostensibly "in their private capacity". Because the workshops are informal and unofficial, they have a bit more room than official forums for wide-ranging discussions and activities pertaining to mutual understanding and cooperation in South China Sea matters. Not the least of the virtues of the workshop series, which started in 1990 with Canadian support, is that officials and scholars from Taiwan and the Chinese mainland take part in it. The fact that all of ASEAN, claimants and non-claimants alike, as well as the Chinese from both sides of the Taiwan Straits, have decided to continue the workshops, funding them themselves after Canada ceased supporting them in 2001, underscores the value that they place on the workshop process. Some of the activities prescribed in the Declaration on the Conduct of Parties in the South China Sea are, in fact, being undertaken within the workshop framework.

A LEGALLY BINDING CODE OF CONDUCT?

There have been public calls for a "legally binding code of conduct" as the next step after the 2002 Declaration on Conduct. The inability of China and Vietnam to agree on the explicit coverage of the Paracels in a proposed code of conduct in the early 2000s prevented the conclusion of a legally binding instrument. If we do not know where the instrument is to apply, it was asked, how can we legally bind ourselves to observing it? In the transcript of her statement at her media conference after the ARF ministerial meeting in July 2010, Secretary Clinton is quoted as saying, "The United States supports the 2002 ASEAN-China declaration on the conduct of parties in the South China Sea. We encourage the parties to reach agreement on a full code of conduct." Others have also called for such a code.

   A "full" code of conduct would be welcome as indicating a further step in the commitment of the parties to the peaceful resolution of the territorial and jurisdictional issues in the South China Sea, the preservation of peace and stability in the region, respect for freedom of navigation and overflight, and the exercise of self-restraint in the area. In substance, however, there does not seem to be much difference between a political declaration and a legal code in terms of enforcement or observance.

While trying to advance the "form" of the undertakings, China and ASEAN, with the encouragement of others, should also seek to build on the "substance" of the 2002 declaration. That declaration emphasizes the peaceful settlement of disputes, confidence building, freedom of navigation and overflight, and, not least, "self-restraint in the conduct of activities that would complicate or escalate disputes and affect peace and stability", including refraining from occupying "presently uninhabited" land features. The declaration calls for confidence-building measures like dialogues among defence and military officials, just and humane treatment of people in danger or in distress, and voluntary notification of "other parties concerned" about "impending" joint military exercises. It prescribes specific cooperative activities of a maritime nature. An agreement subsequent to the declaration could elaborate on these commitments. For example, the "no new occupation" provision could be expanded and applied to the reinforcement of military facilities already on the land features in the South China Sea. The confidence-building measures specified could be the subject of more precise and more detailed agreements and carried out. The cooperative activities could be undertaken in accordance with, again, specific agreements.

SUMMARY OF RECOMMENDATIONS

In summary, these are my recommendations:

1. Let us stop dreaming of a "grand solution" to the South China Sea disputes. It is not possible; dreaming about it only distracts us from doing what can and should be done to manage the disputes and keep the harm that they do to a diminishing minimum.
2. Claimants — Southeast Asians and Chinese alike — should endeavour to align their claims with the provisions and requirements of UNCLOS, to which they are all parties.
3. China and the United States (and others with the capacity and interest to deploy military aircraft and vessels above and in China's EEZ) should seek a common and agreed understanding of what each can and cannot do in the other's EEZ.

4. China and the United States (and other rival powers) should take steps to improve their relations and expand the areas of their common interest so as to contribute to peace and stability in the South China Sea in particular and in the Asia-Pacific in general.
5. The United States should ratify the 1982 UNCLOS.
6. The informal workshops on managing potential conflict in the South China Sea should be continued and encouraged for the sake of networking, cultivating the habit of and capacity for cooperation, cooperating on an operational basis, and building confidence.
7. The Declaration on the Conduct of Parties in the South China Sea should be carried out and built upon through implementing agreements or through a "legally binding" code of conduct or both. The conclusion of such a code of conduct might be pursued, but recognized for what it would be, a message-sending and confidence-building instrument that would strengthen the commitments of the ASEAN countries and China to peaceful and cooperative behaviour in the South China Sea.

2

ASEAN AND THE SOUTH CHINA SEA DISPUTE

Robert C. Beckman

BACKGROUND ON THE SOUTH CHINA SEA DISPUTES

The South China Sea consists of four groups of islands, two of which are in dispute, the Paracels and the Spratlys.

The Paracel Islands consist of two groups, the Crescent Group and the Amphitrite Group. Together they contain over 30 islets, sandbanks or reefs, and occupy about 15,000 square kilometres of ocean. The Paracels are located in the northern part of the South China Sea, approximately equidistant from the coastlines of Vietnam and China (Hainan). In 1974 China forcibly ejected South Vietnamese troops from the Paracels, and since then they have been occupied exclusively by China, but they are also claimed by Vietnam.

The Spratly Islands consist of more than 100 islets, coral reefs, and seamounts scattered over an area of nearly 410,000 square kilometres in the central South China Sea, north of the island of Borneo, east of Vietnam, and west of the southern Philippines. The total land area of all of the islands is less than 5 square miles. The Spratly Islands are claimed in their entirety by China, Taiwan, and Vietnam, while some islands and other features are claimed by Malaysia and the Philippines. Brunei has established a fishing zone that overlaps a southern reef, but it has not made any formal claim.

The Spratly Islands are not critically important for international maritime navigation. They are dangerous for shipping, and no major international shipping lanes pass through them. However, the islands could be important in safeguarding the international shipping lanes, and are often described as having strategic importance. Japan occupied all of the islands during its expansion into Asia in the 1930s and staged its invasion of the Philippines from its submarine naval base on Itu Aba, the largest island in the Spratlys.

The islands were not regarded as very important until the 1970s, when it was agreed at the Third United Nations Conference on the Law of the Sea[1] (UNCLOS) to allow states to claim a 200 nautical mile exclusive economic zone (EEZ) from islands. The prospect of a 200 nautical mile EEZ around the islands triggered a renewed interest in the islands because of potential gas and oil deposits and fisheries resources.

Taiwan has occupied Itu Abu, the largest island, since 1947, except during the period from 1950 to 1956 when it withdrew because of the civil war in China. It has had a garrison on the island since 1963. In the early 1970s other claimants began occupying the islands and other geographic features. The Philippines began occupying islands in the early 1970s and declared a 200 nautical mile EEZ in 1978. Vietnam occupied 6 islands in 1975 and expanded its occupations in the 1980s. Malaysia claimed an EEZ in 1980 and occupied Swallow Reef in 1983. It later occupied other atolls. China was late in the quest to occupy the features. After a military confrontation with Vietnam in 1988, China constructed a base on Fiery Cross Reef the following year.

Following the 1992 Association of Southeast Asian Nations (ASEAN) Declaration on the Conduct of Parties in the South China Sea (DOC), the contest over unoccupied features continued. Tensions peaked in 1995 after China occupied Mischief Reef, which was claimed by the Philippines and is located only 100 miles off the coast of Palawan. The occupation of Mischief Reef caused serious tension between ASEAN and China and led to discussions for a code of conduct which resulted in the 2002 DOC.

It was reported in 1997 that the number of features occupied by each of the claimants in 1996 was as follows: Vietnam 21–24, Philippines 8, China 8–9, Malaysia 3–6 and Taiwan 1.[2] It is not clear whether these figures are accurate or whether the figures changed between 1997 and 2002. A study published by Jamestown Foundation in November 2009 states that Vietnam occupies 21 features, the Philippines 9, China 7, Malaysia 5 and Taiwan 1.

It has been reported that there were no new occupations after the adoption of the 2002 DOC. However, observers have reported that the parties have continued to develop facilities on the features which they occupy.

INTERNATIONAL LAW APPLICABLE TO THE DISPUTE

Relevance of International Law

From an international lawyer's perspective, it is important to understand how the principles of international law on territorial sovereignty and the law of the sea apply to the dispute. The rules and principles of international law will not be determinative in resolving the South China Sea disputes, but they will often influence the conduct of the parties and frame the debate. In addition, the rules of international law have a significant impact on how the international community perceives the legitimacy of the positions of the claimant states on the issues.

Two fields of international law are relevant to the dispute. First, the rules of customary international law on the acquisition and loss of sovereignty over territory are applicable. Second, the 1982 UNCLOS sets out what maritime zones states can claim from territory over which they have sovereignty and the rights and obligations of states in the various maritime zones.

International Law on Acquisition and Loss of Territorial Sovereignty

Territorial Sovereignty is the right to exercise the functions of a state within a piece of territory, to the exclusion of any other state. Territorial sovereignty may be exercised over continental land territory and over islands. The major and intractable disputes in the South China Sea are about which state has the better claim to sovereignty over the islands in the Spratlys and the Paracels.

Acquisition of Territory by the Display of Sovereignty (Occupation or Prescription)

Under traditional customary international law, two of the most common modes of acquiring sovereignty over remote islands are by occupation and prescription.

Occupation applies to territory that is *terra nullius,* that is, territory which is not under the sovereignty of any state and is subject to acquisition by any state. Occupation requires proof of two elements; first, the intention or will to act as the sovereign; and second, the continuous and peaceful display of sovereignty. The requirements for manifestations of territorial sovereignty for tiny, remote uninhabited islands are far less than for land territory.

Prescription applies to territory that was claimed by another state. It is described as the acquisition of territory through a continuous and undisturbed exercise of sovereignty during such a period so as to usurp another state's sovereignty by its implied consent or acquiescence.

In actual practice, the distinction is often blurred, especially with respect to tiny, remote offshore islands. In modern cases such as the *Pedra Branca* case,[3] the court does not examine whether the historical requirements of occupation or prescription have been satisfied. Instead, the court examined the acts of the competing states which evidenced their belief that they had sovereignty over the territory, and the reaction of the competing states to such displays of sovereignty.

The degree of exercise and display of sovereignty required depends upon the nature of the territory. The requirements for remote, inaccessible and uninhabitable islands are much less stringent. A state must put forward evidence that it acted as though it had sovereign authority over the island.

Evidence of the exercise of authority by a state would include licences or orders for the building of a lighthouse or other structures on the island, legislative and administrative acts relating to the island, granting of concessions for mining or fishing, treaties with other states recognizing sovereignty, the exercise of criminal jurisdiction over acts on the island, the investigation of accidents in the waters near the island, the publication of official maps indicating title to the island, control over immigration or access to the island, and markers on the island.

Acquiescence and Protest

An important factor in assessing a state's evidence of sovereignty is the reaction of other states, especially the reaction of another state which also claims sovereignty over the territory. If a second state claims sovereignty over the island and it objects to or protests the displays of sovereignty of the first state, this obviously weakens the claim of the first state. Also, if a second state which claims sovereignty fails to object to acts of sovereignty of the first state of which it has notice, the second state can be deemed to have acquiesced to the sovereignty of the first state.

The issue of acquiescence was a critical factor in the *Pedra Branca* case. The court gave considerable weight to the fact that Singapore performed several acts with respect to Pedra Branca which were evidence that it believed it had sovereignty over the island, and Malaysia failed to object or protest these acts. Therefore, the court in effect held that Malaysia had acquiesced to Singapore's sovereignty.

States in the South China Sea disputes are obviously very aware that they should object to or protest the sovereign acts of another state over a disputed island if they want to protect their own claim and not be deemed to have acquiesced to the sovereignty of the other state. Therefore, the claimants immediately protest when a government official visits a disputed island or when a competing state takes any action with respect to the island that could be interpreted as being an exercise of sovereign authority.

The Critical Date

The critical date is the date on which a dispute arose between two states over sovereignty. If the issue of sovereignty goes to a court or tribunal, the court or tribunal will only examine the actions of the two states before the critical date. It will not consider evidence of the exercise of authority after the critical date. For example, in the *Pedra Branca* case, the court held that the critical date was 14 February 1980, the date of Singapore's diplomatic note protesting the 1979 map which had depicted the island as being within the territorial waters of Malaysia. Any evidence of maps, investigations or patrols after 14 February 1980 were not considered by the court. In other words, once the dispute arises, a state cannot perform further acts in order to try to bolster its case.

The claimants to the South China Sea islands seem to be assuming that the issue of sovereignty will not be decided by a court or tribunal, but by negotiation. They obviously believe that their bargaining positions in such negotiations will be strengthened and their claims to sovereignty bolstered if they can demonstrate that they have occupied the islands and performed acts on them such as the building of lighthouses, ports, research stations, naval stations, airstrips, and tourist facilities. Therefore, they are ignoring the rules of customary international law and the critical date principle.

Geographic Contiguity

The claims of the Philippines, Malaysia and Brunei are not entirely clear, but to some extent they seem to be based on the principle of geographic contiguity. These states seem to be arguing that small islands and other features close to their main territory, within their EEZ or on their continental shelf, should belong to them as a matter of fairness, especially if such features were never actually occupied or effectively administered by another state.

Under customary international law, contiguity is not an independent basis for the acquisition of territory. Effective, peaceful and continuous display of state authority is required to claim authority over islands which are *terra nullius*. It is also required over islands over which other states claim sovereignty.

The issue with respect to the islands in the South China Sea is whether a state contiguous to islands can claim sovereignty over them through occupation and effective control even if they were previously claimed by other claimants. One problem is how China and Vietnam could demonstrate a continuous display of sovereignty over remote islands which they never occupied. Malaysia and the Philippines seem to be assuming that if they actually occupy and construct facilities on such islands, they will be able to usurp any sovereignty previously claimed by the other claimants. This position is weakened by the fact that China, Vietnam and Taiwan have consistently objected to the actions of Malaysia and the Philippines.

Conquest, Cession and Succession

Conquest through armed force was a means by which a state could acquire territory under traditional customary international law. However, since the adoption of the United Nations Charter in 1945, it is not possible to acquire territory through the use of force. Therefore, China cannot argue that it acquired sovereignty over the Paracels by conquest when it took possession in 1974 by driving Vietnam off the islands by using force.

Cession is another method by which sovereignty over territory can be transferred from one state to another. A cession is a formal transfer of sovereignty which is usually done by means of a formal treaty. For example, the British acquired sovereignty over Singapore through a treaty of cession with the Sultan of Johor (or the Temenggong). In the South China Sea disputes, there were no treaties of cession.

Succession is not a traditional means of acquiring territory, but it is relevant in the South China Sea disputes. Vietnam is arguing that it succeeded to the title held by France over the Spratlys and the Paracels as the "successor state" to French Indo-China or Cochin-China. Vietnam is also arguing to some extent that it succeeded after unification to the claims made by South Vietnam, and the People's Republic of China (PRC) is arguing to some extent that it succeeded to the claims made on behalf of China by the Republic of China (ROC) government when it was acting as the government of China before the end of the civil war. When succession applies, the successor state only acquires such title as the predecessor state possessed.

Resolution of the Sovereignty Disputes by an International Court or Tribunal

Under customary international law, a legal dispute between two states cannot be taken to the International Court of Justice (ICJ) or to an international arbitral tribunal without the express consent of the parties to the dispute. If such a dispute is referred to adjudication before the ICJ or to arbitration before an international arbitral tribunal, the court or tribunal decides who has the better claim to sovereignty under international law, and its decision is binding on both parties. For example, in both the *Pedra Branca* case between Malaysia and Singapore and the *Sipadan-Ligitan* case[4] between Indonesia and Malaysia, the two states concerned expressly agreed to resolve the sovereignty dispute by referring it to the ICJ.

States can also use other non-binding modes of third-party dispute settlement such as mediation or conciliation to attempt to resolve the sovereignty disputes, but they are not required to do so. The only binding rule is that under the United Nations Charter, states are obliged to resolve their disputes by peaceful means.

It is generally agreed that it is unlikely that the claimants will agree to resolve South China Sea sovereignty disputes by referring them to an international court or tribunal. This is because of the complexity of the historical disputes, the number of parties involved, the weakness of the claims of some of the states and the economic and strategic importance of the islands. Therefore, if the disputes are to be resolved, it is likely to be through negotiations or some form of non-binding third-party dispute settlement.

Continuing Influence of International Law on Territorial Sovereignty

Even though the claimants agree that the disputes are not likely to go to formal dispute settlement, the rules of international law on territorial sovereignty continue to influence the conduct of the claimant states.

They have continued to attempt to bolster their claims to the features they occupy by carrying out acts to demonstrate their sovereignty, such as conducting naval patrols and constructing scientific research stations, airstrips, naval facilities and tourist facilities. They have also released historical documents, arranged visits for tourists and journalists, and enacted national laws incorporating the features into nearby regional governments for administrative purposes.

By continuing to carry out acts to reinforce and bolster their claims to sovereignty over the islands, the claimants may believe that, as a practical matter, they will strengthen their position in any negotiations. They also continue to object to acts by any other claimant which are inconsistent with their own claims. This is to ensure that they can never be accused of acquiescing to the sovereignty claim of another state. In such cases, the protests or objections are made on the advice of their lawyers in order to protect their sovereignty claim. Such objections and protests should not be interpreted as actions intended to escalate the dispute or as actions reflecting a more hard-line posture.

Relevance of the 1982 UNCLOS

China, Vietnam, Malaysia, the Philippines and Brunei are all parties to UNCLOS. Taiwan is not able to ratify UNCLOS because it is not recognized as a state by the United Nations, but it is likely to accept that it is bound by most of the provisions of UNCLOS under customary international law. Therefore, UNCLOS establishes the legal framework between the claimant states.

There are clear rules (and sometimes not so clear rules) in UNCLOS on many of the issues relating to maritime claims in the South China Sea. If the conduct of the claimants is not consistent with the provisions of UNCLOS, questions will be raised as to the legitimacy of their positions. Finally, some disputes between claimants relating to the application and interpretation of provisions of UNCLOS may be subject to compulsory binding dispute settlement under Part XV of UNCLOS.

UNCLOS has no provisions on sovereignty. UNCLOS assumes that it has been determined which state has sovereignty over a continental land mass or an offshore island. It then sets out what maritime zones can be claimed by states, and the rights, freedoms, jurisdiction and obligations of states in those maritime zones.

Territorial Sea

The territorial sovereignty of a state extends to its land territory and to its airspace, as well as to the 12 nautical mile territorial sea adjacent to its coast, including the airspace above the territorial sea and the seabed and subsoil below the territorial sea. States are entitled to claim a 12 nautical mile territorial sea from the territory over which they have sovereignty, including offshore islands.

The sovereignty of a state in the territorial sea must be exercised subject to the rules of international law, including UNCLOS. The main exceptions to the sovereignty of a coastal state in the territorial sea are the right of innocent passage of ships and the right of transit passage of ships and aircraft in those parts of the territorial sea that are straits used for international navigation as defined in UNCLOS.

Exclusive Economic Zone

States are entitled to claim an EEZ out to a distance of 200 nautical miles from the baselines of the territory from which the territorial sea is measured, including offshore islands. The EEZ is a *sui generis* regime which is not under the sovereignty of the coastal state or part of the high seas. It is a special zone in which coastal states have sovereign rights and jurisdiction to explore and exploit the natural resources. In the EEZ, all other states have the right to exercise high seas freedoms of navigation, overflight and the laying of submarine cables and pipelines, as well as the right to "other lawful uses of the sea relating to such freedoms".

Once it was agreed in the mid-1970s that states could claim a 200 nautical mile EEZ from offshore islands, the potential fishing and hydrocarbon resources made long-forgotten small remote islands potential sources of vast wealth.

Continental Shelf

States also have the sovereign right to explore and exploit the natural resources of the seabed and subsoil on their continental shelf. The continental shelf of a coastal state comprises the seabed and subsoil of the submarine areas that extend beyond its territorial sea throughout the natural prolongation of its land territory to the outer edge of the continental margin, or to a distance of 200 nautical miles from the baselines from which the breadth of the territorial sea is measured where the outer edge of the continental margin does not extend up to that distance.

As in the EEZ, states have the sovereign right to explore and exploit the natural resources of the seabed and subsoil and their continental shelf. If a state's continental shelf extends to a distance less than 200 nautical miles, there is a substantial overlap between the EEZ regime and the continental shelf regime, as both give states the sovereign right to explore and exploit the natural resources of the seabed and subsoil. However, the continental shelf regime is very important for states whose shelf extends beyond 200 nautical miles.

Article 76 of UNCLOS permits states to make continental shelf claims beyond 200 nautical miles out to a maximum of 350 nautical miles or 100 nautical miles from the 2,500-metre isobaths (the line connecting the depth of 2,500 metres). The claim to an extended continental shelf must be made by submitting technical information to the Commission on the Limits of the Continental Shelf established by UNCLOS. The deadline for submission of claims was ten years from the date of entry into force of UNCLOS. At the 11th meeting of the Conference of Parties, parties to UNCLOS decided that the ten years should begin on 13 May 1999. The effect of this decision was to extend the deadline for most states to 13 May 2009. In June 2008, it was decided that states could meet the deadline by submitting "Preliminary Information" instead of a full submission.

The effect of a submission on existing maritime disputes is dealt with specifically in the Rules of Procedure of the Commission. Rule 5(a) Annex I provides that in cases where a land or maritime dispute exists, the Commission shall "not consider" and qualify a submission made by any of the states concerned in the dispute. However, the Commission may consider one or more submissions in the areas under dispute with prior consent given by all states that are parties to such a dispute.

Baselines

All maritime zones are measured from baselines. The normal rule for measuring baselines is use the low-water line along the coast. Article 7 permits the use of straight baselines, first, where the coastline is deeply indented and cut into, or second, if there is a fringe of islands along the coast in its immediate vicinity. In either case,[5] the drawing of straight baselines must not depart to any appreciable extent from the general direction of the coast.

In the *Qatar and Bahrain* case,[5] the ICJ stated that Article 7 should be interpreted strictly. However, most states in East and Southeast Asia have interpreted Article 7 very liberally, and some of the straight baselines employed by China, Taiwan, Vietnam and Malaysia along their coasts are not consistent with a strict reading of Article 7. The Philippines adopted a new baselines law in 2009 establishing archipelagic baselines. Initial reports are that the baselines are in conformity with UNCLOS.

UNCLOS permits an "archipelagic state" to draw straight archipelagic baselines joining the outermost points of the outermost islands and drying reefs of the archipelago. An archipelagic state is "a state constituted wholly by one or more archipelagos, and may include other islands" such as Indonesia and the Philippines. Continental states with offshore archipelagos are not permitted under UNCLOS to draw straight archipelagic baselines. Therefore, straight archipelagic baselines cannot be used in the islands in the South China Sea, such as in the Paracels, even though they are sometimes described as "archipelagos".

Islands, Rocks, Low-tide Elevations and Artificial Islands

An "island" is defined in Article 121 of UNCLOS as "a naturally formed area of land, surrounded by water which is above water at high tide". The normal rule is that islands are entitled to the same maritime zones as land territory, including a territorial sea, contiguous zone, EEZ and continental shelf.

Article 121(3) creates an exception to this rule for very small features. It provides that "rocks which cannot sustain human habitation or economic life of their own shall have no exclusive economic zone or continental shelf". Therefore, it is critically important whether a particular feature is only entitled to a 12 nautical mile territorial sea because it is a "rock" as defined in Article 121(3).

Estimates are that less than 50 of the 150 or more features in the South China Sea are islands as defined in Article 121 because they are naturally formed areas of land above water at high tide. Estimates are also that the vast majority of the 50 or so islands in the South China Sea are so small that they should be classified as rocks which cannot sustain human habitation or economic life of their own.

Most of the geographic features in the South China Sea are not islands because they are below water at high tide. Some are "low-tide elevations", which means that they are below water at high tide but above water at low tide. States are not entitled to claim any maritime zones from low-tide elevations, not even a 12 nautical mile territorial sea. In fact, it is not even clear under international law whether a state can claim sovereignty over a low-tide elevation. In the *Pedra Branca* case, the ICJ stated that international law was not clear whether a state could have sovereignty over a low-tide elevation such as South Ledge. However, it refused to address the issue in that case. In a subsequent judgement in 2012 in a case between Nicaragua and Columbia,[6] the ICJ further clarified its position by expressly stating that "low-tide elevations cannot be appropriated".

Other geographic features in the South China Sea are reefs, shoals and sandbars that are not above water even at low tide. Such features are not subject to a claim of territorial sovereignty, and no maritime zones can be claimed from them.

If a state has used land reclamation or has built structures on a geographic feature so that it becomes above water at high tide, that feature does not become an island. Under UNCLOS, an island must be a "naturally formed" area of land above water at high tide. Such features would be treated as "artificial islands" and would be governed by the rules of UNCLOS on artificial islands, installations and structures. States are not entitled to claim any maritime zones around such features, but they are entitled to declare a safety zone of 500 metres around them.

Therefore, if Article 121 were applied strictly, only a very small number of the islands in the South China Sea would be entitled to an EEZ and continental shelf of their own. Many of the small islands would be rocks within Article 121(3) and would be entitled only to a 12 nautical mile territorial sea and a 24 nautical mile contiguous zone. The majority of the features are not islands because they are not above water at high tide. Such features would not be entitled to any maritime zones of their own, not even a 12 nautical mile territorial sea.

Delimitation of Maritime Boundaries

Articles 74 and 83 of UNCLOS govern the delimitation of the EEZ and continental shelf boundaries between opposite or adjacent states. The wording of both articles are nearly identical and provide that the delimitation shall be effected by agreement on the basis of international law in order to achieve an equitable solution.

Courts have referred to the delimitation method called for in Articles 74 and 83 (and in customary international law) as the "equitable principles–relevant circumstances" method. In more recent cases, a clear two-stage approach has emerged whereby a preliminary strict equidistance line giving full effect to all features is constructed, before the particular facts of the case are examined with a view to assessing whether an adjustment of the line is required in order to achieve an equitable result.

There are overlapping maritime claims in the South China Sea because the EEZ or continental shelf claims of adjacent states overlap. These overlapping boundary claims are complicated by the fact that two or more claimants maintain that the islands in the South China Sea are under their sovereignty. At least some of the disputed islands may be entitled to an EEZ of their own. Therefore, there would be an overlap between the EEZ claim measured from the baselines along mainland coasts and the EEZ claim measured from the baselines of the offshore islands. However, because sovereignty over the offshore islands is disputed, these overlapping EEZ claims cannot be addressed. As with the case of *Pedra Branca*, states must first determine who has sovereignty over the island before they can begin negotiations on how to delimit the maritime boundary.

One provision on delimitation which is important in the South China Sea is the provision in Articles 74 and 83 relating to delimitation of the EEZ and continental shelf providing that states should enter into "provisional arrangements of a practical nature" pending final agreement on the maritime boundary. This provision has been cited by academics to try to convince claimants that they should cooperate on matters of common interest (fisheries management, protection of the environment, search and rescue, for example) pending any resolution of the boundary delimitation issues. The relevant paragraphs of Articles 74 and 83 read as follows:

> 3. Pending agreement as provided for in paragraph 1, the States concerned, in a spirit of understanding and cooperation, shall make every effort to enter into provisional arrangements of a practical nature and, during this transitional period, not to jeopardize or hamper the reaching of the final agreement. Such arrangements shall be without prejudice to the final delimitation.

UNCLOS provides that if agreement cannot be reached through negotiation, delimitation disputes can be referred to the system of compulsory binding dispute settlement in Part XV. For example, in October 2009 Bangladesh invoked Part XV against both India and Myanmar to resolve the overlapping maritime claims in the Bay of Bengal.

However, Article 298 of UNCLOS provides that states have a right to "opt out" of the system for compulsory binding dispute for disputes on the interpretation or application of the provisions on maritime boundary delimitation. Significantly, China has exercised its option to opt out of the

compulsory binding dispute settlement system in UNCLOS for disputes
relating to the interpretation or application of the provisions on maritime
boundary delimitation.

Maritime Boundary Delimitations Involving Islands and Rocks

Although there has been no authoritative ruling on how Article 121(3) is
to be interpreted, international courts and tribunals have on a number of
occasions been faced with the question of how islands should be treated
in the context of the delimitation of maritime boundaries.

Courts and tribunals have often dealt with small islands by treating
them in one of three ways. First, international courts and tribunals have
tended to address the potentially disproportionate effect of offshore islands
by according them reduced effect on the final delimitation line. This is often
achieved by constructing strict equidistance lines and then modifying the
line so as to give the feature concerned only partial effect. Second, some
courts and tribunals have given small islands very little effect by partially
or wholly "enclaving" them. Third, in some cases courts and tribunals
have wholly discounted small islands by not allowing them to be used
as base-points in the construction of the boundary line.

Historic Rights

There are no provisions in UNCLOS which refer to historic rights. There
are references to "historic bays" and "historic title" in three articles.
First, Article 10(6) provides that the provisions in Article 10 on baselines
for bays do not apply to so-called "historic" bays. Second, Article 15
provides that the territorial sea of opposite or adjacent states shall be
delimited according to the equidistance line, but that such provision
does not apply where necessary by reason of "historic title" or other
special circumstances to delimit the territorial seas of the two states
in another manner. Third, Article 298 permits states to opt out of the
compulsory binding dispute settlement system for disputes involving
"historic bays or titles".

The terms "historic bays" or "historic title" are otherwise not dealt
with in UNCLOS. They would be determined by customary international
law. However, given that the term historic title is referred to only in the
context of historic waters in the territorial sea, it is implied that states are
not able to make any historic claims outside the territorial sea regime.

The rights of states to claim sovereign rights to the natural resources outside the territorial sea are set out in the continental shelf and EEZ regimes. Therefore, although UNCLOS does not say so directly, it seems clear that parties to UNCLOS would not be able to make any claims to historic rights or historic waters outside the territorial sea. Given this, most experts would agree that there is no basis whatsoever for China to maintain that its infamous "U-shaped line" can be used to support any claim to historic rights or historic waters outside the territorial sea. This issue will be dealt with in more detail later.

2002 ASEAN-CHINA DECLARATION OF CONDUCT

The 2002 DOC was adopted by the Foreign Ministers of ASEAN and China at the 8th ASEAN Summit in Phnom Penh on 4 November 2002. The DOC states that the parties reaffirm their respect for and commitment to the freedom of navigation in and overflight above the South China Sea as provided for by universally recognized principles of international law, including UNCLOS. In addition, it states that the parties concerned stand ready to continue their consultations and dialogues concerning relevant issues, through modalities to be agreed by them, including regular consultations on the observance of this declaration. It also states that the parties undertake to respect the provisions of the declaration and to take actions consistent therewith. In addition, the final paragraph states that the parties concerned reaffirm that the adoption of a code of conduct in the South China Sea would further promote peace and stability in the region and agree to work, on the basis of consensus, towards the eventual attainment of this objective.

The vagueness of the self-restraint provision in the 2002 DOC has resulted in misunderstandings and increased tension. The provision states that the parties undertake to exercise self-restraint in the conduct of activities that would complicate or escalate disputes and affect peace and stability including, among others, refraining from the action of inhabiting the presently uninhabited geographic features. This suggests that the parties are to refrain from new occupations, and that they should not undertake activities on islands they already occupy if such actions would "complicate or escalate disputes and affect peace and stability". However, the parties seem to have interpreted the self-restraint clause to imply that they can continue enhancing their presence on features they already occupy. In other words, the parties seem to take the position that their actions to build fortifications, structures, runways and tourist facilities on features they currently occupy are not inconsistent with the self-restraint provision.

One of the obvious weaknesses of the 2002 DOC is that it contains no provisions setting out any procedures or mechanisms to ensure that the parties comply with their obligation "to respect the provisions of this Declaration and take actions consistent therewith". Nor does it provide for any mechanism to deal with differences which may arise over the interpretation or application of the provisions in the declaration, especially the self-restraint provision.

The 2009 Extended Continental Shelf Submissions

As mentioned above, Article 76 of UNCLOS provides that coastal states with broad continental shelves have the right to extend their continental shelf claim beyond 200 nautical miles, but they must do so by making a submission to the Commission on the Limits of the Continental Shelf (CLCS), which is a body of scientific experts established under UNCLOS. Under rules of procedure adopted by the CLCS, most states, including those surrounding the South China Sea, were required to submit information to the CLCS by 13 May 2009 if they intended to make a claim for a continental shelf beyond 200 nautical miles.

Several claimant states made submissions to the CLCS in order to meet the 13 May 2009 deadline. When such submissions included areas surrounding features claimed by other states, the states affected, as would be expected, submitted notes verbales to the UN Secretary-General objecting to the submissions in order to protect their legal interests.

In 2009 Malaysia and Vietnam made a joint submission and Vietnam made an additional submission. The Philippines passed new baselines legislation bringing its archipelagic baselines into conformity with the provisions of UNCLOS. It also objected to the submissions of Vietnam and Malaysia, and reserved the right to make its own submission in the direction of the South China Sea.

In its note verbale to the UN Secretary-General, China not only objected to the submissions of Malaysia, Vietnam and the Philippines, but it also attached the infamous map with the U-shaped claim which includes almost the entire South China Sea. This raised old suspicions about the nature of China's claim in the South China Sea. It also brought the United States into the dispute and, arguably, pushed some of the Southeast Asian countries closer to the United States.

How Claims Have Been Clarified

As a result of the actions of the ASEAN claimant states with respect to the extended continental shelf, their claims have been clarified in several respects.

First, the 200 nautical mile outer limits of the EEZ of Malaysia and Vietnam have been declared and their coordinates have been published and circulated. In addition, the adjacent boundaries within 200 nautical miles between Brunei and Malaysia have been clarified by a bilateral agreement between Brunei and Malaysia.

Second, Malaysia, Vietnam and Brunei seem to have taken the position that the islands over which they claim sovereignty in the South China Sea are not entitled to more than a 12 nautical miles territorial sea. This is implied from the fact that they did not claim an EEZ from any of the features in the South China Sea, but only from the baselines along the coast of their mainland.

Third, Malaysia and Vietnam have claimed the area opposite the outer limits of their 200 nautical mile EEZ as extended continental shelf, but left the maritime boundary between their extended shelves undefined. This would give the two states the sovereign right to explore and exploit the natural resources of the seabed and subsoil on the shelf. The water above the extended continental shelf area would be high seas, and access to the fisheries resources in this area would be subject to the UNCLOS provisions on high seas fishing.

Fourth, the Philippines has established archipelagic baselines in conformity with the provisions in Part IV of UNCLOS. Therefore, it can be inferred that it has finally given up on its rectangular territorial claim based on the coordinates in the 1898 Treaty of Paris and has brought its archipelagic claim into conformity with UNCLOS.

Fifth, the Philippines has also clarified its claim to the islands in the Kalayaan Island Group (KIG) and to Scarborough Shoal by stating that these features will be governed by the regime of islands in Article 121 of UNCLOS. This means that that it will measure its 12 nautical mile territorial sea from the islands using the general rule on baselines, which is the low-water line along the coast, and not by archipelagic baselines. Therefore, the Philippines has also clarified that it will not be using the polygon shaped straight lines around the KIG group as a boundary for its maritime zones. This means that the polygon shaped straight lines were merely a convenient way for the Philippines to have indicated which islands in the Spratlys it claimed are under its sovereignty.

Sixth, the claim of China is clarified to a limited extent. By attaching the U-shaped line map to their note verbale objecting to the submissions of Malaysia and Vietnam, China has officially given notice to the international community that this map is significant to its claim in the South China Sea, including the Spratly archipelago. Before 2009, it was not clear whether China had officially based its claim on the map.

Seventh, the wording of China's note verbale also clarified its position in some respects. In its note, China stated that it claimed "sovereignty" over the islands and their "adjacent waters". If China was to clarify that by adjacent waters it means a 12 nautical mile territorial sea measured from the low-water line of each island, this would be consistent with UNCLOS. In its note, China also stated that it claimed "sovereign rights and jurisdiction" in the "relevant waters". If it was to clarify that "relevant waters" means that it is claiming only an EEZ in the waters adjacent to the territorial sea measured from the baselines of each island, this would also be consistent with UNCLOS.

Finally, China's claim is clarified to some extent because of what is not stated in its note verbale. The note verbale makes no mention of "historic rights" or "historic waters". It uses only the language of UNCLOS, which is "sovereignty, sovereign rights and jurisdiction". Therefore, it seems that China is not asserting any historic rights to the waters inside the U-shaped line and that China is not claiming that the waters inside the U-shaped line are its historic waters. Given that some writers in China and Taiwan had made such assertions when discussing the significance of the U-shaped line map, China's position is now clearer.

How the Claims Have Not Been Clarified

The claim of the Philippines remains unclear in two respects. First, it has not set out the outer limit of its 200 nautical mile EEZ in the direction of the South China Sea. However, since it has established its archipelagic baselines, it is likely that it will measure the limit of its 200 nautical mile EEZ from these archipelagic baselines. Second, the Philippines has stated that Scarborough Shoal and the KIG will be governed by the regime of islands in Article 121. It has not clarified whether it intends to treat all of the features as "rocks" that are only entitled to a 12 nautical mile territorial sea, or whether it intends to claim that some of the features are islands entitled to an EEZ and continental shelf of their own.

China's reference in the note verbale to "adjacent waters" and "relevant waters" left its claim ambiguous. However, the main problem with the notes verbale of China was the fact that they said "see attached map" after the vague language, and then attached the infamous U-shaped-line map. This raised serious concerns in many countries, including ASEAN countries, and rekindled old suspicions about the nature of China's claim and intentions in the South China Sea. Critics of China were quick to claim that by attaching the map, China was in effect claiming 80–90 per cent of the South China Sea as either its territorial sea or historic waters, and that such claims were not consistent with UNCLOS or international law. The U.S. media were quick to pick this point up and observers in the United States began to argue that China's assertive actions were a threat to the freedoms of navigation and overflight in the South China Sea.

China's claim is even more ambiguous when one considers the language it used in its note verbale protesting the 2009 Baselines Law of the Philippines. In that note, China stated it has indisputable sovereignty over Huangyan Island and the Nansha Islands "and their surrounding maritime areas". The phrase "surrounding maritime areas" is even more ambiguous than "adjacent waters". Therefore, unless the true intent was lost in translation, it could be concluded that China's policy with respect to the nature of its claim to the waters in the South China Sea has been one of "deliberate ambiguity".

Even Indonesia, which is not a claimant state, believed it necessary to make an official statement concerning China's notes verbale. Indonesia's note verbale of 8 July 2010 raised two concerns. First, that the U-shaped-line map attached to China's note verbale lacks a basis in international law and upsets the balance established in UNCLOS. Second, that China should act consistently in applying UNCLOS, and follow the same reasoning on rocks and islands in the South China Sea as it had articulated with respect to the claim of Japan over Okinitorishima.

In summary, the measures taken by Malaysia, Vietnam and the Philippines have clarified their claims to a significant extent in a manner that is in conformity with UNCLOS. By contrast, the measures taken by China have reinforced fears and suspicions that its claim is inconsistent with UNCLOS and that it is being deliberately ambiguous about the legal basis for its claim. The result is that a large segment of the international community now views China's claims in the South China Sea as illegitimate.

Shelving the Disputes and Developing Jointly

One basic principle of China's policy on the South China Sea since Deng Xiaoping has been "shelving the disputes and developing jointly".

However, this phrase has caused some confusion, as some Chinese scholars claim that what it means is that the overlapping boundary disputes are set aside, but not the sovereignty disputes over the islands. However, a common sense interpretation of the phrase would be that each claimant state maintains that it has sovereignty over the disputed islands, but regarding those territorial sovereignty disputes for which they cannot reach a comprehensive and durable settlement at the moment, they agree to leave the sovereignty issues alone and set aside the disputes. By shelving the disputes, they are not giving up or renouncing their sovereignty claims, but setting them aside.

In the long term, the only viable solution may be for the ASEAN claimants to enter into discussions with China to implement the principle of "shelving the disputes and developing jointly". However, it must be clear from the outset that such arrangements are without prejudice to a final determination of the sovereignty disputes and the related maritime boundaries.

CONCLUSIONS

Although the policy of the claimant states in the South China Sea is heavily influenced by economic and security concerns, the disputes in the South China Sea cannot be fully understood unless they are also analysed in light of the relevant rules of international law, especially UNCLOS.

The claims of most of the claimant states in the South China Sea were unclear prior to 2009. Although the claimant states became parties to UNCLOS in the mid-1990s, they were slow to amend their national laws and practices and bring their claims into conformity with UNCLOS.

As a result of the submissions and notes verbale submitted to the CLCS in response to the 13 May 2009 deadline, the situation has changed dramatically. The measures taken by the claimant states with respect to an extended continental shelf have resulted in the claims of the ASEAN claimant states being clarified in a manner that is consistent with UNCLOS and international law.

The claim of China has been clarified to a limited extent. However, the measures taken by China in response to those taken by the ASEAN claimants have cast further doubt on the legitimacy of its claim and on its consistency with international law. Consequently, China will be under increasing pressure to clarify its claim and bring it into conformity with UNCLOS.

Although the only long-term solution seems to be "shelving the disputes and developing jointly", it will be difficult for the other claimants to negotiate with China on joint development arrangements so long as China's claim is viewed as being inconsistent with UNCLOS. It is hoped that China will review its policy with respect to the U-shaped line and clarify its claim in a manner that is consistent with UNCLOS.

In the meantime, the best course of action seems to be for ASEAN and China to work together in good faith to implement the Declaration of Conduct. It thus seems that although security concerns and economic interests will continue to dictate policy, the principles and rules of international law will continue to influence and frame the debate.

Notes

1. UN Convention on the Law of the Sea, adopted 10 December 1982, 1833 UNTS 397, entered into force 16 November 1994.
2. Mark J. Valencia, Jon M. Van Dyke, and Noel A. Ludwig, *Sharing the Resources of the South China Sea* (Honolulu: University of Hawai'i Press, 1997), p. 8.
3. Sovereignty over Pedra Branca/Pulau Batu Puteh, Middle Rocks and South Ledge (Malaysia/Singapore), 2008, International Court of Justice, judgement of 23 May 2008.
4. Case concerning Sovereignty over Pulau Ligitan and Pulau Sipadan (Indonesia/Malaysia), International Court of Justice, judgement of 17 December 2002.
5. Case concerning Maritime Delimitation and Territorial Questions between Qatar and Bahrain (Qatar *v.* Bahrain), International Court of Justice, judgement of 16 March 2001.
6. Territorial and Maritime Dispute (Nicaragua *v.* Columbia), International Court of Justice, judgement of 19 November 2012.

3

WHY IS THERE A RELATIVE PEACE IN THE SOUTH CHINA SEA?

Mikael Weissmann

The South China Sea (SCS) represents a historical success of conflict prevention and peace building. It has been, and is, the locus of a number of territorial conflicts between China and the members of the Association of Southeast Asian Nations (ASEAN), and a region where regular military clashes have occurred. In Sino-ASEAN relations, the SCS is the most likely flashpoint to escalate into war, or generally undermine otherwise positive developments. To cite, Rodolfo C. Severino, former ASEAN Secretary-General, "[i]f not for the South China Sea, China-ASEAN relations would be hassle free".[1] It is not without reason that the characterization of the Spratlys as "Asia's next flash point" became a standard reference phrase during the 1990s.[2] However, these predictions seem to have been premature, and have so far not materialized. Indeed, although the underlying incompatibilities have not been resolved, not only have the tensions not escalated into a serious military conflict, but such an event has in fact been mitigated, and as this chapter will argue, a more stable peace has developed.

Scholars of neorealism — the dominant research paradigm for analyses of the East Asian security setting — have painted a gloomy picture of the prospects for the South China Sea and the East Asian region in the post–Cold War era, with perpetual conflicts dominating the predictions.[3] Virtually all analysts of U.S. policy have also made similar assessments.[4] However, these predictions seem to have been premature, and have thus far not materialized. Not only is this the case in the South China Sea, but also in the broader East Asian region where instead of perpetual conflict the post–Cold War era has been characterized by integration and a focus on multilateralism and multilateral cooperation. Though less prone to predict conflict, other mainstream international relations theories fail to account fully for the level of peaceful developments. Liberal institutionalism tends to either give the various institutional arrangements in East Asia more prominence than they deserve, or dismiss them simply because they are so different from the Western ones. Constructivism, on the other hand, tends to give more credit to Asian identity building than it deserves.[5]

This chapter will provide an empirical study of the SCS dispute since the end of the Cold War. More specifically, the study focuses on China's role on behalf of peaceful developments in the SCS and in the overarching Sino-ASEAN relations. The overarching relations are included as the SCS dispute is linked with the overall peace-building process between China and ASEAN that has taken place over the past two decades. The two cannot be separated, as the SCS is the most likely dispute to escalate into military confrontations. At the same time, progress in the SCS is very much a manifestation of positive Sino-ASEAN relations. The study is based on empirical data collected during extensive fieldwork between 2004 and 2008 based in China, and interviews in Singapore in 2010. The major part of the empirical material was collected through interviews with elite individuals in China, Taiwan, Hong Kong, Singapore, and Europe.

The study develops an understanding of the role and impact of cross-border interactions that transcend formal conflict prevention, conflict management, conflict resolution, and peace building. Informal processes and their related conflict prevention and peace building mechanisms are of particular interest here. More specifically, the focus is on a number of processes that have been of importance not only for preventing conflict escalation in the SCS, but also for the progression towards peace in Sino-ASEAN relations more generally. Two interlinked processes — elite interactions and regionalization — have been identified as of key importance for the relative peace. Furthermore, the role of the United States will be analysed. In the first section the role of three types of elite interactions are analysed: the South China Sea workshops, Track Two diplomacy and personal networks among the regional leaderships and elites. Thereafter, the study moves on to the role of regionalization. This section is divided into two parts. First, the importance of the Chinese acceptance of multilateralism and the increasing institutionalization of peaceful international relations between China and ASEAN is analysed. Thereafter, the analysis moves to the importance of economic integration and interdependence (EII). In the third section, the role of the United States for the relative peace is evaluated, after which the conclusions are drawn.

INGREDIENTS FOR A STABLE PEACE

The underlying presumption in this study, that different informal processes, and interrelated mechanisms, constitute at least part of the explanation for the relative peace, is based on three observations. Firstly, there is an absence of any security organization or other formalized conflict-management mechanisms to prevent conflict escalation and/or build peace. This indicates that there needs to be some form of more informal mechanisms in existence. Secondly, the importance of informality and informal processes is widely acknowledged. The Asian states are enmeshed in informal and personalized networks in all spheres.[6] On the international level, the importance of informality is underscored by the regional preference for non-legalistic institutions. Moreover, the pan-regional acceptance of the "ASEAN-way" as the diplomatic norm and the importance given to interpersonal interaction between leaders also illustrate the role of informality. Thirdly, some peace and conflict research points to the importance of informality and informal processes, such as informal networks.[7]

Peace is understood as not merely the absence of war, but as a continuum ranging from crisis, through unstable and stable, to durable peace. A durable peace is a situation where inter-party relations have reached a high level of cooperation and reciprocity and war is unthinkable. When peace has been attained, relations have transcended the stage where war *does* not happen and moved into a situation where war is perceived as something that *will* not happen, at least in people's minds.[8] At the unstable peace level, tensions and suspicions between the parties is so high that peace no longer seems guaranteed and the parties perceive each other as enemies. Tensions and suspicion run high, but violence is either absent or only sporadic.[9] At the crisis level, the risk of war is imminent and military action is the preferred, or likely, option. There may be sporadic utterances of violence between the parties, but no regular organized and open violence.

The process that creates peace is understood as dual, including both "the prevention of conditions conductive to violence" and "the promotion of conditions conducive to peace".[10] The former roughly equates to preventing negative relations between groups, and the latter translates into the promotion of positive inter-group relations. In this chapter, the terms "conflict prevention" and "peace building" are used to capture the two aspects. Conflict prevention covers the prevention of negative relations from escalating, while peace building encompasses the development of positive relations between states. In general, conflict prevention covers mechanisms with impact over a relatively short term, while peace building concerns the building of a longer-term peace.

The Relative Peace in the South China Sea

In terms of peace in the SCS, Sino-ASEAN relations have been transformed since the early 1990s when it was best characterized as a most fragile unstable peace. At the time, military forces were seizing claims and a conflict between the Philippines and China over Mischief Reef in 1995 stopped short of military conflict mainly because of the unequal power of the two. Since then, the conflict has moved towards a more stable peace. Despite tensions and unresolved underlying incompatibilities in the SCS, the assessment is that war is most unlikely to happen. This is the case as the SCS situation cannot be separated from the overarching Sino-ASEAN relations. Since the early 1990s peaceful relations between China and ASEAN have been institutionalized and there has been a strong regional integration process leaving the two interlinked and economically interdependent. Thus, as a manifestation of the latter, the conflict is tilting towards a stable peace where war is very unlikely.

This is still the case despite the situation having deteriorated since late 2007, in particular between China and Vietnam and China and the Philippines. These developments do increase the risk for more confrontations, at least if the trend continues. At the same time, their impact so far should not be overestimated. There are signs that China understands that it has pushed too far.[11] It is also clear that diplomacy continues to be the preferred option among all parties, and the general commitment to cooperative approaches aimed at reducing the risk of conflict, joint development, and the protection of the marine environment remains.[12] The regionalization process has continued, with substantial progress particularly in the economic sphere with the implementation of the China-ASEAN Free Trade Area (CAFTA) on 1 January 2010.

Thus, despite the increased tensions, the unstable peace continues to tilt towards a stable peace (although somewhat less so). The parties do not perceive each other as enemies, and in the short-term perspective, the United States continues to be a safeguard for peace. In the longer-term perspective, as long as China continues to focus on its need for economic development there are strong incentives for continuing to develop positive relations with its Southeast Asian neighbours. It should here be noted that China's assertive stance has not come as a shock for an ASEAN that has been deceived by the Chinese "charm offensive", as some analysts suggest.[13] As argued by Dewi Fortuna Anwar, the ASEAN members "were and continue to be fully aware of both the inherent promises and dangers that China present[s]", and it continues to believe "that the best course of dealing with China ... is to engage and integrate it fully into the regional order".[14]

ELITE INTERACTIONS

The proliferation of elite interactions, in particular Track Two diplomacy and personal networks, has been important for peace building and conflict prevention in the South China Sea as well as in Sino-ASEAN relations and the broader East Asian region. The elite interactions have increased the regional ability to prevent conflicts from arising and escalating. They have been an important force for regional trust and confidence building and for the development towards a regional identity through East Asian community building.

In regards to the South China Sea dispute, the informal South China Sea workshops have been of particular importance. These workshops have been promoting cooperation and confidence building and have been building understanding and trust among the different parties. The importance of these workshops should be understood in the context of the thick web of Track Two frameworks that developed in the region in the 1990s. The frameworks are interlinked: they interact both formally and informally; they discuss similar issues and largely have overlapping participants.[15] This creates synergy effects and strong links to the Track One level. These mechanisms will be explored in more depth in the following sections on the proliferation of Track Two diplomacy and on personal networks.

The South China Sea Workshops

In the early 1990s the SCS was the region's most critical flashpoint, and there was no forum through which this conflict could be efficiently handled. At the time, the "Informal Workshops on Managing Potential Conflicts in the South China Sea" (SCSW) were the only mechanisms for reconciliation, and the only feasible forum through which China could engage and cooperate with ASEAN on the South China Sea dispute. The aim of the workshops was to "informally manage potential conflicts in the South China Sea through the promotion of cooperation within the context of promoting confidence-building measures and preventive diplomacy".[16] The workshops were most important between 1990 and 1999, before the ASEAN code of conduct was developed and China agreed to hold talks with ASEAN on this matter. During the 1990's ten annual workshops and a large number of other working-group meetings were held.[17] With the exception of the first workshop, all relevant regional states were participating.[18]

The policy impact of the SCSWs has been high. Although the SCSWs are examples of Track Two diplomacy, they share many of the features of Track 1.5 workshops. From the beginning it was explicitly stated that the workshops should be "a platform for policy-oriented discussions, not only for academic exchanges of views".[19] The workshops focus on policy streams through the way participants are selected, where the emphasis is on senior officials rather than on academics.[20] Thus, the workshops normally gathered senior foreign-ministry-level officials from all participating states. The high-level participation ensured a direct link back to the decision-makers and other relevant authorities concerned with the SCS. This was the case although the officials were participating in their "private capacity", which in practice meant little less than preventing the participants from making binding statements or agreements.[21]

The SCSWs did help the participants to reach a better understanding of each other's positions as they opened up for both information exchange and formal as well as informal communication with each other. This understanding consequently decreased the risk for miscalculations, which is important to prevent unnecessary and unintentional conflict escalation. Moreover, the workshops ensured the existence of channels of communication between the parties, which raised the ability to defuse tensions and prevent conflict escalation. Prevention of such escalation is critical for the SCS, since it is a flashpoint where the parties not only have military forces present, but where military confrontations have been a regular occurrence.

The SCSWs have been a successful forum for policy innovation and pre-negotiation, serving as a possible starting point for official negotiations. In fact, many of the features that later on appeared in official statements and joint declarations had previously been discussed in the informal workshops. Being both Track Two and informal, the SCSWs did not have the same restrictions as official negotiations. Already at the second workshop in Bandung, West Java, in 1991 — the first workshop with Chinese participation — the involved parties agreed to settle the conflict peacefully, thereby avoiding the use or the threat of force. The participants also agreed to exercise restraint and to develop cooperative programmes and projects regardless of the territorial disputes.[22]

The workshops have also worked as catalysts for cooperation within a range of different functional areas.[23] Through its Technical Working Groups and Group of Experts Meetings, a number of projects have been established in areas such as ecosystem monitoring, biodiversity, sea level, and tide monitoring. Functional frameworks have been established. For example, a special study group on joint development in the South China Sea was set up in 1998, which addressed the sensitive and conflict-ridden issue of access to natural resources. Taken together, these projects have had positive outcomes in building confidence and trust between the parties. As argued by Hasjim Djalal, these measures "are meant to promote a spirit of cooperation among the claimant-countries. It is in part because of them that no violent conflict has taken place since 1988."[24]

In conclusion, the SCSWs have been important for safeguarding the relative peace during the 1990's, both by preventing conflict escalation and by setting the stage for peace-building initiatives. They have been a driving force for peaceful developments in the SCS as a forum for pre-negotiation and policy innovation. The workshops have created a meeting place in which the relevant officials have been able to meet in an informal setting, thereby allowing for the building of relationships and trust among them. The workshops have also been significant for the development of personal networks among the participants. This network building was important, as there were limited linkages between China and ASEAN during the 1990s. The workshops have also smoothed relations through technical cooperation at a time when conflict was tense and the official lines of communication between China and the other parties were limited. In short, the SCSWs thereby not only contributed to the prevention of conflict escalation, but also constituted an important part of the peace-building process in the SCS.

Personal Networks among Regional Leaders and Elites

The existence of personal relations between regional leaders and elites has been crucial for the building of mutual trust and understanding.[25] Most interviewees, particularly in East Asia, called personal relationships among regional leaders "extremely important".[26] Indeed, it was even argued that personal contacts and relations between the top leaders are "a key" to friendly interstate relations as it "reflects relations between countries".[27] It is also clear that the Chinese leaders themselves attach high importance to leader and elite interactions, which have been richly described in a memoir by Qian Qichen, former Minister of Foreign Affairs. A good example here is found in his detailed account of how China restored formal ties with Indonesia.

The combined forces of regionalization and the proliferation of Track Two processes have driven the network building. The unprecedented number of meetings has led to a situation where top leaders, officials, and other regional elites have extensive points of contact. Through the socialization in these meetings, webs of personal networks have been built among the participants. The socialization and the networks have not only increased confidence and trust among their members; it has also contributed to the building of a nascent regional identity. As argued by a senior member of a Chinese government think tank, the identity-building process has been important, given the "need for a regional identity" if "mutual confidence" should be achieved in such a diversified region as East Asia with its differing political systems, levels of economic development, culture, and ethnicity.[28]

It should be emphasized that the development of personal relations between the Chinese and the ASEAN leaders is a new phenomenon. China has traditionally not had personal relations with Southeast Asian countries. This new trend came after China introduced its "good neighbourhood policy", which has resulted in good relations with all its Southeast Asian neighbours.[29] The ASEAN+3 (APT) process has been of foremost importance for this network and trust-building exercise, as the summits are "a very good opportunity for top leaders to develop a mutual understanding plus getting to know each other better".[30]

The importance of personal networks goes beyond the top leaders. Through the multilateralism and the institutionalization of the regionalization process — in particular the APT process — lower-ranking officials socialize with their counterparts as well. The importance given to informal socialization can be seen in different ASEAN-related meetings where efforts are made to ensure that participants get the opportunity to interact informally. The lower-level socialization does increase the mutual understanding and develops confidence and trust at all bureaucratic levels and in different policy sectors. As foreign policy today includes actors and bodies outside the top leadership and the foreign ministry, it is essential to include all levels and sectors. It is important that individuals at all levels be determined to avoid confrontations and prevent issues and tensions from escalating or spreading.

The benefit of elite socialization and elite networks is also noticeable within the respective states. Here, the networks build an efficient link between Track Two and Track One policymaking circles. This is an important aspect in the Sino-ASEAN setting where the link between Track Two and Track One is unclear, as the two tracks often overlap. Moreover, in China the linkages to Track One have increased in recent years, as the Chinese leaders have become more receptive to new ideas.[31] Personal networks also contribute to keep channels of communication open between parties in conflict, as illustrated by the informal communication that predated the South China Sea workshops. The personal networks also facilitate back-channel negotiations, as can be seen in the setting up of the SCSWs.

Track Two Diplomacy

In looking beyond the SCS, Track Two diplomacy has proliferated in East Asia during the last two decades, from three or four Track Two channels in the whole Asia-Pacific in 1989,[32] reaching 268 in 2008 after having passed 200 in 2005.[33] The reason for this trend is an increasing interest, both within and outside the region, to engage in dialogues aimed at developing a more secure and stable neighbourhood and to work for continued economic prosperity. The Track Two style fits the region very well as it corresponds to the region's important norms of informality, consensus building, consultation, face saving, and conflict avoidance. Another key factor for the proliferation is China's shift from being a reluctant (non-)participant, to becoming one of the driving forces in Track Two dialogues in the region.

For conflict prevention and peace building, the benefits of the proliferation of Track Two diplomacy can be found in their impact through enhanced mutual understanding (even when the parties are hostile), increased transparency, and the development of mutual trust.[34] These changes occur even when there is a lack of concrete policy outcomes. As Chinese scholars with extensive Track Two experience have observed, since officials are included, the Track Two processes build trust between policymakers and make them more informed, in turn leading to them making more knowledgeable decisions.[35] Both trust and informed decisions are important for conflict prevention, as they increase the ability to successfully handle and defuse tensions and disputes before they escalate beyond control. Track Two dialogues also have a more direct peace impact when official dialogues are stalled, or when a government wants a "benign cover" to try out new policy ideas.[36] The latter is seen in the case of the SCSWs. In addition, they are also important for long-term peace building through their spillover effect on regional identity formation.

A number of Track Two institutions stand out for their role for the relative peace. The ASEAN Institutes of Strategic and International Studies (ASEAN-ISIS) and the Council for Security Cooperation in the Asia Pacific (CSCAP) have been of utmost importance. Their impact goes beyond trust, confidence, and network building, as they have worked in symbiosis with Track One forums. They form a part of the ASEAN Regional Forum "two-track approach", where,

> Track One activities will be carried out by ARF governments. Strategic institutes and non-government organizations in the region, such as ASEAN-ISIS and CSCAP, will carry out Track Two activities.... The synergy between the two tracks would contribute greatly to confidence building measures in the region. Over time, the Track Two activities should result in the creation of a sense of community among participants of those activities.[37]

Thus, the two institutions have had a direct impact on policy through their close working relationship with official institutions. They have also been forerunners in the institutionalization of East Asian regionalization and community building.

CSCAP was formally launched in 1993 as the result of a series of conferences on regional security issues in the early 1990s. It has since been of foremost importance for regional trust and confidence building, preventive diplomacy, and cooperation on non-traditional security issues. With two formalized channels, it can influence ARF on a wide array of topics drawing on its working groups. In other words, CSCAP has not only been a facilitator of elite socialization, but has also contributed to semi-official engagement on a range of issue areas. That said, over time CSCAP has ceded some of its roles, as many of its areas eventually have become institutionalized within the APT process.

ASEAN-ISIS has not only played a fundamental role in the development of ASEAN, but has also been a positive force for developing peaceful relations between ASEAN and China. It has fostered capacity building for cooperative security and preventive diplomacy, and has provided valuable advice to governments in East Asia on a range of issues affecting regional peace and security in Southeast Asia.[38] This includes recommendations to create the ARF, to strengthen the ASEAN Secretariat, and to push for a realization of an ASEAN Free Trade Area (AFTA). In turn the ASEAN Secretariat has been important, particularly within ASEAN, but also in the organization's work to engage China as a collective. The ARF has become the institutionalized forum in which common concerns for the whole region are addressed. It has been an excellent platform for elite interactions. It has also built a link between Track One and Two levels by institutionalizing meetings between the heads of ASEAN-ISIS and the ASEAN Senior Officials. In conclusion, ASEAN-ISIS has been an important catalyst for building a coherent ASEAN, which is important for the level of success in ASEAN's relations with external actors. The success is most clearly manifested in the APT process, in the development of free trade agreements with its East Asian neighbours, and in the development of good intra-ASEAN relations, all of which have been important for the long-term peace-building process between China and ASEAN, as we will see in the section on regionalization below.

Other Track Two processes have been developed within the APT framework. Following a proposal by South Korean President Kim Dae Jung in 1998, two research institutes focussing on East Asian affairs were established as the East Asian Vision Group (EAVG) and the East Asian Study Group (EASG). Since 2003, largely as a result of the work of the EAVG and the EASG, three other Track Two processes have been established: the East Asia Forum, the Comprehensive Human Resources

Development Program for East Asia, and the Network of East Asian Think-tanks (NEAT). These processes have played an important role for peace building by being a driving force in the East Asian regionalism project and in East Asian community building.

All Track Two processes facilitate the gathering of policymakers in low-key informal settings, which allow for relatively open and frank discussions on security issues. Even if the general discussions in the open forum tend to be rather formal, there is room for informal, off-the-record discussions during coffee breaks, dinners, excursions, etc. To cite a regular CSCAP participant:

> That is pretty much how it is!… There is a table, you present a paper. You do not mention Taiwan, then the Chinese would walk out. All business [is] on the sidelines. [It is] very Asian, very consensual. No debate [at the main table, and] all positions [are] decided beforehand. [There are] [s]ome open discussions, but most of it at the sidelines, at the coffee table, etc.[39]

The unofficial discussions and socialization are important for network building. They also work as trust and confidence building mechanisms and as indirect conflict prevention by allowing the participants to test their ideas without committing to them officially. This not only encourages new thinking, but also allows for increased knowledge about, and understanding of, the underlying logic and interests behind official positions, statements, and actions. Through these exchanges, confidence and trust is being built. Occasionally, deep trust is developed, not least as the participants share many experiences and characteristics, and frequently are each other's counterparts. Repeated interactions also discourage cheating, as there are mutual gains from upholding a certain level of sincerity. At a minimal level, your ability to assess the other's level of sincerity will have increased, as through interactions you learn whom to, and whom not to, trust. In this way, unofficial discussions also decrease the likelihood of confrontations due to misunderstandings or miscalculations. The development of confidence, trust and networks between, at least some, individuals is central to the ability to implement direct conflict-preventive measures.

Elite Interactions and the Relative Peace

The proliferation of elite interactions has been of great importance to the building and upholding of the relative peace in the SCS and between China and ASEAN. Both the short-term conflict-prevention and the long-term peace-building impacts have been high. The Track Two frameworks have played an important role for the enhancement of understanding and the building of confidence and trust since the end of the Cold War. In this context, the role of the Track Two processes for network building and as a facilitator for elite socialization is obvious. The elite interactions have built mutual understanding and trust among the regional elites and leaders. It has also altered both how they perceive each other and how East Asia as a region is perceived. This has been an important component for the building of a shared (regional) identity among the elites. The interactions have also created a platform for pre- and back-channel negotiations, by creating the trust, channels and settings needed for such measures. Finally, the Track Two frameworks have worked as an important catalyst for regional cooperation.

For the SCS disputes, the SCSWs played an essential role during the critical 1990s period by promoting cooperation and confidence building among the parties. The workshops were also important for increasing the understanding between the parties at a time when there were otherwise limited interaction. The SCSWs worked as a framework, together with the increasingly thick web of Track Two frameworks in the rest of East Asia, for conflict prevention and peace building in the SCS. The workshops can, in this respect, be understood as pre-negotiations and a forum for policy innovation for future Track One negotiations and/or agreements. Through the workshops, continued inter-party dialogues could be assured and, thereby, the hopes for an eventual peaceful resolution could be kept alive.

REGIONALIZATION

As set out above, the developments in the SCS dispute cannot be separated from the overall Sino-ASEAN relations. As observed by Rodolfo C. Severino, "good Sino-ASEAN relations decrease the risk of conflict in the South China Sea. At the same time, bad relations in the South China Sea are a problem for the overall relations."[40] The key factor for the positive developments in Sino-ASEAN relations, and in turn for conflict prevention and peace building in the SCS, is the strong regionalization process that has been happening since the end of the Cold War. From a peace perspective, two aspects of the regionalization process in particular stand out: the acceptance of multilateralism and institutionalization of peaceful relations, and economic integration and interdependence.

Chinese Acceptance of Multilateralism and the Institutionalization of Peaceful Relations

China's acceptance of multilateralism and the interlinked institutionalization of peaceful Sino-ASEAN relations have, together with the APT-process, been important for the gradual move towards a stable peace. Of particular importance for peace is the general acceptance and institutionalization of the "ASEAN-way", which works as a structure defining how international relations and diplomatic practices are to be conducted. This, in turn, influences and constrains actual behaviour. In constructivist terms, the "ASEAN-way" has created a normative and ideational framework that all East Asian states need to consider and relate to in their decision-making processes. This is the case even though the principles are not necessarily followed.

The institutionalization of peaceful relations between China and ASEAN can be traced back to the Tiananmen incident in 1989 when ASEAN pursued a diplomatic campaign to engage rather than isolate China.[41] ASEAN's "constructive engagement" strategy was to become a reciprocal process, with China moving from a great-power oriented foreign policy to "soft power" diplomacy to counteract the perception of China as a threat.[42] This rapprochement has been a long-term identity-altering process for both parties, who have reinterpreted their interests and transformed their behaviour towards each other. The rapprochement is fundamental for the understanding of why there have been attempts to manage the SCS, and why these attempts have been successful. Without the mutual aim of building peaceful relations, there would have been little incentive for either side to ensure that the SCS did not negatively affect their overall relations.

The 1997 Asian financial crisis was another milestone for the institutionalization of peaceful relations, being a critical juncture not only for ASEAN's perception of China, but also for the levels of communication and diplomatic respect.[43] In 1997 the first APT summit was held between China, South Korea, Japan, and the ASEAN members. This was the initiation of the APT process, which was to become one of the driving forces for East Asian regionalization as well as the institutionalization of peaceful relations between China and ASEAN. The importance of the APT process for East Asian peace lies in its inclusiveness. Being a broad cooperative process, the APT became *the* platform for cooperation, reconciliation, and community building in East Asia. Seen from the perspective of regional peace, the states have been able to use this platform in "avoiding [the need for] conflict avoidance", that is, positive interstate relations have developed to such an extent that there is less need for deliberate efforts to avoid confrontations over conflictual issues.[44] This role is important as ASEAN "is not much of a mediator", which makes APT "a place to reassure each other [that one is] not trying to be dangerous."[45]

Parallel with the institutionalization of peaceful relations, there has been increasing Chinese acceptance of multilateralism. In the early 1990's, China was both inexperienced and unwilling to participate in multilateral frameworks. It was only reluctantly that China joined the ASEAN regional forum (ARF) in 1994. This was, to quote Ren Xiao, a leading Chinese expert on Sino-ASEAN relations, "a remarkable development", as China at the time had "little experience in multilateral processes, except those within the United Nations system".[46] Through participation, over time the "mindsets towards multilateral approaches" changed.[47] China became more positive and proactive in its engagement in multilateral frameworks. It started to develop what is best described as "an open mind", and "changed its mindset to the idea of security dialogues".[48] Given that ASEAN consistently has been trying to enmesh China into the regional order and to get it to accept some regional norms and practice, such as multilateral engagement and the ASEAN way, these changes were highly appreciated.[49]

Since 2000 China has moved beyond being a participant and has become a proactive actor in multilateral settings. The underlying Chinese logic is that an understanding of China and its benign intentions will make the Asian actors change their perceived interests and behaviour in a direction that is favourable to China. For example, in 2001 China launched the Bo'ao Forum as part of its strategy to reassure Southeast Asia of its benign intentions. In addition, the signing of the Declaration on the Conduct of Parties in the South China Sea in 2002 and the 2003 accession to the Treaty of Amity and Cooperation were part of the same strategy.

The move towards, and acceptance of, multilateralism has over time become institutionalized. Institutionalization has, together with multilateralism, been key "[t]o make the region a more secure one".[50] It has been argued that, "there is a need to develop regional institutions" in order to "prevent conflicts".[51] It should here be emphasized that institutions should not be equated with regional organizations in a traditional (Western) sense here. Institutions are, to cite Robert O. Keohane, "persistent and connected sets of rules (formal and informal) that prescribe behavioural roles, constrain activity, and shape expectations".[52] They do not need to be formalized in the legal sense, and "may include organisations, bureaucratic agencies, treaties and agreements, and informal practices that states [as well as non-state actors] accept as binding".[53] The foremost example of the institutionalization of Sino-ASEAN relations can be found in the APT process, which is "a set of complex meeting/dialogue mechanisms of cooperation, moulded ASEAN-style consultations" with dialogue at various levels and on a wide range of issues.[54]

The APT process has not only driven cooperation to unprecedented levels, it has also turned the ASEAN way into an institution in its own right. Despite its non-legalistic nature, the ASEAN way does fulfil the requirements set out for an institution: it implies a "persistent and connected sets of rules" that "prescribe behavioural roles, constrain activity, and shape expectations",[55] which "states accept as binding".[56] Consequently, the ASEAN way has worked as an ideational and normative structure, which has both guided and constrained the diplomatic practice and interstate relations across East Asia, including between China and ASEAN.

To sum up, the Chinese acceptance of multilateralism and institutionalization of peaceful relations have been a precondition for the Sino-ASEAN peace-building process. Through the creation of structural frameworks with forums, dialogues, and accepted diplomatic norms and practices (the ASEAN way), the institutionalization has stabilized the regionalization process and made it permanent and regular. The institutionalization has been an important part of ASEAN's engagement of China and served to increase its stakes in regional peace and stability. Moreover, it has assured that the "China threat" does not become a self-fulfilling prophesy.[57] The long-term objective of engaging China aimed "to lock China into regional multilateral institutions, which will not only moderate but also gradually transform Chinese regional behaviour"[58] has been successful: China's behaviour has become more moderate and it has become accustomed to, and compliant with, engagement in multilateral forums. Moreover, China has accepted the ASEAN way as the diplomatic principle and has started to consider its neighbours' interests. This has been a reciprocal process between China's "soft power diplomacy" and ASEAN's "constructive engagement" policies.

Applied to the SCS disputes, both the changes in perception and the Chinese acceptance of multilateralism were necessary for success in the overall negotiation processes. Without these changes, the talks on a regional code of conduct that started in 2000 would most likely not have been possible. These negotiations benefited from the trust and confidence that had developed between the parties. Since the SCS is a multiparty issue, it required a multilateral setting, at least to avoid unbalanced bilateral negotiations with China. The difference is most clearly seen in the differences in developments before and after the 1995 Mischief clash. Before the clash, the SCS dispute was stalemated at a high conflict-intensity level, with no mutual trust or confidence. Rather, the involved actors did their utmost to secure their claims. After the incident, the ASEAN members succeeded in taking a common stance in their dealings with China, thereby forcing it to deal with the ASEAN members on a multilateral basis, as opposed to its preferred bilateral approach.

Economic Integration and Interdependence

Beneath the above processes lies a significant process of economic integration and interdependence (EII) in East Asia. The whole region, with the possible exception of North Korea, seeks peace, security, and prosperity. The focus on economic growth and prosperity has been a common policy goal across East Asia, driving the regionalization process. It is not without reason that Ali Alatas, former Indonesian Minister for Foreign Affairs, equated ASEAN+3 with "peace plus prosperity".[59]

In East Asia, the proliferation of EII is a relatively recent phenomenon. Central for this to take off was the founding of the Asia-Pacific Economic Cooperation in 1989 and the agreement on an ASEAN Free Trade Area in 1992. Since the early 1990's the EII has increased dramatically, with bilateral trade between China and ASEAN increasing fifteenfold between 1991 and 2005 when it reached US$130.3 billion.[60] The EII goes beyond trade volume, with China taking the bold step of arranging for the China-ASEAN Free Trade Area (CAFTA) that was signed in November 2002, coming into force 1 January 2010.[61] The process of implementation is important beyond its economic benefit, as it forms part of China's diplomatic policy to win trust among the ASEAN members by "giving more and taking less" (*Duo Yu*

Shao Qu).[62] It is also an important catalyst for the overall regionalization and community-building process, having been described as "an initial step towards the realisation of an East Asian community".[63]

EII has both direct short-term conflict-prevention potentials and a longer-term peace-building impact. In the short term, it has had a moderate impact by increasing the cost of military conflict thereby increasing the incentive to pursue non-conflict paths. This has been an important incentive for the states to avoid confrontations or conflict escalation over what the parties perceive as non-essential issues. With the increased EII, the problems in the SCS have simply become less central on the agenda.[64] The benefits of economic cooperation simply overshadow the problems in the SCS since none of the parties want to risk undermining the benefits from economic cooperation by triggering an escalation of conflict in the South China Sea. This has made conflict avoidance the preferred path.

For long-term peace building, EII has been significant in promoting conditions conducive to peace, both by itself and through spillover effects. It has been important as a driving force for regionalization and the institutionalization thereof. As argued by a senior analyst in a Chinese government think tank, "[a]ll East Asian countries take East Asian economic cooperation as [a] first step in the East Asian community building process."[65] That is, it works as an important platform for East Asian identity building and, in turn, influences how the participants perceive and behave towards each other and how they construct their interests. The interaction in the economic sphere has also built trust and understanding, which in turn has spread to other more sensitive issue areas. This applies both through spillover, as predicted by functionalist theories (although there have been no infringement on sovereignty), and through trust and understanding on a more informal and personal level, which is important for successful negotiation and communication. Overall, when accounting for all the direct and indirect effects of economic integration and interdependence, its role for the relative peace has been high.

Building Trust and Transforming Relations

The regionalization process has since the early 1990s fundamentally transformed relations in the region, including how the states perceive each other and construct their interests. The relative importance of the conflicts in the SCS on the greater Sino-ASEAN agenda has decreased and conflict avoidance has become the preferred path. The importance of the SCS was downplayed, and the shared interest of ensuring a peaceful resolution has been emphasized. This way, regionalization has also had a moderate conflict-preventive impact by preventing negative relations in the SCS from escalating.

Regionalization has created unprecedented interactions between China and ASEAN, which has also been an important trust-building exercise. As argued by a Hong Kong strategic thinker, in East Asia trust is "depending on reciprocity" and there is "no good and easy way to build trust. It takes time and is not built quickly."[66] Here China has gradually built trust and confidence by repeating its behaviour, gaining credibility among the ASEAN members. This altered the perceptions of others over time and the interpretations of each other's interests have been transformed. A joint understanding has developed that the actors share certain interests, and that they all benefit from cooperation. In addition, through a mutual and reciprocal confidence and trust building process, the level of trust between China and ASEAN has reached unprecedented levels. Currently, the two actors not only have an agreed interest in cooperation, but also the trust and confidence needed to do so successfully.

There have been nascent developments towards a shared regional identity, because of the increasingly deep integration and the active work for an East Asian community. These developments have altered the ideational and normative structures within Sino-ASEAN relations, which have made possible a reassessment of interests with regard to the SCS and in how to pursue these interests. In theoretical terms, the identity-building process has affected how the actors define their interests, how they perceive their counterparts, and how they behave. These types of changes do occur, and have already done so, regardless of whether the regional identity-building exercises are successful. The process itself has altered the social identities of the parties, given that identities are continuously being reconstructed. The identities, in turn, influence interest, perceptions, and behaviour. That said, the greater the development of common norms and values, the better for peace. So far, the process has been moving in a positive direction. Indeed, the changes in the early 2000s, when China acceded to the Treaty of Amity and Cooperation and signed the 2002 declaration on the SCS are clear examples of this. These transformations are still valid, despite the more assertive stance taken by the Chinese since 2007. The multilateral frameworks that have been developed are still there, and the integration and the East Asian community-building process have been continuing. Overall the relations are still good, though there has been an increased caution about Chinese intentions and a certain increase on the perceived importance of keeping the U.S. presence in the region, which will be discussed in the next section.

The general acceptance and institutionalization of the ASEAN way is an important manifestation of the relative peace, as it captures the ideational and normative transformations that have taken place. The regional integration and interdependence, in the economic and other spheres, have also created an incentive for avoiding confrontation. Equally important is the cost of losing the mutual trust that has been gradually built over time through the Sino-ASEAN engagement process. This trust forms the basis of Sino-ASEAN relations and both sides are taking great efforts to ensure continuous positive relations.

Overall, regionalization has been of great importance for the relative peace in the SCS and in the overarching Sino-ASEAN relations. It has been the foremost peace-building process, being a long-term process that both promotes and encompasses the development of positive relations between states and non-state groups. In fact, East Asian community-building is the promotion of conditions conducive to peace in its clearest form. In addition to its long-term role, it has had a moderate conflict-preventive impact.

THE ROLE OF THE UNITED STATES

There is a consensus among strategic thinkers of varying schools of thought that the United States has played a role in the South China Sea, although they differ in their interpretation of the American influence. From a constructivist perspective, the United States is "thought to be important", it is therefore "induced with centrality" and the United States might is assumed.[67] The perception of the United States as a safeguard against a rising China has had a stabilizing effect, by creating a feeling of security within ASEAN. This feeling has created more space for ASEAN to "constructively engage" China, as the feeling of security has limited the fear of becoming more dependent on China. It has also been beneficial for China in its attempts to engage with ASEAN without creating fears about its intentions.

The perception of the United States as a central and powerful actor results in its presence creating a framework for acceptable behaviour. In practice this framework only affects behaviour at the margins in the case of the SCS. As the United States' interest is limited to the preservation of the status quo and the freedom of navigation, its involvement can only be expected in extreme cases.[68] Indeed, in the case of the SCS, the United States has not recognized any of the claims of the parties, and there are no commitments to peace beyond a potential intervention if the situation in the SCS would endanger the freedom of navigation.[69] In theoretical terms, the United States is reluctant to get involved beyond conflict prevention, and it has done little to resolve the underlying issues. This lack of interest was made clear when the United States declined to offer its Philippine ally support during the 1995 Mischief Reef incident.[70] Still, despite the limitations of U.S. engagement in the SCS, it has had a moderate indirect effect for relative peace building by creating space for the development of positive relations. It would be an exaggeration to say that the United States has been a precondition for peace, but it has, without question, been a catalyst.

For conflict prevention, the United States did play a particular role during the early 1990s, when the SCS dispute was at its most critical. During this period it acted as a stabilizing force by its efforts to prevent an escalation into war and as a balancer of Chinese military power.[71] However, when assessing the underlying explanations for the lack of war during the 1990s, it should be remembered that the Chinese military was still relatively weak. Most importantly, China had at the time no blue-water capability to project force into the South China Sea. Consequently, it lacked capacity for any long-term forward presence in the South China Sea. Thus, it is highly questionable whether China would have been able to secure remote areas in the SCS, including the Spratlys or the Paracel Islands. Since Sino-ASEAN relations were transformed in the latter part of the 1990s, the United States has been of little conflict-preventive influence. The American role was limited to ensuring that the Chinese avoid any hasty military actions in the SCS. Put simply, the conflict intensity level of the SCS dispute has not corresponded to a real risk of an escalation large enough to trigger a U.S. reaction.

CONCLUSION

It is clear that both the SCS and Sino-ASEAN relations have transformed from being Southeast Asia's next flashpoint into a relatively stable peace. In the SCS dispute, peace can best be described as situated between the unstable and stable level. Indeed, the probability of war is small, but not to the extent that the level of peace has transcended the stage where war *does* not happen and moved into a situation where war is perceived as something that *will* not happen. At the same time, the tensions are not so high as to define it as unstable peace. As a manifestation of Sino-ASEAN relations, the SCS disputes tilt towards a stable peace.

The stability of the peace is dependent on how much faith one puts into China's commitment to peaceful settlements of the South China Sea disputes and the continuing progression of East Asian regionalization and community-building processes. The assessment here is that Sino-ASEAN relations have transformed to the extent that in the current climate, war is increasingly unthinkable. Some issues remain unresolved, but the positive relations have built solid conditions conducive for peace. Central to this assessment is the trust gradually built up at length between China and ASEAN, the institutionalized regionalization through the APT process, and the acceptance of the ASEAN way. To the extent that there have been negative developments since 2007, they have been balanced out with the U.S. commitment to safeguarding peace and the fact that ASEAN has already taken a long-term perspective on China's rise. As argued by Shaun Breslin, ASEAN considers "China's continued rise an inevitable fact of economic life.... Just as financial markets discount future economic shocks — for example, oil price rises — by dealing with them before they occur, so ASEAN leaders have discounted China's future economic rise."[72]

Two interlinked types of processes have been important for the relative peace: elite interactions and regionalization (see Table 3.1). The proliferation of elite interactions has been important in the building and upholding of the relative peace in the SCS and in the overarching Sino-ASEAN relations. Both the conflict-prevention and peace-building impacts have been high.

Table 3.1
Matrix of the Relative Importance of the Identified Processes

Type of process	The Relative	(Short Term) Conflict	(Long Term) Peace
Elite interactions	HIGH	HIGH	HIGH
Regionalization	HIGH	MODERATE	HIGH
The U.S. Role	MODERATE	LOW	MODERATE

This is the case despite regionalization being the most important process for peace building. The Sino-ASEAN and East Asian regionalization processes have been key to the relative peace, moving relations towards a stable peace between China and ASEAN. It is a concrete example of how negative relations are minimized by increasing the level of positive relations. In addition to its long-term impact, it has also been of moderate importance for conflict prevention.

Together, elite interaction and regionalization have successfully transformed the way China and ASEAN perceive and behave towards each other. The development of shared identities is seen most clearly in the identification with the ASEAN way and in the shared goal of transforming EII and the APT process into an East Asian community. The transformation of perceptions and behaviour is particularly obvious in the shifting view of China — from threat, to partner — by ASEAN and its members. The combination of "comprehensive engagement" by ASEAN and China's "soft power" approach with the aim of becoming accepted as a responsible regional power (including taking the interests of others into account and to accept multilateral engagement with its neighbours) has been highly important for the transformation of these perceptions. Here, the trust-building process is, in itself, a peace-building mechanism, as it increases positive relations and builds conditions for a stable peace. Moreover, it is also a mechanism for conflict prevention since the risk of quickly losing the trust it built at great length gives China a strong incentive to avoid actions that could be perceived as threatening by ASEAN. The transformed perceptions and behaviours, together with the shared identities, work as a structure. They define acceptable state behaviour, how behaviour and interests are to be communicated and legitimized, and what is within the realm of possible behaviour in the first place. In addition, as a result of the engagement, both parties' ability to cooperate has been substantially enhanced.

Lastly, the United States has been positive for the relative peace. The United States has been of moderate importance for peace building by generating a feeling of security in Southeast Asia, thereby creating space for ASEAN to engage China and vice versa. The United States has also created a framework for acceptable behaviour among the regional actors. However, the impact has been more limited in this case, as its commitment has been both narrow and ambiguous. Its overall conflict-preventive impact is assessed as low, as relations between the parties, with exceptions in the 1990s, have been at a level where their behaviour does not endanger U.S. interests. Together with the moderate peace-building impact, the United States has been of moderate importance for the relative peace. To argue that there would have been war without the United States is to overestimate its role, but its presence has been positive for the development of peaceful relations between China and ASEAN, including the relative peace in the SCS.

Notes

A version of this chapter has been published in *Asian Perspective* 34, no. 3, pp. 35–69. ("The South China Sea Conflict and Sino-ASEAN Relations: A Study in Conflict Prevention and Peace Building"). The author wishes to thank *Asian Perspective* for allowing re-publication.

1. Interview, Singapore, 7 December 2010.
2. Andrew Tanzer, "Asia's Next Flash Point?", *Forbes* 150, no. 10 (10 October 1992): 96–100.
3. See, Richard Betts, "Wealth, Power, and Instability: East Asia and the United States after the Cold War", *International Security* 18, no. 3 (1993): 34–77; Barry Buzan and Gerald Segal, "Rethinking East Asian Security", *Survival* 36, no. 2 (1994): 3–21; Aaron L. Friedberg, "Ripe for Rivalry: Prospects for Peace in a Multipolar Asia", *International Security* 18 (1994): 5–33; David C. Kang, "Acute Conflicts in Asia after the Cold War: Kashmir, Taiwan, and Korea", in *Asian Security Order: Instrumental and Normative Features*, edited by Muthiah Alagapp (Stanford: Stanford University Press, 2003); David C. Kang, "Getting Asia Wrong: The Need for New Analytical Frameworks", *International Security* 27, no. 4 (2003): 57–86; S. Peou, "Withering Realism? A Review of Recent Security Studies on the Asia-Pacific Region", *Pacific Affairs* 75, no. 4 (2002): 575–86.
4. Melvin Gurtov, *Pacific Asia? Prospects for Security and Cooperation in East Asia* (Lanham: Rowman & Littlefield, 2002), p. 191.
5. For an in-depth review of mainstream international relations theories, see Mikael Weissmann, *Understanding the East Asian Peace: Informal and Formal Conflict Prevention and Peacebuilding in the Taiwan Strait, the Korean Peninsula, and the South China Sea 1990–2008* (Gothenburg: Peace and Development Research, School of Global Studies, University of Gothenburg, 2009), chap. 2; Daojiong Zha and Weixing Hu, *Building a Neighborly Community: Post–Cold War China, Japan, and Southeast Asia* (Manchester: Manchester University Press, 2006), chap. 2.
6. Allen Carlson and J.J. Suh, "The Value of Rethinking East Asian Security: Denaturalising and Explaining a Complex Security Dynamic", in *Rethinking*

Security in East Asia: Identity, Power, and Efficiency, edited by J.J. Suh, Peter J. Katzenstein, and Allen Carlson (Stanford: Stanford University Press, 2004); Peter J. Katzenstein, "Introduction: Asian Regionalism in a Comparative Perspective", in *Network Power: Japan and Asia*, edited by Peter J. Katzenstein and Takashi Shiraishi (Ithaca, NY: Cornell University Press, 1997).

7. Lowell Dittmer, Haruhiro Fukui, and Peter Nan-Shong Lee, "Informal Politics in East Asia" (Cambridge: Cambridge University Press, 2000); Leung Kwok and Dean Tjosvold, eds., *Conflict Management in the Asia Pacific: Assumptions and Approaches in Diverse Cultures* (Singapore: John Wiley, 1998); Mikael Weissmann, "Informal Networks as a Conflict Preventive Mechanism", in *Conflict Prevention and Conflict Management in Northeast Asia*, edited by Niklas Swanström (Uppsala & Washington: Central Asia-Caucasus Institute & Silk Road Studies Program, 2005); Mikael Weissmann, "Peacebuilding in East Asia: The Role of Track 2 Diplomacy, Informal Networks, and Economic, Social, and Cultural Regionalisation", in *Conflict Management, Security and Intervention in East Asia: Third-Party Mediation in Regional Conflict*, edited by Jacob Bercovitch, Kwei-Bo Huang, and Chung-Chian Teng (London: Routledge, 2008).

8. Pierre Allan and Alexis Keller, eds., *What Is a Just Peace?* (Oxford: Oxford University Press, 2006), p. 111.

9. Michael Lund, *Preventing Violent Conflicts: A Strategy for Preventive Diplomacy* (Washington, DC: United States Institute of Peace Press, 1996), p. 39.

10. John Burton, *Conflict: Resolution and Provention* (Basingstoke: Macmillan, 1990), p. 3.

11. Interviews with strategic thinkers, Singapore, December 2010.

12. Clive Schofield and Ian Storey, *The South China Sea Dispute: Increasing Stakes and Rising Tensions* (Washington: Jamestown Foundation, 2009), p. 42.

13. Christian Caryl, "Panda-Hugger Hangover", *Foreign Policy* (2010).

14. Dewi Fortuna Anwar, "Between Asean, China and the United States", *Jakarta Post*, 30 August 2010.

15. Hasjim Djalal and Ian Townsend-Gault, "Managing Potential Conflicts in the South China Sea: Informal Diplomacy for Conflict Prevention", in *Herding Cats: Multiparty Mediation in a Complex World*, edited by Chester A. Crocker, Fen Osler Hampson, and Pamela Aall (Washington, DC: United States Institute of Peace Press, 1999), p. 121.

16. Hasjim Djalal, "Preventive Diplomacy and the South China Sea", in *The Next Stage: Preventive Diplomacy and Security Cooperation in the Asia-Pacific Region*, edited by Desmond Ball and Amitav Acharya (Canberra: Strategic and Defence Studies Centre, Research School of Pacific and Asian Studies, 1999), p. 195.

17. Hasjim Djalal, "The South China Sea: The Long Road Towards Peace and Cooperation", in *Security and International Politics in the South China Sea: Towards a Co-Operative Management Regime*, edited by Sam Bateman and Ralf Emmers (London: Routledge, 2009), pp. 179–82; Ian Townsend-Gault,

"The Contribution of the South China Sea Workshops: The Importance of a Functional Approach", in *Security and International Politics in the South China Sea: Towards a Co-Operative Management Regime*, edited by Sam Bateman and Ralf Emmers (London: Routledge, 2009).

18. After the original funder Canada cut its funding in 2001, it was decided at a special meeting in Jakarta in August 2001 to continue the workshops in an "informal, unofficial and track-two way, focusing on building confidence and cooperation while avoiding controversial, political and divisive issues"; Hasjim Djalal, "Managing Potential Conflicts in the South China Sea", in *Conflict Resolution and Peace Building: The Role of NGOs in Historical Reconciliation and Territorial Issues*, edited by So Ng-Ho Kang et al. (Seoul: Northeast Asian History Foundation, 2009), p. 77. Donations from government and non-governmental funders have funded these workshops. Since 2001, nine workshops have been organized on an annual basis, most recently in Bandung in November 2010. In practice, these workshops have mainly been a framework for technical cooperation.

19. Djalal and Townsend-Gault, "Managing Potential Conflicts", p. 117.

20. Townsend-Gault, "The Contribution of the South China Sea Workshops", pp. 195–96.

21. Djalal and Townsend-Gault, "Managing Potential Conflicts", p. 117.

22. Djalal, "Preventive Diplomacy and the South China Sea", p. 46.

23. Townsend-Gault, "The Contribution of the South China Sea Workshops".

24. Institute of Southeast Asian Studies, "Entering Unchartered Waters? ASEAN and the South China Sea Dispute (Conference Summary)" (Singapore: Institute of Southeast Asian Studies, 2011).

25. Interviews with strategic thinkers in China, Taipei, Hong Kong, South Korea, Japan, United Kingdom, Sweden, and Denmark, 2004–8.

26. Interviews, China: November 2004–January 2005, July 2006–June 2007, September 2007, July–December 2008; Taipei: March–May 2007; Hong Kong: December 2007; South Korea: February–March 2008; and Japan: March 2007.

27. Interview with senior member of a Chinese government think tank, Shanghai, China, 15 December 2006.

28. Interview, Shanghai, China, 15 December 2006.

29. Ibid.; cf. Gregory Chin and Richard Stubbs, "China, Regional Institution-Building and the China–Asean Free Trade Area", *Review of International Political Economy* (2010).

30. Ibid.

31. Interview with a senior member of a government think tank, Shanghai, China, 15 December 2006, and with a China expert, United Kingdom, 12 June 2008.

32. Paul Evans, "The Dialogue Process on Asia Pacific Security Issues: Inventory

and Analysis", *Studying Asia Pacific Security: The Future of Research, Training and Dialogue Activities* (Toronto: Joint Centre for Asia Pacific Studies, 1994): 297–318.

33. Data from Japan Centre for International Dialogue and Exchange, Research Monitor <http://www.jcie.or.jp/drm/> (accessed October 2010).

34. Interview with senior member of government think tank affiliated with a number of Track Two frameworks including NEAT and CSCAP, Shanghai, China, 12 May 2007. The same line of argumentation was raised in interviews with Track Two participants from East Asia as well as Europe.

35. Interviews with scholars with extensive experience from Track Two processes, Fudan University and Shanghai Institute of International Studies, Shanghai, China, 14–15 December 2006. This idea was also recurrent in the interviews conducted in China between November 2004 and December 2008 and in Singapore in December 2010.

36. Ralph A. Cossa, "Track Two Diplomacy: Promoting Regional Peace, Stability", *U.S. Foreign Policy Agenda* 3, no. 1 (1998): 54.

37. ASEAN Senior Officials, "The ASEAN Regional Forum: A Concept Paper", p. 113, quoted in Desmond Ball, *The Council for Security Cooperation in the Asia Pacific: Its Record and Its Prospects* (Canberra: Strategic and Defence Centre, Research School of Pacific and Asian Studies, Australian National University, 2000), p. 48.

38. Sheldon W. Simon, "Evaluating Track II Approaches to Security Diplomacy in the Asia-Pacific: The Cscap Experience", *Pacific Review* 15, no. 2 (2002): 167–200.

39. Interview, United Kingdom, January 2008.

40. Interview, Singapore, 7 December 2010.

41. David Shambaugh, "China Engages Asia: Reshaping the Regional Order", *International Security* 29, no. 3 (2004/5): 64–99.

42. David C. Kang, *China Rising: Peace, Power, and Order in East Asia* (New York: Columbia University Press, 2007), p. 274; Allen S. Whiting, "Asean Eyes China: The Security Dimension", *Asian Survey* 37, no. 4 (1997): 299–322.

43. See, e.g., Alice D. Ba, "China and ASEAN: Renavigating Relations for a 21st-Century Asia", *Asian Survey* 43, no. 4 (2003): 622–47; Ren Xiao, "Between Adapting and Shaping: China's Role in Asian Regional Cooperation", *Journal of Contemporary China* 18, no. 59 (2009): 303–20.

44. Interview with strategic thinker, Hong Kong, China, December 2006.

45. Ibid.

46. Xiao, "Between Adapting and Shaping", p. 304.

47. Interview with member of government think tank, Shanghai, China, 15 December 2006.

48. Interview with member of government think tank, Shanghai, China, December 2006.

49. Shaun Breslin, "Comparative Theory, China, and the Future of East Asian Regionalism(s)", *Review of International Studies* 36, no. 3 (2010): 709–29. Also see Alice D. Ba, "Who's Socialising Whom? Complex Engagement in Sino-ASEAN Relations", *Pacific Review* 19, no. 2 (2006): 157–79.

50. Interview with senior scholar, Fudan University, Shanghai, China, 14 December 2006.

51. Ibid.

52. Robert O. Keohane, *International Institutions and State Power: Essays in International Relations Theory* (Boulder, CO: Westview, 1989), p. 3.

53. Steven L. Lamy, "Neo-Realism and Neo-Liberalism", in *The Globalisation of World Politics*, 2nd ed., edited by John Baylis and Steve Smith (Oxford: Oxford University Press, 2001), p. 189.

54. Zha and Hu, *Building a Neighborly Community*, p. 133.

55. Keohane, *International Institutions and State Power*, p. 3.

56. Lamy, "Neo-Realism and Neo-Liberalism", p. 189.

57. Interviews with senior experts on East Asian security from Beijing, Shanghai, Hong Kong, and Singapore, Beijing: July 2006–June 2007; Shanghai: November–December 2006, May 2007; Hong Kong: December 2006.

58. Zha and Hu, *Building a Neighborly Community*, pp. 121–22.

59. Ali Alatas, *"ASEAN Plus Three" Equals Peace Plus Prosperity* (Singapore: Institute of Southeast Asian Studies, 2001).

60. Liao Shaolian, "China-Asean Economic Relations: Progress and Prospects", in *Harmony and Development: ASEAN-China Relations*, edited by Hongyi Lai and Tin Seng Lim (Singapore: World Scientific, 2007), pp. 139–44; John Wong and Sarah Chan, "China-ASEAN Free Trade Agreement: Shaping Future Economic Relations", *Asian Survey* 43, no. 3 (2003): 507–26.

61. See, Chin and Stubbs, "China, Regional Institution-Building".

62. Zha and Hu, *Building a Neighborly Community*, pp. 181–89.

63. Zhenjiang Zhang, "ASEAN-China Relations and Development of East Asian Regionalism", in *Harmony and Development: ASEAN-China Relations*, edited by Hongyi Lai and Tin Seng Lim (Singapore: World Scientific, 2007): 92–95.

64. Interview with member of government think tank, Shanghai, China, 15 December 2006.

65. Ibid.

66. Interview, Hong Kong, China, December 2006.

67. Interview with East Asian expert, United Kingdom, 10 January 2008.

68. Interviews with strategic thinkers in China: November 2004–January 2005, July 2006–June 2007, September 2007, July–December 2008; Taipei: March–May 2007; Hong Kong: December 2007; South Korea: February–March 2008; United Kingdom: October 2007–June 2008; Singapore: December 2010.

69. Interview with East Asian security expert, United Kingdom, 8 November 2008.

70. Ian Storey, *The United States and ASEAN-China Relations: All Quiet on the Southeast Asian Front* (Carlisle Barracks, PA: Strategic Studies Institute, U.S. Army War College, 2007).

71. Timo Kivimäki, Liselotte Odgaard, and Stein Tonnesson, "What Could Be Done?", in *War or Peace in the South China Sea?*, edited by Timo Kivimäki (Copenhagen: NIAS Press, 2002): 131–64; Liselotte Odgaard and Stein Tønnesson, "Potentials for Containing Violence: Deterrence and Codes of Conduct", in *Territorial Disputes in the South China Sea. A Report to the Finnish Foreign Ministry*, edited by Timo Kivimäki (Helsinki & Copenhagen: CTS-Conflict Transformation Service, 2001).

72. Breslin, "Comparative Theory, China, and the Future of East Asian Regionalism(s)", p. 725.

Part Two
ASEAN's View on the South China Sea

4

ASEAN CLAIMANTS' POSITION IN THE SOUTH CHINA SEA

Hasjim Djalal

The long road towards peace and cooperation in the South China Sea (SCS) started back in the late 1980s. This was after several decades of disputes and confrontation that began soon after the end of World War II when countries around the SCS first started making claims to sovereignty over features within the sea. In the late 1980s and before the conclusion of the Cambodian war through the 1991 Paris Peace Agreement, I recognized that prospects for peace and cooperation may finally have come to Southeast Asia, although there was still potential for worrying developments and conflicts in the SCS.

The countries around the SCS have a long history of confrontation and very little experience of cooperation. Armed clashes between China and Vietnam have occurred primarily in 1974 with the latest in 1988. Multiple territorial claims to islands existed, as well as claims to national maritime zones of jurisdiction, particularly in and around the Spratly Islands group. The island disputes were bilateral, trilateral or even, in some instances, multilateral. The rapid economic development of the countries around the SCS, particularly China, led to a scramble for the natural resources of the SCS, both living and non-living.

Strategic issues were also at stake. The strategic significance of the SCS to non-littoral countries could not be ignored. The sea-lines of communications through the area are significant both for the region and for world trade and the global economy. Consideration needed also to be given to increasing problems of pollution and the safety of navigation as well as to the protection of the marine environment and fragile marine ecosystems.

Then there were the political factors that inhibited the process of cooperation. The SCS is surrounded by countries that are vastly different from one another, in land size, population, per capita income, employment in fisheries, fish catch and consumption of fish per capita. Political systems also markedly varied from the communist/socialist countries of the northern littoral, namely China and Vietnam, to the non-communist southern and eastern insular countries (Malaysia, Singapore, Indonesia, the Philippines, and Brunei Darussalam). There was also the complicating factor of Taiwan/Chinese Taipei as a claimant. An important geographical fact is that the insular countries control maritime approaches to and from the coasts of the mainland SCS countries.

THE INTERESTS OF MAJOR POWERS

The SCS is one of the most strategic waterways in the world. The approaches to the SCS, especially the Straits of Malacca-Singapore, Sunda-Karimata, Balabac, Mindoro, Bashi, and Taiwan Straits are located in non-communist countries. These approaches are important for the passage of military and commercial vessels, including and especially oil tankers. The Soviet Union, and now the Russian Federation, placed great importance on the right of "transit passage" through the Malacca and Singapore Straits, as well as through the surrounding waters in the SCS area, primarily because these passages were important for communication between western and eastern Russia through the warm waters of the South Seas.

For Japan, the SCS and its approaches, especially the Straits of Malacca and Singapore, are extremely important since more than eighty per cent of its oil imports are transported through these waterways. These waterways are also extremely important to Japanese trade with Southeast Asia, South Asia, Africa, the Middle East and Europe. Japanese interest in the preservation of peace and cooperation in the SCS may increase as the result of its new orientation and increasingly intensive economic, trade and investment relations with the Association of Southeast Asian Nations (ASEAN), South Asian and Middle-Eastern countries.

The United States has always been interested in the area because it offers the shortest route from the Pacific to the Indian Ocean, and because it is essential for the movement of U.S. fleets, both for its own global strategy or for defending its allies in the region. The United States also has large trade, economic and investment relations with the countries around the SCS. In May 1995, the United States Department of State announced the American policies on the South China Sea which basically were as follows:

1. The United States urges peaceful settlement of the issue by the states involved in a manner that enhances regional peace, prosperity and security;
2. The United States strongly opposes the threat or use of military force to assert any nation's claim in the South China Sea, and would view any such use as a serious matter;
3. The United States takes no position on the legal merits of competing sovereignty claims and is willing to help in the peaceful resolution of competing claims if requested by the parties;
4. The United States has a strategic interest in maintaining maritime line of communication in the region and considers it essential to resist any maritime claims beyond those permitted by the United Nations Convention on the Law of the Sea;
5. The United States strongly supports multilateral security dialogue and, in particular, Indonesia's ongoing effort to develop a peaceful solution to the South China Sea disputes, and urges all involved to work diligently within the framework provided by Indonesia.[1]

CONFLICTING TERRITORIAL AND JURISDICTIONAL CLAIMS

Both China and Vietnam claim territorial sovereignty over the Paracel group of islands situated southeast of Hainan. It was occupied by the former regime of South Vietnam until China took it by force in 1974. Vietnam still maintains a claim over the islands in spite of its occupation by China. Both China and Vietnam rely on historical records to support their respective territorial claims to the Paracels. Except for its possible impact on the situation in the SCS as a whole, the Paracels are generally regarded as a bilateral matter between China and Vietnam.

The Spratly Islands are the main source of territorial dispute. Some of the islands, rocks, and reefs in the group are presently occupied by Vietnam (22), the Philippines (11), China (14), Malaysia (10) and Taiwan (1). Brunei Darussalam claims certain portions of the nearby sea as its exclusive economic zone (EEZ) or continental shelf but does not occupy any feature.

China claims the South China Sea islands for historical reasons. It has also based its claim on a map produced in 1947 by the Republic of China, indicating nine undefined, discontinued and dashed lines. This claim was renewed in 1958 in which China proclaimed a twelve-nautical-miles territorial sea and declared that "no foreign vessels for military use and no foreign aircraft may enter China's territorial sea and the airspace above it without the permission of the government of the PRC".[2] China claims all the features encompassed by those nine undefined and dashed lines, although it began to occupy some of them only recently. There was no definition of those dashed lines, nor were their coordinates stated. Therefore the legality and the precise locations indicated by these lines are not clear. It was presumed, however, that China's claim, at least initially, was limited to the islands, the rocks, and perhaps the reefs, but not the whole sea enclosed by those nine undefined dashed lines. Some recent Chinese writers seem to imply that China also claims the "adjacent sea" of the islands and rocks, but again the concept of "adjacent sea" has not been clearly defined.

Taiwan's claim in the South China Sea was basically similar to that of China. The Chinese claim was originally described in the Taiwanese/ Kuomintang (KMT) map of 1947. Therefore, the positions of the participants from China and Taiwan in the SCS Workshops were sometimes very similar. Taiwan has occupied Itu Aba, the largest island in the group, since 1956.

Vietnam's claim is also basically historical. It claims the Paracel Islands as well as the whole Spratly group together with all its continental shelf. Again, the boundary lines of the claim are not clearly identified, either by description or by coordinates. The claim also covers quite an extensive area of the South China Sea, and Vietnam has also occupied a considerable number of features.

The Philippines' claim is based on the so-called "proximity" principle and "discovery" of the islands concerned by a Philippine explorer Thomas Cloma in the 1950s. Unlike the Chinese claim, the Philippine claim clearly defines the coordinates and therefore is quite identifiable. However, the coordinates are not measured from base-points on land, but from fixed positions at sea. The Philippines has also occupied a number of islands and rocks.

The Malaysian claim is primarily based on the continental shelf principle and is clearly defined by coordinates. It occupies islands that it considers to be situated on its continental shelf. Equally, Brunei's claim seems to have been based also on the principle of EEZ and continental shelf, although the boundary lines are drawn almost parallel from, and are the continuation of, two points at sea at the hundred fathoms depth contour that were announced in 1958 by the British as the continental shelf boundaries between Brunei and Sarawak and North Borneo (Sabah).

All or most of these claims overlap with one another and some of them with several other claims. All the claimants, with the exception of Brunei, have occupied several rocks and reefs. There is no clear pattern of occupation. Some Chinese occupations have been quite far to the south. The significance of the various conflicting claims is very clear. It is basically a scramble for space and resources, either living or oil and gas, which are believed to be abundant in the area. Exploration efforts are continuing for oil and gas and fishery resources are being exploited. Conflicts have arisen in the past and may arise again in the future.

INDONESIAN INITIATIVE

Indonesia is not a claimant to any islands or rocks in the Spratly group. But if the Chinese/Taiwanese dashed lines of 1947 are taken into consideration and continuously connected, then the Chinese/Taiwanese claims could also intrude upon Indonesia's EEZ and continental shelf as defined in the 1982 United Nations Law of the Sea Convention (UNCLOS), and as demarcated in the Indonesian-Malaysian Agreement of 1969 and Indonesian-Vietnam Agreement of 2003. China, however, has assured Indonesia that it does not have any maritime boundary problems with Indonesia in the South China Sea.

Indonesia took the initiative to try to manage the potential conflicts in the area and to promote actual cooperation among the claimants. Indonesia saw that the end of the Indochina War in 1989–90 provided the opportunity to transform an environment of bickering and confrontation into one of cooperation. When the end of the Cambodian conflict was in sight in 1990, ASEAN and Indochina seemed ready for economic development and cooperative relations. Development efforts needed peace, stability and cooperation. The countries of Indochina later joined ASEAN. However, with regard to the SCS, it was essential to seek ways and means of preventing potential conflicts from erupting into armed conflagration.

I thought that a sense of community in the South China Sea area should be developed. There was the basis of cooperation in UNCLOS, especially in the EEZ regime (Articles 61–67) and the "Enclosed or Semi Enclosed Seas" concepts as stipulated in Article 122 and 123. Article 123 stated that:

> States bordering an enclosed or semi-enclosed sea should cooperate with each other in the exercise of their rights and in the performance of their duties under this Convention. To this end they shall endeavour, directly or through an appropriate regional organisation: 1) to co-ordinate the management, conservation, exploration and exploitation of the living resources of the sea 2) to co-ordinate the implementation of their rights and duties with respect to the protection and preservation of the marine environment 3) to co-ordinate their scientific research policies and undertake where appropriate joint programmes of scientific research in the area, and 4) to invite, as appropriate, other interested states or international organisations to co-operate with them in furtherance of the provisions of this article.

It was difficult at that time to see whether ASEAN had a perspective on SCS. However, there was a strong conviction in Indonesia and in ASEAN that we should concentrate on promoting development, particularly economic development, as well as the ASEAN and Southeast Asian principles of resilience and cohesiveness. We did not want to see a repeat of the disturbances that had occurred before in Southeast Asia and in the SCS area.

At the same time, the issues of the Paracels and the Spratlys were attracting attention and posing a threat to Southeast Asian stability. I had developed contact with Professor Ian Townsend-Gault of the University of British Columbia in Vancouver who was willing to seek Canadian support to help manage potential conflicts in the South China Sea informally if the countries around the SCS were interested. The Canadian International Development Agency (CIDA) was later willing to support all the meetings. The South China Sea Informal Working Group (SCS-IWG) was established in Vancouver and the Centre for Southeast Asian Studies, which I had established and directed in Jakarta, would collaborate and help develop the agenda for the meeting, prepare background papers, and arrange for the participation of "resource persons".

In view of this, at the end of 1989 I travelled around the ASEAN capitals to find out what we could do together about the SCS within the context of preventive diplomacy. For that purpose, I prepared a basic working paper. Out of this trip, I found out that:

1. Practically everybody thought that we should do something;
2. There was apprehension that territorial disputes could pose major difficulties in developing cooperative efforts;
3. In view of difficult and sensitive territorial issues, it would be better if the approach were informal, at least at the initial stage; and
4. There was a notion that ASEAN members should coordinate their views and positions first before they engaged non-ASEAN states in such efforts.

Consequently, I felt that regardless of the territorial disputes, we should always try to find ways to manage potential conflict and to find an area or areas in which everyone could agree to cooperate, no matter how small or how insignificant it might seem. We should be guided by the idea that despite potential conflict, there was always an opportunity for cooperation. At that time, I had three basic objectives:

1. To manage the potential conflicts by seeking an area in which everyone could cooperate;
2. To develop confidence-building measures or processes so that the various claimants would be comfortable with one another, thus providing a conducive atmosphere for the solution of their territorial or jurisdictional disputes; and
3. To exchange views through dialogue on the issues involved in order to increase mutual understanding.

It would be a major achievement for the region to work together to transform the habit of confrontation into a habit of cooperation. This could be achieved sooner if we had programmes designed to achieve it. Therefore, it was important to find a common denominator, no matter how slow the process might be or how small was the result at the beginning. Patience was important then as it still is today.

THE WORKSHOP PROCESS

Despite many concerns and reservations at that time, all of us in ASEAN agreed to try to manage the potential conflicts in the SCS and to convert them as much as possible to cooperation. We all agreed informally to come to the First Workshop on the South China Sea in Bali in 1990. This was basically a meeting among ASEAN participants only. The following areas were identified for discussion at the first meeting: (1) territorial and sovereignty issues, (2) political and security issues, (3) marine scientific research and environmental protection, (4) safety of navigation, (5) resource management, and (6) institutional mechanisms for cooperation. We also discussed whether and how to include other non-ASEAN countries in the discussion on the South China Sea, particularly Vietnam, China, Taiwan (Chinese Taipei), Laos and Cambodia. The workshop was acknowledged as a platform for policy-oriented discussions, not only for an academic exchange of views.

Each ASEAN country was asked to prepare a specific paper and to take a leading role in discussions. Malaysia was to lead the discussion on territorial and sovereignty issues; Singapore on political and security issues; Indonesia on marine scientific research and environmental protection; the Philippines on safety of navigation; Thailand on resource management; and Brunei Darussalam on institutional mechanisms for cooperation. Since this was the first exploratory meeting, there was no statement issued at the end of the meeting, although informal records were prepared by the organizer.

The first workshop laid the groundwork and it was apparent that there were quite a few areas where participants were prepared to cooperate. In preparing the second workshop, I thought that China and Taiwan should be included as they have claims in the SCS and also occupied some features in the area. But it was not easy at that time to bring China into the discussion, primarily because China considered that the SCS issues should not be "regionalized" or "internationalized", and that China would discuss whatever problems it had directly and bilaterally with the countries concerned. In China's view, its claims to sovereignty over the SCS islands were "indisputable". In addition, it would be difficult for China to sit down with Taiwan in international meetings like the South China Sea Workshop if these were "formal" meetings. But, by the second workshop in Bandung in 1991, it had become an all inclusive group; not only Vietnam and China were invited and participated but also Taiwan. Even landlocked Laos was invited. Cambodia was invited later after the political situation there became clearer.

Thus, by the second workshop in Bandung in February 1991, we were able to bring China, Vietnam, Laos, and Chinese Taipei into the workshop process. The Bandung meeting went into more detail with the topics mentioned above, including the problems of sovereignty over the Spratlys and the Paracels, the roles of major non-SCS powers in the region, as well as confidence-building measures. More technical discussions took place on marine scientific research, marine environmental protection, safety of navigation, and on resource management. Some ideas to establish a secretariat as well as to formalize the meeting were mentioned. More significantly, the participants attending the Bandung meeting agreed to issue a statement saying that the SCS disputes should be settled peacefully, that force shall not be used to settle the disputes, and that the parties to the disputes shall exercise restraint in order not to exacerbate the potential conflicts. This statement was a precursor to a much more formal ASEAN Declaration on the South China Sea in Manila in July 1992, which provided guiding principles for efforts to manage potential conflicts in the SCS through cooperation.

By the third workshop in Yogyakarta in 1992, more specific discussions took place on the various topics. By this time, I felt that devising cooperative projects would have to be worked out in more detail by specific Technical Working Groups (TWGs) and Group of Experts Meetings (GEMs). Thus, the meeting in Yogyakarta agreed to establish two TWGs, namely the TWG on Marine Scientific Research and the TWG on Resources Assessment. Some participants continued to consider that it was necessary to establish a secretariat for the workshop process as well as to formalize the process. There was no consensus to establish a secretariat because many participants were not yet willing to institutionalize or formalize the process. In addition, there were also many technical reasons for not establishing the secretariat. It was generally felt that the Centre for Southeast Asian Studies (Pusat Studi Kawasan Asia Tenggara) in Jakarta should continue to be the focal point for the workshop process.

With regard to formalizing the workshop process, some countries also had difficulties, particularly China, primarily due to its problem in sitting down with Taiwan/Chinese Taipei in a formal process. Thus, the informal set-up of the workshop process was a necessity and perhaps the only possibility for bringing in China and Chinese Taipei together. Moreover, it was generally thought that discussions and ideas could flow more freely in an informal process. In a more formal meeting participants would be extremely constrained by the policies of their respective governments.

The fourth workshop in Surabaya in 1993 discussed the participation of non-SCS countries. It agreed that non-SCS participation would be allowed on a case-by-case basis to implement specific agreed programmes of cooperation. In the meantime, the TWG–Marine Scientific Research (MSR) had already begun discussions in Manila and the TWG–Resources Assessment (RA) had been convened in Jakarta. The Surabaya meeting discussed the results and recommendations of the two TWG meetings and agreed to convene a follow-up meeting of the TWG-MSR in Singapore. It also agreed to establish the TWG–Marine Environmental Protection (MEP) and the TWG–Legal Matters (LM) and discussed the possibility of establishing the TWG–Safety of Navigation, Shipping and Communication (SNSC). Finally, the participants also indicated that the workshop series had reached a stage where it would have to concretize programmes or projects to realize cooperative efforts through a step-by-step approach.

The fifth workshop in Bukittinggi in 1994 approved some specific projects, which had been formulated by the Technical Working Groups, particularly a programme for cooperation on the study and conservation of biodiversity in the SCS. The Bukittinggi Workshop also agreed, among others, to authorize me to seek support and funding for the project proposal on biodiversity; to convene another meeting of the TWG on Marine Scientific Research to finalize proposals on sea level and tide monitoring, and on a database, information exchange and networking; and to convene the first meeting of the TWG on Legal Matters in Thailand. The workshop also further discussed confidence-building measures, including discussion in detail on the need for non-expansion of existing military presence in the South China Sea.

The sixth workshop in Balikpapan in 1995 approved the two project proposals drawn-up by the TWG on Marine Scientific Research, namely "study on tides and sea level change" and "regional cooperation in the field of marine science data and information network in the SCS". The participants also agreed to forward these project proposals to their respective authorities for their consideration and support in their implementation. I was asked to solicit support from various sources for these projects.

The seventh workshop in Batam in 1996 further discussed the problems of implementing the agreed project proposals. Since 1995 there have been some difficulties in implementation, not only because of the financial problems but also because of political issues. Practically all the countries in the SCS have indicated a willingness to participate in the implementation of the agreed programmes either in providing expertise, facilities or some financial assistance. But China believed that the implementation of the agreed programmes should be left to national institutions alone, particularly due to the sensitive nature of the issues dealing with territorial and sovereignty claims. It was only at the eighth workshop meeting in Pacet, Puncak, in December 1997, that the participants agreed to jointly implement the agreed programmes for cooperation. I was asked to continue to approach various international, regional and national agencies, governmental or non-governmental, to support the implementation of the agreed programmes.

The ninth workshop in Ancol, Jakarta, in 1998, continued discussion on implementing the agreed projects. A representative of the United Nations Environmental Programme (UNEP) indicated to the meeting that UNEP could help with the implementation of some components of the Biodiversity Project. The meeting also continued discussion on the Code of Conduct for the South China Sea. On the safety of navigation, the participants agreed to recommend to their respective authorities to consider ratification of the Rome Convention on the Suppression of Unlawful Acts Against the Safety of Maritime Navigation, 1988, of the International Convention on Civil Liability for Oil Pollution Damage, 1992, of the International Convention on the Establishment of International Fund for Compensation for Oil Pollution Damage, 1992, and of the International Convention on Oil Spill Pollution and Preparedness, Response and Co-operation, 1990.

The tenth workshop in Bogor in 1999 noted that the atmosphere of cooperation had improved, despite some difficulties. The workshop also discussed and endorsed the recommendations of the various meetings of the TWGs and GEMs. The issues of the formulation of the Code of Conduct for the South China Sea and the issues of implementation, as well as linkages with other activities, continued to be the subjects of discussion. In order to avoid difficulties with regard to implementation of a biodiversity expedition in the South China Sea, it was agreed to conduct the expedition in and around the undisputed Indonesian islands of Anambas.

The eleventh workshop was held in Cengkareng in March 2001. This meeting, while discussing and endorsing the reports and recommendations of the various TWGs and GEMs, was also confronted with the decision of Canada, for reasons unknown to us, not to extend its financial support to the workshop process beyond the current support (early 2001). In view of this situation, the 11th Workshop decided unanimously to make all efforts to continue the process and to hold a Special Meeting to explore various options to continue the process.

The Special Meeting, which took place in Jakarta in August 2001, agreed to continue the workshop activities in an informal, unofficial and Track Two way, focusing on building confidence and cooperation while avoiding controversial, political and divisive issues. The workshop could continue to be held in Indonesia, but if Indonesia is not in the position to hold such a workshop, it could be held in other places, at the expense of the host authorities concerned. With regard to funding, the workshop process should seek voluntary donations from participating authorities, voluntary donations from the non-governmental organizations, foundations or private companies from the SCS region, and voluntary donations from the non-governmental organizations, foundations or private companies from outside the SCS region, provided no political conditions were attached. It was also decided that the workshop process should function more as a think-tank group and should develop implementable projects, taking into account the limited availability of financial and human resources. They also agreed to recommend the establishment of a Special Fund to be administered by Pusat Studi Asia Tenggara (the Centre for Southeast Asian Studies) in Jakarta.

In the meantime, the Anambas Expedition to study biodiversity in the South China Sea was conducted on 11–22 March 2002, financed by voluntary contributions from the participants. The expedition discovered a number of previously unknown marine species. The scientific results of the expedition were published in the *Raffles Bulletin of Zoology* in Singapore in March 2004.

The twelfth workshop in Jakarta in October 2002 agreed to continue efforts to manage the potential conflict in the SCS and to implement agreed projects by their own means and with voluntary support from various sources. They also agreed to establish the Special Fund for this purpose.

The thirteenth workshop was held in Medan in September 2003. It discussed the preparation for the Palawan Biodiversity Expedition as a continuation of the Anambas Expedition. It continued discussion on the Database Information Exchange and Networking (coordinated by China),

Sea Level and Tide Monitoring Project (coordinated by Indonesia), and Training Programme for Marine Ecosystem Monitoring (coordinated by the Philippines). It was agreed to revise the projects in the light of comments by participants. The workshop discussed further the development of the Special Fund.

The fourteenth workshop held in Batam in November 2004 reviewed the projects so far planned, namely (1) Marine Science Data and Information Networking, (2) Biodiversity Studies, (3) Study of Tides and Sea Level Change, (4) Training Programme for Marine Ecosystem Monitoring, (5) Training Programme for Seafarers, (6) Fisheries Stocks Assessments, (7) Hydrographic Survey, and (8) Search and Rescue and Illegal Acts at Sea including Piracy and Armed Robbery at Sea.

China reported that it had convened a working group meeting in Hainan in September 2004 to discuss the Marine Database Programme and, in light of the discussion, had revised the programme. The workshop decided to endorse the revised proposal and requested China to continue with the preparation to implement the project. With regard to the Palawan Biodiversity expedition, the Philippines informed the workshop that it has changed the implementation of the expedition from a Track Two activity to a Track One activity and had widened the area of the expedition to also include Luzon. This announcement created problems, and the workshop decided not to continue discussion on this matter since Track One activity was outside the purview of the workshop. As it turned out, some participants later withdrew their participation in the Luzon-Palawan expedition. The workshop also asked Indonesia to continue with the preparation for the study of sea level rise and asked Malaysia to initiate works on cooperation with regard to search and rescue. At this occasion, Chinese Taipei proposed the establishment of SEAONE for training purposes to promote ocean science research. China had difficulties with this proposal and, due to lack of consensus, the proposal was not discussed further, noting that Chinese Taipei could initiate the programme itself by inviting all other participants to make use of it.

The fifteenth workshop was held in Anyer, Banten, in November 2005. The workshop discussed and endorsed the results of the TWG meeting on the Database Information Exchange and Networking project, held in Tianjin, China, on 11–12 October 2005. The workshop also discussed and endorsed the result of the TWG meeting on the Study of Tides and Sea Level Change and their impact on coastal environments in the SCS, held in Anyer, Banten, Indonesia, on 22–23 November 2005, and agreed to begin its implementation. All participants acknowledged the importance of the workshop process as a confidence-building measure and a preventive diplomacy mechanism which was still relevant to the current situation. In addition, after the implementation of the biodiversity project in Anambas (and later in Palawan), it encouraged China, Chinese Taipei, the Philippines, and Vietnam to consider the possibility of conducting biodiversity expeditions that will include the northeast and northwest areas of the South China Sea in order to complete the picture of biodiversity in the SCS as a whole.

The sixteenth workshop was held in Bali in November 2006. It discussed regional cooperation in the field of marine science and information, and China undertook to organize a technical training course on constructing a website and sub-website with data on the SCS area. Equally, Indonesia was continuing its preparation for cooperation on the study of sea level change and the coastal environment in the SCS affected by potential climate change. The participation of certain authorities, as in the 15th Workshop, was already covered by the Special Fund which was established in 2004.

The seventeenth workshop was held in Yogyakarta in November 2007. It discussed the various programmes, particularly regarding the impact of global climate change on the South China Sea. It was agreed that the workshop process is still relevant to maintain peace, stability, and cooperation in the region and it shall remain informal, with participants attending the workshop in their personal capacities, and that the workshop will continue to work on the basis of consensus.

The eighteenth workshop was held in November 2008 in Menado, North Sulawesi, Indonesia. An important achievement of this workshop was an agreement by China and Chinese Taipei to work out a joint proposal on the training and education programme on ocean and maritime issues among the South China Sea Workshop participants. This joint proposal was submitted and agreed at the nineteenth workshop in Makassar in November 2009. This first part of the joint programme was implemented by Chinese Taipei in 2010 and the result of the training programme was reported to the twentieth workshop in Bandung in November 2010. China would implement the second part of the joint programme in 2011.

A new issue, however, came into the picture in the form of conflicting submissions to the Continental Shelf Commission of the limit to the continental margin in the South China Sea by Vietnam, Malaysia and the

Philippines. The Vietnamese and Malaysian submissions were criticized by China and the Philippines, whilst the Philippines submission was primarily criticized by Malaysia. At the same time, a more assertive Chinese policy in the South China Sea also raised some concern among ASEAN countries.

DIALOGUE BETWEEN THE PARTIES

We have also encouraged more discussions and dialogues among parties to the territorial disputes to find the basis for a solution that would be acceptable to all concerned. The bilateral dialogue between China and the Philippines in August 1995 produced an eight-point code of conduct between them. Similarly, bilateral dialogue between Vietnam and the Philippines has also produced a nine-point code of conduct, which in many respects was similar to the China and the Philippines code of conduct. I understand there has also been dialogue between China with Vietnam and Malaysia, and between Malaysia and other claimants, although the dialogues have not led specifically to bilateral codes of conduct.

In this context it is encouraging to note the signing of bilateral agreements between China and Vietnam on 25 December 2000 regarding the maritime boundaries between the two countries in the Gulf of Tonkin, covering the boundaries of their respective territorial seas, EEZs, and continental shelves, and another Agreement on Fishing Cooperation in the Gulf. There is no agreement yet, however, regarding the delimitation of contiguous zones between the two countries. The Fishing Cooperation Agreement is interesting because it establishes a "common fishing area", or some kind of "joint development zone" in the gulf and a "buffer zone" for small fishing boats. The agreement also covers the right of passage of Vietnamese vessels through the Qiangzhou Strait between Hainan and mainland China, which China so far has always regarded as part of its internal waters.

Equally interesting, on the same day, the Foreign Ministers of the two countries signed a Joint Statement regarding relations between the two countries, which is tantamount to a bilateral code of conduct. In the statement, the two sides recalled their "time-honoured traditional friendship", comprehensive cooperation, mutual trust, equality and mutual benefits between them. They reaffirmed that they will follow the guidelines and principles of the United Nations Charter, the five principles of peaceful coexistence, and the principles of international relations, independence, sovereignty, full equality, mutual respect and non-interference. They agreed to regularly hold high-level meetings, exchange visits, and continue to broaden cooperation in economic, commercial, scientific and technical cooperation. They also agreed to strengthen cooperation and coordination at multilateral, regional and international forums, to carry out multilevel military exchanges and expand cooperation in the security field, as well as many other areas of cooperation.

Specifically on maritime issues, and apparently with the disputes in the SCS in mind, the two countries will continue to seek everlasting solutions acceptable to both sides through peaceful negotiation. Pending that solution, the two sides "will not take action to complicate or aggravate disputes, nor will they resort to force or threat of force". They will consult each other "in a timely manner in case of disputes and adopt a cool and constructive attitude to handle them properly in order not to allow disputes to impede the normal development of bilateral ties".

It appears that in formulating any code of conduct, several elements should be included, such as (1) Peaceful settlement of disputes, (2) Prohibition against the use of force or threats of force, (3) The exercise of self-restraint, (4) Development of confidence-building measures (CBMs), (5) Cooperation, (6) Consultation, (7) Transparency, (8) Respect for international law and freedom of navigation in the South China Sea, and (9) The area of application of the code.

At this moment, it appears that ASEAN countries would like to elevate the status of the Declaration of Conduct into a more legally binding instrument than simply a non-binding "declaration".

JOINT DEVELOPMENT CONCEPT

One of the most important issues in the South China Sea was the question of joint development (JD) or joint cooperation (JC). I personally supported this approach in overcoming the territorial problems. We even formed a Special Technical Working Group on Resources Assessment and Ways of Development (TWG-RA) to deal with this topic and the TWG met twice in Jakarta in July 1993 and in 1999. The TWG-RA also established an SG to better understand the concept, and this SG had met twice in Vientiane in June 1998 and in Tabanan, Bali in July 1999.

The TWG-RA agreed that JD had excellent potential and that we should study the various concepts or models of joint development around the world in order to learn from them what could be applied to the SCS. I believed the concept should be formulated with agreement on at least four points:

1. The "zone" where the joint development will take place;
2. The "nature", the "subject" or the "topics" of the cooperation (fisheries, minerals, gas, oil, environment, marine scientific research, marine parks, etc.);
3. The "mechanism" for such joint development, which could be an authority or a loose coordinative organization or arrangement; and
4. "Who" shall participate in such joint-development or joint-cooperation activities: governments, companies or corporations.

These four points, it seemed to me, were the sine qua non of joint development. In 1996 I suggested several principles for joint development and attempted to find out and define the "zone" where every participant, at least those having overlapping claims, could cooperate on the basis of UNCLOS. Theoretically this was that part of the SCS beyond 200 miles from undisputed coastlines or islands — the so-called "donut hole". On the basis of various comments and reactions by participants, I submitted a revised proposal in 1998 to the participants directly concerned, which in essence reduced the zone and the number of possible participants. For some reasons, discussion of the JD or JC concept stalled in the workshop. However, some bilateral agreements have been reached on joint development, such as between Malaysia and Thailand and between Malaysia and Vietnam in the Gulf of Siam, and between China and Vietnam in the Gulf of Tonkin.

CONCLUSION

Preventive Diplomacy

In view of our experience with developing cooperation to promote preventive diplomacy in the SCS, some conditions for successful efforts would seem to be:

1. Realization by the parties to the disputes that conflict, especially armed conflict, will not settle the disputes and will not bring benefits

to any/either party; in fact they only bring mutual damage or loss to the parties. I feel that the parties to the disputes in the SCS are now aware of this.

2. Political will is required to settle the disputes peacefully and to prevent the disputes escalating into armed conflicts. The parties must realize that their interests lie in finding a solution to the disputes rather than in prolonging them. I feel that we still have to do a lot to strengthen political will, although some progress has been made.

3. The parties should not legislate any territorial claims, especially in areas where claims are clearly disputed. Legislating territorial claims and seeking support through public opinion tends to harden the position of all sides and makes it more difficult to seek solutions or compromises, or even temporary solutions such as joint development. I feel that this point still needs to be appreciated.

4. There is a need to increase "transparency" in national policy, legislation and documentation, with more frequent meetings among the legal officers of the various regional countries in order to exchange documentation and information, including with legislative planning.

5. Successful efforts often begin with informal activities, either through the Track Two or informal Track One processes. After such efforts have had some success, a more formal Track One approach could be attempted. This was the case with the Cambodian issue (which started with informal "cocktail parties"), the Southern Philippines and the South China Sea Workshops. Preventive diplomacy requires patience, tenacity and consistent efforts.

6. Preventive diplomacy should be undertaken by all parties who have an interest in the solution to the problem, both regionally and internationally. Solutions that take into account only national and regional interests but ignore the interests of states outside the region are not necessarily an effective solution for the long run. I feel that this point is slowly being appreciated.

Basic Principles

In managing potential conflicts, it is important to take into account several basic principles, such as:

1. To use an "all inclusive approach" and not exclude any directly interested countries or parties.

2. To start with less-sensitive issues which participants feel comfortable discussing without incurring the animosity of their respective governments or authorities.

3. The participants should be senior enough or eminent persons in their government, although they are participating in the process in their private capacity.

4. The structure of the process should not be institutionalized by creating a permanent or well-organized mechanism. The process should be kept as flexible as possible.

5. Differences should not be magnified and cooperation should be emphasized.

6. In view of the delicacy and sensitivity of some issues, it is wise to start with what is possible and follow a step-by-step approach and take into account the principle of cost effectiveness.

7. It should be understood that the process of managing potential conflicts is a long-term continuing process where lack of immediate concrete results should not be cause for despair or frustration.

8. Objectives should be kept clear and simple. The South China Sea Workshops have clear objectives: to learn how to cooperate and to implement cooperation. The goal is to build confidence through dialogue and cooperative programmes.

9. The roles of the initiator, the interlocutor, or the convener of the process, as well as the roles of disinterested supporters and sponsors, are crucial. The key persons must be impartial, have patience and dedication, as well as tenacity and sufficient knowledge of the delicate issues involved, and be able to retain the respect and the continued support and cooperation of all participants.

Current Prospects

The current situation of the workshop process on managing potential conflicts in the SCS could be summarized as follows:

1. Discussion on territorial and jurisdictional issues, after several meetings, has stalled in the workshop process, because of the objections of China and certain other participants. China and Vietnam, however, have reached bilateral agreement on maritime delimitation in the Gulf of Tonkin, and Indonesia and Vietnam have reached bilateral agreement on the delimitation of their continental shelf boundary in the SCS.

2. Discussion and bilateral dialogues among parties concerned have achieved results. As indicated above, there is already an eight-point Code of Conduct between the PRC and the Philippines and a nine-point Code of Conduct between the Philippines and Vietnam. In fact the six-points basis for settlement of disputes agreed upon by the second workshop in Bandung in July 1991 and the five-point ASEAN Declaration on the SCS in Manila in July 1992 became elements for the formal ASEAN-China Dialogue resulting in the Declaration on the Conduct of Parties in the South China Sea, adopted in Phnom Penh in 2002.

3. Discussion on confidence building with regard to military activities has also slowed down, although there is still agreement to continue discussion on this matter.

4. Discussion on formulating cooperation in technical matters has made a lot of progress in the various Technical Working Groups. In fact, three projects of cooperation have been agreed, namely on biodiversity, climatic change and sea-level monitoring, as well as on preparing a database and networking. A biodiversity expedition took place in 2002 in the Anambas area, followed by the Philippines biodiversity expedition near Palawan Island.

5. The efforts to develop cooperation through joint development have also produced concrete results, such as the agreement between China and Vietnam on the common fishery area in the Gulf of Tonkin in 2002. An agreement between China and the Philippines to conduct a joint exploration survey for oil between the oil companies of the two countries was signed in Beijing in 2004, and a similar agreement for three years on marine seismic undertakings between the oil companies of China, the Philippines and Vietnam was signed on 14 March 2005.

Throughout the discussion of South China Sea issues, China has played a key role. I am happy to note that China has moved away from being reluctant and sceptical to become an ardent supporter of the workshop process. China's neighbours in the SCS have responded positively, and the policy of the Southeast Asian countries of "constructive engagement" with China seems to be working. China and its neighbours in Southeast Asia may see closer relations and cooperation in the future.

One of the successes of the efforts to manage the potential conflicts in the SCS would be the absence or continued absence of armed conflict in the area. Yet, precisely the absence or the prolonged absence of conflicts in the area would also be one of the reasons for the argument that the workshop process would no longer be needed. This argument could also be used as an excuse not to implement agreed projects of cooperation, which have been so painstakingly discussed and formulated. I personally believe that this reasoning is dangerous, because I do not share the view that we have to wait until disputes erupt into actual armed conflict before we do something about it. If disputes erupt into armed conflict, then the efforts to manage potential conflicts in the SCS would have failed.

Concluding Remarks

There are good opportunities for promoting cooperation in various areas and developing confidence-building measures and processes for the SCS. The more discussion takes place on relevant issues, the better are the prospects for managing potential conflict in the area. The prognosis for the future would be much worse if South China Sea countries were not prepared to talk about the issues and to transform these talks into cooperation.

It has indeed been a long road towards peace and cooperation in the South China Sea, but it has all been worthwhile. In this context, I hope that Indonesia, together with all its partners in the South China Sea Workshop, will continue to exercise wisdom and leadership, albeit informally, in taking the initiative to promote peace, stability and cooperation in the SCS and South East Asia in general. There are also good prospects for the model of the South China Sea Workshops to be used to deal with similar problems, including in the East China Sea and the Sea of Japan or East Sea.

Notes

1. These policies were mentioned in House of Representatives Resolution No. 114 of the 104 Congress, First Session, submitted by Congressman Gilman of the Foreign Affairs Committee and in the Statement of the U.S. Department of State on the Spratlys and the South China Sea on 10 May 1995.
2. Point 3 of the Declaration of the People's Republic of China on China's Territorial Sea, dated 4 September 1958. This point was repeated in Article 6 of the Chinese Law No. 55/1992 on Territorial Sea and the Contiguous Zone of China, passed by the 24th meeting of the Standing Committee of the 7th Congress of the PRC on 25 February 1992.

5

AN ASEAN PERSPECTIVE ON THE SOUTH CHINA SEA
China-ASEAN Collision or China-U.S. Hegemonic Competition?

Aileen S.P. Baviera

THE SOUTH CHINA SEA AND ITS THREE PROBLEMATIQUES

Among the reasons why a resolution of the territorial and maritime resource disputes in the South China Sea seems to be nowhere in sight are that there is not one, but many disputes in question; not two but many actors involved; and not one particular issue but several strategic interests at stake. The South China Sea disputes can be described as the confluence of three problematiques.

Primarily, the disputes are a contest for sovereignty and control over specific areas of land and water, as well as over economic resources (fisheries, oil and gas), involving two or more of altogether six claimant parties (Brunei, China, Malaysia, the Philippines, Taiwan, and Vietnam). Successful claimants hope to enjoy benefits arising from sovereignty and sovereign rights, as recognized under international law, but such rights and benefits may only be fully enjoyed if uncontested. For this to happen, the different sets of countries whose claims overlap must negotiate boundary limits to reduce/remove the overlaps, or, failing to do so, they should agree to resource-use arrangements and other rules governing activities in disputed areas, that may be pursued even in the absence of a definitive determination of sovereignty or boundaries.

Mistrust of neighbours has clearly been an obstacle to an early resolution of the disputes, attributable to power asymmetry or to historical enmities. However, in some cases strong domestic opposition to any compromise, the absence of a clear-cut national policy, and inadequate capacity to move forward with the technical and legal aspects of the claims have also prevented sustained efforts at dispute management.

Secondly, the disputes are a microcosm of the dilemma in security relations between China on the one hand and the Association of Southeast Asian Nations (ASEAN) on the other hand (four of the claimant-states being members of ASEAN, and Taiwan not having the juridical personality to participate in state-level interactions on this issue). The weaker states (ASEAN) realize they must band together to strengthen their influence over the stronger power (China), but fear that this will lead to a perception of ganging up against China and thus elicit greater hostility than may already exist. On the other hand, the stronger state (China) can leverage division among the weaker ones (ASEAN) but finds power asymmetry to be a double-edged sword, as weak states standing on their own may refuse to engage at all in what is perceived as not being a level playing field, leaving the strong state without an arena for leveraging.

The disputes have indeed been referred to as a litmus test of China's attitudes and long-term intentions as a rising power (whether peaceful and self-restrained or dominating and aggressive) towards its smaller Southeast Asian neighbours. In corollation to this, the disputes challenge the countries of ASEAN to define the extent to which they are ready to collectively engage China and to accommodate its growing influence and importance in the region, especially with respect to its military presence and role in their shared ocean spaces. As important as ASEAN unity may be in ensuring a solution that is peaceful and that does not end in hegemonic control by one power, the reality is that ASEAN states do not have a unified position or strategy for addressing this dilemma. In the overall scheme of Southeast Asia–China relations, there are in fact other important aspects of ties (e.g., economic cooperation, coordination on non-traditional security issues, socio-cultural linkages) that both the ASEAN and Chinese sides feel should not be held hostage to the disputes, resulting in a generally low sense of urgency in addressing the disputes per se.

Thirdly, the disputed geographical features and waters happen to be located alongside strategic waterways — navigational routes that are important because of the traffic of commodities on which the major economies of East Asia depend (particularly oil from the Middle East), but vulnerable because of the existence of choke points where freedom and safety of navigation may be impeded by a number of actual or potential threats (e.g., piracy and armed robbery at sea, terrorist activity, natural hazards).

Protection of trade routes, as in earlier times, continues to be a major justification for big powers to want to establish a large maritime presence and a long naval reach over the world's oceans. More importantly, the number, strength, and combined capabilities of one's naval assets continue to be the main measure of global military power and influence (i.e., the ability to wage interventions in distant lands in defence or promotion of one's interests), where the intent is both to control the seas and to deny access to others who would. Thus, apart from the littoral states and parties to the territorial and maritime disputes, established and aspiring maritime powers such as the United States, China, and to a lesser extent India and Japan have a compulsion to show the flag in the South China Sea, which extends into the East China Sea and Pacific Ocean in the east and into the Indian Ocean in the west. Clearly, increase in strategic competition between the region's big powers will be a complicating factor in the resolution of the disputes.

In all three problematiques, China plays the pivotal role, respectively (1) as proponent of apparently the most expansive territorial claim, (2) as the region's most ambitious and rapidly modernizing military power, and (3) as currently the only credible source of a potential strategic challenge to the United States' naval primacy. The further complication to this situation is that from China's official perspective, the entire South China Sea — marked on its maps by nine dotted lines fringing the coasts of all the other littoral states — is an area where it holds "indisputable sovereignty" over islands and adjacent waters, and which various other states are simply encroaching on.[1] China appears to believe that the disputes themselves should be subject only to Chinese initiatives at bilateral resolution, albeit (China says) in accordance with international law, including respect for the freedom of navigation. However, it concedes that regional stability is a joint responsibility for which instruments such as the multilateral Declaration on the Conduct of Parties (DOC) signed between China and ASEAN can make a contribution.

This chapter examines how the territorial and maritime jurisdiction disputes in the South China Sea, rather than inching closer to resolution, are at risk of becoming embroiled in the brewing strategic competition between China and the United States, because of the assertive stance once more being taken by a rising China vis-à-vis its territorial claims, the growing distrust such behaviour elicits from many of China's neighbours, and the United States' desire to regain diplomatic ground and military influence in East Asia that it believes may have been lost to China during the previous United States' administration.

TO THE BRINK AND BACK AGAIN

Much has already been written about China's recent acerbic behaviour in the South China Sea, as well as its increased military confidence and evidence of resurgent nationalism in the last few years. These recent developments stand in sharp contrast to what had been touted as China's successful charm offensive in Southeast Asia since 2000. Aside from China, and often in reaction to it, other claimants and even extra-regional powers have also weighed in on the issue, through actions and policy declarations that have had as their consequence a rise in the political temperature in the region.

If one were to classify triggers of tensions in the last two or three years, these mainly involve conflict over (1) exploration/exploitation of oil and gas resources,[2] (2) fishing activities,[3] (3) the passage of laws that impinge on the disputed areas, whether for purposes of strengthening one's claims or bringing them in line with international legal obligations,[4] (4) military presence and activities perceived as exacerbating threat perceptions,[5] (5) actions seen as directed at internationalizing the disputes and involving third parties,[6] and (6) other statements, actions, and policies that signal assertions of sovereignty.[7]

One significant development came in April 2010, when U.S. sources reported a statement by State Councillor Dai Bingguo that China viewed the South China Sea as part of its "core interests".[8] This was taken to mean that, like other Chinese core interests Taiwan and Tibet, Chinese use of force to address the disputes could not be ruled out. It also signalled that China would not tolerate any interference from the United States on this matter.

Secretary of State Hillary Clinton further claimed that Dai Bingguo made similar remarks during the U.S.-China Strategic and Economic Dialogue in May in Beijing.

However, among various sources there is some confusion as to what had actually been said — one explanation being that the "core interest" statement was mentioned not with regard to the South China Sea per se but with general reference to sovereignty and territorial integrity; another that it was in the context of opposition to United States' surveillance activities in the Chinese exclusive economic zone (EEZ), specifically the area surrounding Hainan. Even Chinese academics expressed disbelief that such a statement was made by their officials to specifically refer to the whole South China Sea. The U.S. edition of *China Daily*, an official People's Republic of China (PRC) paper seen as mainly addressed to an international audience, offered a nuanced explanation in August 2010 that confirms the statement but indicates that its target was solely the United States, coming as a reaction to the announcement of United States' arms sales to Taiwan and President Barack Obama's meeting with the Dalai Lama earlier in the year.

Whether the supposed Chinese statement was accurately quoted or interpreted, the U.S. response came months later, articulated by Secretary of State Hillary Clinton at the ASEAN Regional Forum (ARF) meeting in Hanoi on 23 July 2010. She said that, "The United States has a *national interest* [emphasis mine] in freedom of navigation, open access to Asia's maritime commons, and respect for international law in the South China Sea." Clinton also said "We oppose the use or threat of force by any claimant" and declared U.S. support for a collaborative diplomatic process towards resolution of the disputes. Specifically, she called for a binding regional code of conduct to be signed, something that ASEAN was pushing for but that China was perceived to have been delaying since the signing of the 2002 China-ASEAN Declaration of Conduct in the South China Sea. The United States also offered to provide support towards a resolution of the dispute, although, as expected, China immediately rejected the offer.

Foreign Minister Yang Jiechi, China's representative at the ARF meeting, reacted sharply to Clinton's remarks, especially resenting the fact that the representatives of twelve countries — including the four ASEAN claimants and Indonesia — spoke in similar tones in the run-up to Clinton's statement, in what China suspects was an orchestrated move against it. Yang said of American involvement, "It will only make matters worse and the resolution more difficult. International practices show that the best way to resolve such disputes is for countries concerned to have direct bilateral negotiations."

Subsequently, the United States, China and ASEAN have all stepped back from statements and actions that may further add fuel to the tensions created by the apparent juxtaposition of "Chinese core interest" versus "American national interest". Chinese officials have tried to distance themselves from this statement of "core interest" — some saying it had never been official policy — and in time ceased mention of it altogether. (Although to deny that it was said or that it is China's policy would not have been politically possible.) Instead, there were frequent iterations of China's commitment to the DOC and assurances to ASEAN of its non-hegemonic intentions over the long term. The above-mentioned commentary in the *China Daily* on 2 August 2010 even attempted to refine the position and assuage regional concerns by publishing three qualifications, to wit:

> China must avoid the possible misunderstanding on the concept of "core national interests". First of all, with its surging national power, China should cautiously define its core interests as security, just as defensive realism argues. It will not be in China's interest to define interest as power, like those classic realists did. Second, there are different layers in core national interests. Issue [*sic*] "related to" core interest is sensitive and important, but they are not core interest or "red line".... Third, there are many ways to handle issues involving national core interests, not just military means.

The United States, perhaps sensing that an even more active intervention in the dispute management processes beyond the ARF statement would be seen as counter-productive by ASEAN, also moderated its tone. For instance, Assistant Secretary of State for East Asian and Pacific Affairs Kurt Campbell was quoted as saying to journalists in Tokyo in October 2010 that it would be "inappropriate" for the United States to play a direct role in the DOC talks. China and the United States also seem to have downplayed their differences over the South China Sea issue during the ASEAN Defence Minister's summit in Hanoi. The United States could however claim a successful impact of Secretary Clinton's statement, as it appears to have nudged China and ASEAN to announce a resumption of code of conduct discussions as early as December 2010. More discreetly, the United States has continued to strengthen bilateral security ties with other claimants and affected ASEAN states.

Southeast Asia's response to U.S. interest in the territorial disputes signalled at the ARF was cautious because they needed to avoid antagonizing China, but also perhaps because among themselves there was unlikely to emerge a unified position on what a U.S. role might be. It was clear that Vietnam, then Chair of ASEAN, ARF meeting host, as well as China's toughest rival in the South China Sea sovereignty claims, had used the opportunity of its ASEAN chairmanship to encourage a stronger United States' engagement on the issue, but there were few indications that ASEAN was of one mind on what exactly this would entail. Indeed, officials from the region came out with a number of seemingly contradictory statements in the wake of Clinton's ARF bombshell, indicating the difficulties that may arise from a more active U.S. role and the balancing it would require from ASEAN.

Philippine Foreign Secretary Alberto Romulo, queried by Philippine media on his reactions, said that "it's between ASEAN and China" (per Philippine Foreign Ministry sources, referring to the DOC), while President Benigno Aquino in a subsequent speech before the U.S. Council for Foreign Relations in September 2010, said that the Philippines welcomed Secretary Clinton's statements. Termsak Chalermpalanupap, director of ASEAN's Political and Security Directorate, also expressed in a published article his belief that "as far as the DOC is concerned", "ASEAN and China can handle their differences without the involvement of a third party", even while he "welcomed" "expressions of support for the early implementation of the DOC projects from outsiders". During a visit by Defence Secretary Robert Gates to Jakarta following the ARF meeting, Indonesia indicated it welcomed a U.S. role in resolving these disputes but subsequently, during the ASEAN retreat in Lombok on 15–17 January 2011, Indonesia expressed concern that United States and Japanese involvement in the disputes may further complicate ASEAN's discussion with China.

During the ASEAN-U.S. summit in September 2010, amidst some expectation of greater mutual support and follow-through statements on how to handle the disputes and the U.S. role, the public press releases indicated no mention of Secretary Clinton's earlier call, nor any direct reference to the South China Sea. The final communiqué instead merely "reaffirmed the importance of regional peace and stability, maritime security, unimpeded commerce, and freedom of navigation, in accordance with relevant universally agreed principles of international law, including the United Nations Convention on the Law of the Sea (UNCLOS) and other international maritime law, and the peaceful settlement of disputes". Similarly, at the Hu Jintao–Barack Obama summit of 19 January 2011, the Joint Statement referred to cooperation for peace, stability, and prosperity in the Asia-Pacific, and recognition of the United States as an Asia-Pacific nation, but made no mention of Southeast Asia or the South China Sea (unlike specific references to the Korean peninsula, Sudan, Iran, among others). However, there may have been more significance in what was not said, as Hu Jintao also described Taiwan and Tibet as "core issues" for China, but did not refer to the South China Sea.

China has since increased assurances to ASEAN of its peaceful intentions, and agreed to resume dialogue with ASEAN on the regional code of conduct. After eight years of very little progress on the implementing guidelines for the DOC, let alone its evolution into a legally binding Code of Conduct (COC), a fifth meeting of the working group on DOC implementation was held from 21 to 23 December 2010, and a following meeting was set for March 2011. However, a principal bone of contention in the talks remained unresolved: China's opposition to a provision in the declaration about ASEAN members engaging in consultations among themselves prior to meeting with China. In China's eyes, it was bad enough that it had to discuss the matter with all of the ASEAN states present. If Beijing could have its way, it would discuss the disputes bilaterally only with other claimant countries. It argues that the Spratlys issue "does not concern the four ASEAN claimants collectively, or ASEAN as a group". Yet, having already acceded to the DOC in 2002, it is bound to continue consultations with ASEAN. China's stance is seen by many as an attempt to prevent increased coordination and unity in the positions of the ASEAN countries.

Foreign Minister Marty Natalegawa of Indonesia, then chair of ASEAN, emphasized the need for a speedier process and real breakthroughs on the disputes, but so far ASEAN proposes only to upgrade the code of conduct discussion from Working Group to ASEAN Senior Officials level. Even Vietnam, now no longer ASEAN Chair, appears to have pulled back from the evidently growing tendency towards confrontation of the last few years. During a visit of Chinese Premier Wen Jiabao to Hanoi on 28 October 2010, China reported that Vietnam had agreed to pursue proper handling of the South China Sea territorial rights issue.

The return to the COC discussions does not necessarily give cause for optimism that there can be an early outcome favourable to all parties concerned. The reason is that the management of the disputes now lies in the shadow of a more strategic challenge, that of growing U.S.-China maritime competition in East Asia. If optimists then felt that there were enough shared interests among the claimants and littoral states for pragmatic positions to prevail (provided successful confidence-building measures were in place), from today's vantage point, the claimants and littoral states may find more obstacles with the interests of the great powers having to be taken into consideration.

THE U.S.-CHINA MARITIME COMPETITION OVERLAY

The escalation of tensions and more confrontational positions that we have seen in the last several years have not been limited to the United States, China and some ASEAN countries in the South China Sea alone. Sharp Sino-Japanese disputes over the Senkaku islands and tensions over oil exploration activities in the Chunxiao fields which straddle overlapping EEZs of the two countries were simultaneously taking place. Of particular note was the reported ramming of a Japanese coastguard vessel by a Chinese fishing boat, followed by Japan arresting the fishing captain and subsequently suffering non-military retaliation by China even after the vessel and captain had been released. Notably, the incident between China and Japan merited a reiteration by the United States of its alliance commitment to the defence of Japanese territory (in contrast to its neutrality in the South China Sea).[9]

There were also disagreements between the United States and China over the handling of renewed tensions on the Korean peninsula that added to rancour in the region, and a tit-for-tat conduct of military exercises, including China's largest, involving coordinated actions of its major fleets in areas close to Okinawa and the islands that are disputed with Japan. Apparently of great concern to the United States was China's development of a submarine base on Hainan Island and confirmation of its intentions to deploy a carrier battle group. Efforts by the United States and Japan to involve India in an East Asian regional security role to act as a balancer to Chinese influence were also indicative of growing power competition.

This seeming spiral of instability affecting both the East China Sea and the South China Sea could be traced to (1) China's rapidly developing naval capability and its new assertiveness, (2) renewed interest on the part of the United States to defend, promote, and assert its naval primacy and role as the pre-eminent Asia-Pacific power (given major setbacks in its diplomatic influence in East Asia during the previous U.S. administration), and (3) the uneasy dynamic between these two. The outcome in the rest of the region is growing apprehension over the first, leading to a greater appreciation of the need for the second, while fearful of getting caught in the crossfire of the third.

There are indications that China's programme of naval modernization has had better-than-expected results in the eyes of worried Western analysts. Some observers now believe that China's ballistic and cruise missile capabilities may already have eroded joint U.S.-Taiwan air defence capabilities in the Taiwan Straits. The United States also fears that some nations are investing new capabilities that "could threaten our primary means of projecting power, our bases and our sea and air assets", in reference to China's anti-access strategy and development of anti-ballistic missiles. Increased transparency has moreover given us insight into internal debates about the future roles of Chinese maritime power that to some extent add to existing apprehensions among its neighbours, e.g., why there is a need to have aircraft carriers, whether the defence of Taiwan and territorial claims in the South China Sea and East China Sea, or protection of EEZ resources and commercial sea lanes are the main justification for naval and air modernization; or whether China's power projection in far areas of the world are a requisite for an anticipated role in global security, e.g., anti-piracy missions in the Gulf of Aden.

The U.S. actions and reactions are in turn shaped by its own maritime strategic interests and power projection goals, including a need to become more relevant to regional diplomatic initiatives that may in time help grow a new regional security architecture (East Asia Summit, ASEAN Regional Forum, among others) for the Asia Pacific. Its emphasis on the global maritime domain has been obvious, underscored by several policy declarations, e.g., the 2005 Strategy for Maritime Security which emphasized awareness of the maritime domain, access to the maritime commons, freedom of military navigation as well as unimpeded economic development and commerce, among other things. The Proliferation Security Initiative (PSI), Container Security Initiative (CSI), Regional Maritime Security Initiative (RMSI), Combined Task Force 150, Global Maritime Partnership (also known as Thousand Ship Navy) are but some of the American initiatives to take the lead in maritime security governance. Such programmes have had a mixed record of acceptance and rejection by littoral states, the latter explained by discomfort at allowing the United States such a leadership role, reservations as to whether these are considered appropriate under international law, or conflicts with territorial sovereignty.[10]

Meanwhile, the United States continues to contest China's interpretations of its EEZ as an area where foreign military activity would require its consent. China's view is that U.S. surveillance activities undertaken by its spy planes or ships in or above the EEZ may be considered hostile. The U.S. policy is to deliberately exercise what it considers "high seas freedom" in foreign EEZs. This seeming irreconcilable difference in interpretation is and will continue to be a key obstacle to U.S.-China maritime cooperation, and therefore to peace and stability in the general South China Sea region. China, however, assures the United States and other ocean users that it will abide by international law and will respect freedom of navigation and overflight according to international law.

As has become more evident following its 2008 financial crisis, U.S. primacy in the Asia-Pacific which has traditionally relied on naval presence close to regional hotspots, will become more dependent not just on the political cooperation but on the material support of traditional allies and new security partners in the region. The 2010 National Security Strategy includes "investing in the capacity of strong and capable partners". Regional small and middle powers have in recent years been more forthcoming in their welcome of the American presence, perhaps concerned that the combination of U.S. internal economic woes and decline in influence on the one hand, and China's growing strength and assertiveness on the other hand, can spell greater uncertainty. The greater acceptability of the Obama government (in contrast to unilateralist, militarist George W. Bush), the renewed interest it has thus far demonstrated towards East Asian engagement, even the growing confidence of democratic Indonesia and Vietnam to interact with the United States on the world stage, are some factors that also contribute to more positive attitudes towards the United States among governments in the region. In Southeast Asia's predominantly maritime environment, renewed U.S. engagement has taken the form of increased defence cooperation (agreements, joint exercises, capability-building assistance) with its allies such as the Philippines, Thailand and quasi-ally Singapore, but more so with new partners Vietnam, Indonesia, and to a lesser extent Malaysia and Brunei.

Apart from closer engagement with the United States, some regional states have embarked on their own beefing up of naval, coastguard and air capabilities. Vietnam, for instance, announced an 8.5 billion dollar economic and defence development plan that would turn the Spratlys into an "outer defence stronghold". In December 2010, Russia signed an arms deal to provide Vietnam six "Kilo" class submarines, which will give Hanoi the most powerful submarine fleet in Southeast Asia. On the other hand, Malaysia already took delivery of its first two submarines, one of which has completed an underwater test-firing exercise of an anti-ship missile in the South China Sea in 2010. Indonesia is reportedly planning to buy billions of dollars of American-made military aircraft, once the U.S. embargo on military sales to it is lifted. Assistant Secretary of State Kurt Campbell, visiting Manila in January 2011, explicitly offered the Aquino government cooperation in territorial defence and maritime security.

Both the vigorous military acquisitions and enhanced military ties with the United States, as well as initiatives to bring in external powers through the East Asia Summit (United States, Russia, India, Australia and New Zealand in addition to the ASEAN+3) are part and parcel of ASEAN states' hedging against a more assertive China.[11]

When ASEAN and China now turn their attention to the South China Sea, including through revived consultations on the Declaration/Code of Conduct, the strategic environment will be somewhat different from before. Events since 2009 have undone a large part of China's earlier painstaking efforts at building trust and assurances with its neighbours, thus agreement to cooperate on certain activities might be more difficult in the making. Moreover, another 800 lb gorilla, while remaining seated outside the fence, has given notice that it would be happy to butt in when needed.

CHALLENGES AHEAD FOR ASEAN

In this complex and rather less predictable environment characterized by growing contradictions between the United States and China in the Asia-Pacific maritime theatre, China and ASEAN will have to squarely face a number of issues to move the process of dispute management forward.

New challenges for ASEAN have arisen from the recent turn of events, including the following questions: (1) What might be the future scenarios and implications of a U.S. role? (2) Should the South China Sea disputes be resolved bilaterally as China prefers, or multilaterally, by relying largely on initiatives of the claimants, of regional formations (ASEAN+1), or with support of a broader international community of stakeholders (United States and United Nations)? And (3) in addressing the disputes as well as the related questions of maritime security, will international law (including coastal states' rights and obligations) prevail or will it be trumped by great power politics?

The Role of the United States

As in past occasions, rising tensions among great powers gives ASEAN cause to worry; but manageable competition between them places ASEAN in a tactically advantageous position. With respect to the South China Sea, the United States is for the first time eager to be seen as a player, for now by supporting a "collaborative diplomatic process" that will place ASEAN at the core (while working with Vietnam, the Philippines, and other stakeholders to strengthen maritime capabilities and partnerships). China, on the other hand, precisely fearful of such intervention by the United States, is once more urged on to the track of direct consultations with ASEAN, under increased pressure from the realization that failure at achieving some sort of significant compromise will likely push ASEAN claimants closer to the United States. In this context, U.S. expression of support for moving the process forward is to be welcomed: it brings China back to the dialogue table and increases the costs of failure for China; it should likewise force ASEAN to come up with a more coherent position lest the opportunity to make new progress be squandered.

It is unlikely that ASEAN will allow the United States to weigh in directly on the Declaration of Conduct or Code of Conduct discussions with China. Rather, a more likely role would be for the United States to encourage ASEAN and China to persist with multilateral dialogue and consultations while it works with individual countries to build security linkages, particularly with an eye to assisting China's neighbours in capacity building for the promotion of maritime security. The unstated expectation is that this is in exchange for their acquiescence to continuing U.S. primacy in the region's maritime domain.

There are probably quarters in Southeast Asia that recognize that renewed U.S. interest in the territorial disputes is driven by its own goals of re-engagement and sustaining its primacy in the long term, and believe that Washington stands to gain more in a situation of continued low-level tensions and mistrust between China and ASEAN. But even granting the possibility of ASEAN and China concluding an agreement on the management of disputes, the United States would still want to ensure that the arrangements that would emerge would not put its own interests at risk, particularly with respect to possible restrictions on freedom of navigation and the conduct of military activities.

That said, there are a number of new multilateral mechanisms now involving the United States where it will have opportunities to promote its maritime security goals. Aside from the ASEAN–United States Summit, there are the ASEAN Defence Ministerial Meeting Plus (ADMM+), the ASEAN Regional Forum, and the East Asia Summit. Several ASEAN states would be happy to see the United States more fully engaged, with the qualification that ASEAN may see such engagement as temporary insurance against uncertainties caused by a rising China, while the United States may see it as an offer of leadership for the long term. The U.S. and Chinese governments will have to understand that ASEAN's current tactical hedging or "soft-balancing" may not necessarily be the same as nor should it lead to strategic balancing or containment behaviour.

Processes of Dispute Management and Resolution: Whither the DOC?

For ASEAN the key objective in the South China Sea remains to prevent or mitigate any military threat from China or any other claimant that would upset the status quo and lead to regional instability, thus explaining ASEAN's preference for confidence-building measures as the first step. Beyond the disputes themselves, going by its history, tradition, and *raison d'être*, ASEAN would wish to prevent the rise of any regional hegemon that would impose its interests on smaller states. For ASEAN claimants (Philippines, Vietnam, Malaysia, Brunei), as well as for China and perhaps Taiwan, in addition to the above, the pragmatic objective is to maximize or optimize access to fisheries and hydrocarbon resources as well as obtain recognition of claimed maritime jurisdiction zones.

Given that there are different objectives for various stakeholders, a singular, linear approach to the successful resolution of the disputes (e.g., via confidence building and an ASEAN-China DOC) may not reasonably be expected to go smoothly. Moreover, the overlay of great power strategic competition and even domestic political developments such as heightened nationalism may mean that ASEAN does not have the luxury of time to do things in its customary, gradualist, and step-by-step way.

Failure to make progress on the DOC guidelines reflected not just the differences in the positions of China and ASEAN, but the absence of a strong push by the ASEAN governments themselves. This was most notable in the lack of any reference to the South China Sea issue during recent ASEAN Summits' Chairman's Statements. The ASEAN-China Joint Working Group (JWG) on the Implementation of the DOC which was established in 2004 has as of this writing convened five times. The main task of the JWG, according to its terms of reference, is to study and recommend measures to translate the provisions of the DOC into concrete cooperative activities that will enhance mutual understanding and trust. Thus far, the priorities set by the JWG include marine scientific research, protection of the marine environment, safety of navigation and communication at sea, search and rescue operations, humane treatment of all persons in danger or distress, fight against transnational crime as well as cooperation among military officials. While the second meeting in Sanya in 2006 reached some agreement on such activities, the lack of trust has prevented any real progress from taking place. In other words, China and ASEAN seem to need confidence-building measures (CBMs) before they can do these proposed CBMs, a catch-22 situation.

Few of the current proposals appear to address the real bones of contention — which, stripping away the basic disagreement over sovereignty, are the contest for fishing grounds, competing oil and gas claims, and threat perceptions arising from military presence and activity. The concentration on functional cooperation as a confidence-building process in the framework of the DOC may have made sense before the July 2010 ARF, but to give this China's and ASEAN's sole attention may be misplaced since then. There are new factors that now need to be taken into consideration, including evidence that China's central leadership may now be weaker than before while various groups and institutional interests may have become more influential in driving foreign policy, that China's maritime power capabilities have significantly advanced even in the years since ASEAN and China signed but failed to implement the DOC, that a U.S. re-prioritization of the Asia-Pacific will be constrained by domestic demands to set right its own crisis-ridden economy (and now, renewed attention to the explosive instabilities in the Middle East and North Africa).

What might make more of a difference in China-ASEAN management of the disputes would be agreements on how to prevent armed confrontation; measures to mitigate the effects of increasing militarization in the region; policies to dissuade or regulate fishing activities in disputed areas; seriously exploring the possibility of joint oil and gas exploration; and efforts to unify understanding among the governments of littoral states on commonly acceptable interpretations of crucial Law of the Sea provisions, to ensure that the rule of law shall prevail.

Between China's insistence on bilateral discussions, and ASEAN's preference for a collective or coordinated approach among its members towards China, there may be the possibility — even desirability as well as necessity — of taking a more diversified and multi-track strategy driven by simultaneous but disaggregated objectives. Table 5.1 is a rough and non-exhaustive attempt to illustrate the parallel processes that may be undertaken.

In principle, three levels of action are possible: bilateral negotiations between relevant pairs of disputing states (including but not limited to China) where the nature of the dispute is a matter of vital concern only to them; multilateral consultations on measures necessary for the preservation of regional peace and stability, as well as maritime security and implementation of the UNCLOS; and a "minilateral" process among the claimant states focused on military-conflict prevention and cooperation in joint development of resources.

The territorial disputes are considered the potential flashpoint in the South China Sea, for which reason much attention has been given on this. However, the management of the disputes are also very much related to the questions of implementation of the Law of the Sea, regional maritime security cooperation, and, more broadly speaking, ocean governance. There is a need to elevate ASEAN's (and China's as well as other stakeholders') perspective on the South China Sea from focusing excessively on territorial disputes back to a diplomacy on ocean governance — encompassing the economic, development, security, and environmental imperatives of managing it as a semi-enclosed sea, rights and obligations pertaining to which have been stipulated in UNCLOS.

Even while the disputes have prevented cooperation among littoral states in the South China Sea from taking place, there have been a number of initiatives at regional cooperation in the last decade alone, and thickening discourses on maritime security focused on other problems — e.g., sea lane

Table 5.1
Possible Parallel Processes to Address South China Sea Issues

Objective	Modality	Pros	Cons	Conditions for success
Delimitation of boundaries where only 2 claims overlap (e.g., China-Vietnam continental shelf, Philippines-Malaysia, Malaysia-Brunei in the south) Agreement on resource conservation or exploitation in areas where only 2 claims overlap	Bilateral	Easier to negotiate when only 2 parties are involved Encourages flexible approach, e.g., designation of functional zones	Taiwan is disregarded Power asymmetry may result in inequitable solutions China may not recognize other pairs of bilaterals (e.g., Phil-Malaysia, Vietnam-Malaysia) Non-transparent, exclusivist; thus may fuel mistrust by those excluded from the process Can cover only peripheral areas and not occupied Spratlys	Need for security guarantees and trust-building measures between two parties Have an impartial third party to monitor process Provide transparency and assurances to parties that may be indirectly affected

Multilateral (ASEAN-China)	Implementation of Declaration of Conduct, CBMs/cooperation projects based on agreed principles	Helps reduce the impact of power asymmetry in negotiations	Taiwan is disregarded (or a formula for participation in certain functional activities may be negotiated between Taiwan and the PRC)	Need for mechanisms and resources to support implementation
	Building a non-traditional security regime, e.g., marine biodiversity conservation, search and rescue, anti-piracy	Greater transparency helps build cohesion and trust	Multilateral agreement will take a longer process to negotiate due to need to consult many national stakeholders, thus strong continuous commitment by leaders is needed	Focus on a few, selected high-impact, low-risk/cost cooperative activities
		Focuses on functional cooperation for mutual or common benefit		Need efforts to strengthen stakes of ASEAN's non-claimants
	Initiatives to achieve common understanding of UNCLOS/ applicable international law	Favours long-term commitments by parties and boosts community building if successful	Low level of interest and commitment of ASEAN non-claimants needs to be overcome	ASEAN-level coordination is imperative to emphasize regional security and stability objectives
			Risk of process being dominated by China	Requires ASEAN and Chinese agreement on strategic goals

continued on next page

Table 5.1 — _cont'd_

Objective	Modality	Pros	Cons	Conditions for success
Binding code of conduct focused on military CBMs and conflict prevention	'Minilateral' (Claimants only — China, Vietnam, Philippines, Malaysia, Brunei, Taiwan) or other appropriate 'minilaterals'	Focus on existential threats and vulnerabilities (e.g., security, oil and gas competition) rather than CBMs/atmospherics	Tends to divide, thus may weaken ASEAN if not managed properly	Need mechanisms for monitoring compliance with military CBMs
Functional cooperation in specific areas of more than 2 overlaps, e.g., oil and gas, fisheries		Driven by pragmatic as well as strategic interests No ASEAN-level coordination is necessary, except for transparency	Difficult due to sensitivity of issues to sovereignty	'Minilaterals' to report back to ASEAN, ASEAN+1 Strong political commitment at highest levels

safety and security, maritime search and rescue, marine environmental protection. In Southeast Asia, attempts by certain extra-regional states to take control of maritime security management (e.g., the RMSI and PSI proposals of the United States; Japan's proposed ASEAN+3 regional coastguard) may have been flatly rejected by some parties, yet regional navies and enforcement agencies have shown willingness to cooperate on such matters as information sharing (the Information Fusion Center in Singapore), capacity building (Regional Cooperation Agreement on Combating Piracy and Armed Robbery against Ships in Asia or ReCAAP),[12] and gradually higher and more complex levels of cooperation, such as the MALSINDO (Malaysia-Singapore-Indonesia) anti-piracy Malacca Straits Patrol that covers the territorial waters of the three countries, and the MALSINDO Plus Thailand Eyes in the Sky programme of coordinated air patrols.

This broader agenda of ocean governance on the one hand and maritime security regime-building on the other hand may have important implications for the eventual resolution of the disputes, particularly in terms of encouraging cooperative multilateral security frameworks based on shared interests and mutual benefit.

CONCLUSION

This chapter argues that the environment for addressing the territorial, maritime jurisdiction and related resource disputes in the South China Sea has changed in recent years due to increasing strategic competition between the United States and China, and increasing wariness of an assertive China by regional states, particularly in the maritime domain. U.S. involvement in a supporting capacity can have a positive as well as negative impact, but there appears to be little consensus in the region towards it. There is a need to revisit whether priorities set by ASEAN and China since the 2002 DOC remain valid, and whether the overall approach is sufficient to move the process forward.

The author raises more questions than answers, but hopes they are the right questions relevant to the conjuncture. The chapter also poses some alternative or additional approaches — specifically refocusing dialogue from confidence-building activities to the real issues of contention (fisheries, energy, military threats); parallel but coordinated bilateral, multilateral and "minilateral"/claimants' diplomacy addressing varied objectives and involving different sets of parties; and finding opportunities for resolution in the broader cooperation agenda of ocean governance and maritime security regime-building.

Notes

Based on a paper presented at a Workshop on "Entering Uncharted Waters: ASEAN and the South China Sea Disputes", Institute of Southeast Asian Studies, Singapore, 18 February 2011.

1. The most significant recent Chinese assertion of "indisputable sovereignty" is the PRC government's note verbale, submitted in reaction to the joint submission by Vietnam and Malaysia to the U.N. Commission on the Limits of the Continental Shelf, which states that it "has indisputable sovereignty over the islands in the South China Sea and the adjacent waters, and enjoys sovereign rights and jurisdiction over the relevant waters as well as the seabed and subsoil thereof". China attached to this note verbale its famous map (dating to 1947) in which nine dotted lines enclose the SCS. For an international lawyer's interpretation, see Robert Beckman, "South China Sea: Worsening Dispute or Growing Clarity in Claims?", *RSIS Commentaries*, S. Rajaratnam School of International Studies, 16 August 2010.

2. Vietnamese reports say China had conducted seismic surveys of areas near the Paracel islands encompassing Vietnam's continental shelf in early 2010 ("Vietnam Protests Chinese Seismic Study on Paracel Islands", 5 August 2010 <http://www.monstersandcritics.com/news/asiapacific/news/article_1575710.php/Vietnam-protests-Chinese-seismic-study-on-Paracel-Islands>. China also warned the Philippines to cease exploration activities in the Reed Bank, which is 150 kilometres away from the Spratlys <http://www.energy-daily.com/reports/China_warns_against_SChina_Sea_oil_exploration_999.html>. In 2007 China reportedly used intimidation and threat of the use of force against international oil companies Exxon Mobil Corp and BP to halt exploration activities they were doing under license by Vietnam in China's claimed areas (*Wall Street Journal* via Dow Jones Newswires, 24 July 2008 <http://www.eoearth.org/article/Energy_profile_of_South_China_Sea>.

3. Vietnam complained of its fishing boats and equipment being seized and it being fined by China in areas which Vietnam considers traditional fishing grounds. China has been unilaterally imposing an annual fishing ban in the South China Sea during the summer months, ostensibly for conservation purposes. See, "Vietnam to Protest China Fishing Ban in the South China Sea", *Nanyang Post*, 6 May 2010 <http://www.nanyangpost.net/>.

4. The Philippines passed a new Archipelagic Baselines Law on 11 March 2009, mending its earlier baselines to conform to UNCLOS, while declaring a regime of islands around Scarborough Shoal and the part of the Spratlys (Kalayaan Islands) that it claims. Vietnam, China and Taiwan protested the new law. Also, submissions in May 2009 by Vietnam and jointly by Vietnam/Malaysia of the proposed extended continental shelf limits to the UN Commission on

Limits of the Continental Shelf (CLCS), were protested by China as "illegal and invalid". See Zhang Xin, "Change Tack with Sea Strategy: China Experts", *China Daily*, 13 February 2011 <http://www.chinadaily.com.cn/china/2009-05/13/content_7771886.htm>. In its protest, China sent a note verbale to the United Nations to which it attached a map showing its extensive claims enclosed in the famed nine dotted lines. Indonesia, concerned that the Chinese map appears to include its Natuna gas fields, once more sought clarification from China. The Natunas were considered undisputed until China in the 1990s released a map with unclear maritime boundaries indicating Natuna might be part of its territory. Chinese armed presence has also been reported in Indonesian EEZ. See <http://www.globalsecurity.org/military/world/war/spratly.htm>.

5. On 9 March 2009, five Chinese vessels shadowed and harassed the USNS Impeccable 75 miles south of Hainan island. China accused the United States of engaging in spying activities within its EEZ while the United States said its surveillance ship was conducting routine operations in international waters. The incident harks back to 2001, when this issue came to public attention with the U.S. EP-3 spy plane incident close to China's Hainan province. Vietnam also protested Chinese anti-piracy drills held in February 2010 in the Paracels. See <http://www.defence.pk/forums/china-defence/93916-vietnam-protests-chinas-military-exercise-south-china-sea.html>. In July 2010 China held large-scale military exercises coinciding with U.S. drills in the Sea of Japan. See <http://www.voanews.com/english/news/China-Conducts-Military-Exercise-in-South-China-Sea-99615779.html>. In August the United States and Vietnam held joint naval exercises of a non-combatant nature. See <http://www.bbc.co.uk/news/world-asia-pacific-10925061>.

6. Vietnam organized international conferences on the South China Sea consecutively in 2009 and 2010. China, wary of growing military ties between the United States and Vietnam exemplified by the USS John McCain providing search and rescue training for Vietnamese soldiers in the South China Sea, accused Vietnam of "internationalizing" the disputes.

7. For example, in August 2008, Malaysia's then Deputy Prime Minister, Datuk Seri Najib Tun Razak, paid a visit to Swallow Reef (Pulau Layang-Layang), to assert Malaysia's sovereignty. Taiwan protested the visit.

8. The statement was reported to have been made by Dai Bingguo, in a meeting with visiting U.S. Deputy Secretary of State James Steinberg and the US National Security Council's Jeffrey Bader in March 2010. Also present at the meeting was Assistant Minister of Foreign Affairs Cui Tiankai. See <http://www.nytimes.com/2010/04/24/world/asia/24navy.html?_r=1&scp=1&sq=South%20China%20Sea%20as%20part%20of%20Chinas%20core%20interests%22&st=cse>.

9. Hillary Clinton stated after meeting with Japanese Foreign Minister Seiji Maehara in Hawaii on 29 October that the islands do fall within the scope

of the treaty. See <http://e.nikkei.com/e/fr/tnks/Nni20100923D23NY148.htm>.

10. The new U.S. National Security Strategy places a lot of emphasis on the maritime domain and strengthening its forward position through alliances and partnerships spread geographically. In its QDR 2010, the United States referred to a mission of maintaining "forward stationed and forward deployed forces, rapidly employable capabilities scattered throughout the globe, providing allies and friends protection crisis through missile defenses, defensive information operations and counter-terrorist operations". Concerned that for the first time since the end of the Cold War, a potential peer competitor was emerging that could erode U.S. defence superiority and primacy in the Asia-Pacific, deterrence and strategic denial of sea control to competitor states remained part of the strategy.

11. However, given the fact that between and among ASEAN states there are still extant territorial and boundary issues, some of which (e.g., Ambalat, Preah Vihear, Malaysia-Brunei) have resulted in or brought the parties quite close to armed conflict, then the concern must be registered that any arms-buying spree may lead to greater risks of destabilization in the future.

12. ReCAAP is the "first government-to-government agreement that addresses the incidence of piracy and armed robbery in Asia. The ReCAAP initiative aims to enhance multilateral cooperation among sixteen regional countries. The sixteen countries include the People's Republic of Bangladesh, Brunei Darussalam, the Kingdom of Cambodia, the People's Republic of China, the Republic of India, the Republic of Indonesia, Japan, the Republic of Korea, the Lao People's Democratic Republic, Malaysia, the Union of Myanmar, the Republic of the Philippines, the Republic of Singapore, the Democratic Socialist Republic of Sri Lanka, the Kingdom of Thailand, and the Socialist Republic of Viet Nam. The Agreement was finalised on 11 November 2004 in Tokyo, and came into force on 4 September 2006." See <http://www.recaap.org/>.

References

Ross, R. "China's Naval Nationalism: Sources, Prospects, and the U.S. Response". *International Security* 34, no. 2 (2009): 46–81.

Storey, I. "China-ASEAN Summit: Beijing's Charm Offensive Continues". *China Brief* 6, no. 23 (2007).

———. "China's Missteps in Southeast Asia: Less Charm, More Offensive". *China Brief* 10, no. 25 (2010) <http://web1.iseas.edu.sg/?p=952>.

Valencia, M. "The South China Sea: Back to the Future?" *Global Asia* 5, no. 4 (2010).

Wong, K. "Diving in Changing Times: Malaysia's Submarine Programme". *RSIS Commentaries* no. 121, 27 September 2010 <http://www.rsis.edu.sg/publications/Perspective/RSIS1212010.pdf>.

Wu, S. and Zou K. *Maritime Security in the South China Sea: Regional Implications and International Cooperation*. Burlington, VT: Ashgate, 2009.

Part Three
China's Position

6

CHINA'S STANCE ON SOME MAJOR ISSUES OF THE SOUTH CHINA SEA

Wang Hanling

China has not issued any official document announcing its comprehensive policy on the South China Sea (SCS) issue, nor have the other SCS littoral states. However, China's stance on some major issues of the SCS has been clearly illustrated in its official documents and statements. This chapter illustrates China's basic stance on the SCS based on the historical records, official documents, statements, and state practice concerned.

CHINA'S INDISPUTABLE TERRITORIAL SOVEREIGNTY OVER THE XISHA (PARACEL) AND NANSHA (SPRATLY) ISLANDS AND THEIR ADJACENT WATERS

China was the first to discover and name the islands of the Xisha and Nansha Islands and the first to exercise sovereign jurisdiction over them. This is supported by ample historical and jurisprudential evidence and has long been recognized by the international community.

Major Historical Evidence Supporting China's Sovereignty over Nansha Islands

China the First to Discover and Name the Nansha Islands

The discovery by the Chinese people of the Nansha Islands can be traced back to as early as the Han Dynasty. Yang Fu of the East Han Dynasty (AD 23–220) made reference to the Nansha Islands in his book entitled *Yiwu Zhi* (Records of Rarities), which reads: "Zhanghai qitou, shui qian er duo cishi", or "There are islets, sand cays, reefs, and banks in the South China Sea, the water there is shallow and filled with magnetic rocks or stones." Chinese people then called the South China Sea Zhanghai and all the islands, reefs, shoals, and isles in the South China Sea, including the Nansha and Xisha Islands, Qitou.

General Kang Tai, one of the famous ancient Chinese navigators of the East Wu State of the Three Kingdoms Period (AD 220–280), also mentioned the Nansha Islands in his book entitled *Funan Zhuan* (or Journeys to and from Phnom, the name of an ancient state in today's Cambodia). He used the following sentences in describing the islands: "In the South China Sea, there are coral islands and reefs; below these islands and reefs are rocks upon which the corals were formed."

In numerous history and geography books published in the Tang and Song Dynasties, the Nansha and Xisha Islands were called Jiuruluo Islands, Shitang (literally meaning atolls surrounding a lagoon), Changsha (literally meaning long ranges of shoals), Qianli Shitang, Qianli Changsha, Wanli Shitang, and Wanli Changsha among others. Reference was made to the Nansha Islands in over one hundred categories of books published in the four dynasties of Song, Yuan, Ming and Qing in the name of Shitang or Changsha.

There were more detailed descriptions of the geographical locations and specific positions of the various islands of the Nansha Islands in the Yuan Dynasty. For instance, Wang Dayuan, a prominent Chinese navigator in the Yuan Dynasty, wrote about the Nansha Islands in his book entitled *Abridged Records of Islands and Barbarians* in these words: "The base of Wanli Shitang originates from Chaozhou. It is tortuous as a long snake lying in the sea. Its veins can all be traced. One such vein stretches to Java, one to Boni [or Burni, a kingdom which then existed in what is now Brunei in the vicinity of Kalimantan] and Gulidimen [another kingdom on Kalimantan], and one to the west side of the sea toward Kunlun [Con

Son Islands, located outside the mouth of the Mekong River some 200 nautical miles away from Saigon] in the distance." Wanli Shitang here refers to all the islands in the South China Sea, including the Nansha Islands. In the *Consolidated Map of Territories* and *Geography and Capitals of Past Dynasties* published in the Ming Dynasty, one of the words "Shitang" denotes today's Nansha Islands.

The *Road Map of the Qing Dynasty* marks the specific locations of all the islands, reefs, shoals, and isles of the Nansha Islands where fishermen of China's Hainan Island used to frequent, including seventy-three named places of the Nansha Islands.

China the First to Develop the Nansha Islands

Chinese people started to develop the Nansha Islands and engage in fishing on the islands as early as the beginning of the Ming Dynasty. At that time, fishermen from Haikou Port, Puqian Port, Qinglan Port and Wenchang County went to the Nansha Islands to fish sea cucumbers and other sea products.

The 1868 *Guide to the South China Sea* has accounts of the activities of the Chinese fishermen in the Nansha Islands. According to the guide, "fishermen from Hainan Island went to Zhenhe Isles and Reefs and lived on sea cucumbers and shells they got there. The footmarks of fishermen could be found in every isle of the Nansha Islands and some of the fishermen would even live there for a long period of time. Every year, there were small boats departing from Hainan Island for the Nansha Islands to exchange rice and other daily necessities for sea cucumbers and shells from the fishermen there. The ships used to leave Hainan Island in December or January every year and return when the south-westerly monsoon started." Since the end of the Qing Dynasty, fishermen from Hainan Island and Leizhou Peninsula of China have kept going to fish on the Nansha Islands. Most of the fishermen come from Wenchang County and Qionghai County. One or two dozen fishing boats from these two counties would go to the Nansha Islands every year.

The *Road Map* is another strong piece of evidence to the development of the islands on the South China Sea by the Chinese people since the Ming and Qing Dynasties. The *Road Map* served as a navigational guide to the Chinese fishermen for their trips to the Xisha and Nansha Islands for productive activities there. It was a result of the collective work of many people on the basis of their navigational experience. The first road map was produced in the Ming Dynasty and it was constantly improved subsequently. It showed the navigational routes and courses from Qinglan, Wenchang County, Hainan Island or Tanmen Port of Qionghai County to the various isles of the Xisha and Nansha Islands.

The development and productive activities of the Chinese fishermen on the Nansha Islands after the founding of the Republic of China in 1912 have been recorded in both Chinese and foreign history books. Okura Unosuke of Japan wrote about his expedition to Beizi Island in 1918 in his book *Stormy Islands*, which reads: "he saw three people from Haikou of Wenchang County when the expedition team he organised arrived in Beizi Island". In 1933 Miyoshi and Matuo of Japan saw two Chinese people on the Beizi Island and three Chinese people on the Nanzi Island when they made an investigation trip to the Nansha Islands. It is also recorded in *A Survey of the New South Islands* published in Japan that "fishermen planted sweet potato on Zhongye Island and those fishermen from the Republic of China resided on the islands and grew coconuts, papaya, sweet potato and vegetables there."

China the First to Exercise Jurisdiction over the Nansha Islands

The exercise of jurisdiction by the Chinese government over the Nansha Islands is also manifested in a series of continued effective government actions. After Emperor Zhenyuan of the Tang Dynasty (AD 785–805) came to the throne, China included the Nansha Islands in its administrative map. It did so more conscientiously in the Ming and Qing Dynasties. A wealth of official documents of the Chinese government, its local history books and official maps have recorded the exercise of jurisdiction by the successive governments of China over the Nansha Islands. *Geography Book of the History of the Yuan Dynasty* and *Map of the Territory of the Yuan Dynasty with Illustration* both include the Nansha Islands within the domain of the Yuan Dynasty. The *History of the Yuan Dynasty* has accounts of the patrol and inspection activities by the navy on the Nansha Islands in the Yuan Dynasty.

The inscription on the memorial tablet of the tomb of General Qian Shicai of the Hainan Garrison Command of the Ming Dynasty reads: "Guangdong is adjacent to the grand South China Sea, and the territories beyond the Sea all internally belong to the Ming State." "General Qian led more than ten thousand soldiers and fifty huge ships to patrol tens of thousands of li on the South China Sea." All these descriptions clearly testify to the ownership by China of the Nansha Islands in the Ming Dynasty. The Hainan Garrison Command of the Ming Dynasty was responsible for inspecting and patrolling as well as exercising jurisdiction over the Xisha, Zhongsha and Nansha Islands.

In the Qing Dynasty, the Chinese government marked the Nansha Islands on the authoritative maps and exercised administrative jurisdiction over these islands. The Nansha Islands were marked as Chinese territory in many maps drawn in the Qing Dynasty, including a "Map of Administrative Divisions of the Whole China" of the 1724 *Map of Provinces of the Qing Dynasty*, a "Map of Administrative Divisions of the Whole China" of the 1755 *Map of Provinces of the Imperial Qing Dynasty*, the 1767 *Map of Unified China of the Great Qing for Ten Thousand Years*, the 1810 *Topographical Map of Unified China of the Great Qing for Ten Thousand Years* and the 1817 *Map of Unified China of the Great Qing for Ten Thousand Years*.

Between 1912 and 1949 when China was a republic, the then Chinese government took a series of active measures to safeguard its sovereignty. For instance, it furnished the Chinese fishermen and fishing boats that engaged in fishing on the Nansha Islands and their adjacent waters with China's national flags. It organized trips to the Nansha Islands for a survey of their history and geography. And it authorized a map-printing and toponymic agency to rename and approve the names of all the islands in the South China Sea, including the Nansha Islands, individually and collectively.

Between 1932 and 1935 the Chinese government set up a Committee for the Review of Maps of Lands and Waters of China, which was composed of officials from the Headquarters of the General Staff, the Ministry of Internal Affairs, the Ministry of Foreign Affairs, the Navy Command, the Ministry of Education and the Mongolian and Tibetan Affairs Commission. This Committee examined and approved 132 names of the islands in the South China Sea, all of which belonged to the Xisha, Zhongsha (Macclesfield Bank) and Nansha Islands.

In 1933 France invaded and occupied nine of the Nansha Islands, including Taiping (Itu Aba) and Zhongye (Thitu) Islands. The Chinese fishermen who lived and worked on the Nansha Islands gave firm resistance against the invasion and the Chinese government lodged a strong protest with the French government.

All the names of the islands, isles and reefs in the South China Sea, including the Nansha Islands, were unambiguously marked on the *Map of the Islands in the South China Sea* compiled and printed by the Committee for the Review of Maps of Lands and Waters of China in 1935.

During World War II, Japan launched a war of aggression against China and occupied most of China's territory. In 1939 Japan occupied the islands in the South China Sea, including the Nansha Islands. It was explicitly provided in the Cairo Declaration, the Potsdam Proclamation and other international documents that all the territories Japan had seized should be restored to China, and naturally they included the Nansha Islands. In December 1946 the then Chinese government sent senior officials to the Nansha Islands for their recovery. A takeover ceremony was held on the islands, a monument erected in commemoration of it, and the troops were sent over on garrison duty. In line with the Cairo Declaration and the Potsdam Proclamation, the Ministry of Internal Affairs of China, in consultation with the navy and the government of Guangdong Province, appointed Xiao Ciyi and Mai Yunyu Special Commissioner to the Xisha and Nansha Islands respectively in 1946 to take over the two archipelagos and erect marks of sovereignty on the islands. In 1947 the Ministry of Internal Affairs of China renamed 159 islands, reefs, islets, and shoals in the South China Sea, including the Nansha Islands. It subsequently publicized all the names for administrative purposes.

In 1952 the Japanese government officially stated that it renounced all its "right, title and claim to Taiwan, Penghu Islands, as well as Nansha and Xisha islands", thus formally returned the Nansha Islands to China. After the founding of the People's Republic of China, the Nansha Islands were incorporated into Guangdong Province and Hainan Province successively and the Chinese government has all along maintained sovereignty over the Nansha Islands and taken effective actions for that.

China has a series of legislation concerning the territory of the South China Sea. On 4 September 1958, the Chinese government proclaimed the breadth of its territorial sea to be twelve nautical miles which applied to all territories of the PRC, "including … the Dongsha Islands, the Xisha Islands, the Zhongsha Islands, the Nansha Islands". The 1992 Law of the People's Republic of China on the Territorial Sea and the Contiguous Zone provides, "The land territory of the People's Republic of China includes … the Dongsha Islands, the Xisha Islands, the Zhongsha Islands and the Nansha Islands, as well as all the other islands belonging to the People's Republic of China" (Article 2). In addition, Article 14 of the 1998 Law on the Exclusive Economic Zone and the Continental Shelf of the People's Republic of China provides, "The provisions in this Law shall not affect the rights that the People's Republic of China has been enjoying ever since the days of the past." In 1983 the Chinese Toponymy Committee was authorized to publicize the approved names of the islands, reefs, islets and shoals in the South China Sea.

There are many other examples of safeguarding sovereignty by the Chinese government over these islands. For example, in response to the reports that the spokesperson of the Vietnamese Foreign Ministry indicated that the departments concerned in Vietnam were conducting feasibility studies on organizing tours to the Nansha Islands, China made the following statement on 17 October 2003:

> The Chinese side maintains a consistent position on issues concerning the South China Sea. China has indisputable sovereignty over the Nansha Islands and the adjacent waters. We hope that the countries concerned could earnestly observe the bilateral agreement and the spirit of China-ASEAN Declaration on the Conduct of Parties in the South China Sea and refrain from any action possibly complicating the current situation so as to commonly maintain peace and stability in the region of the South China Sea.[1]

On 17 February 2009 the Philippine Congress passed an Act to Define the Archipelagic Baselines of the Philippines (an Act to Amend Certain Provisions of Republic Act No. 3046, As Amended by Republic Act No. 5446, to define the Archipelagic Baselines of the Philippines, and For Other Purposes). The Act includes Huangyan Island (Scarborough Reef) and some islands and reefs of Nansha Islands as Philippine territory. On 18 February 2009 the Ministry of Foreign Affairs of China issued a statement reiterating that Huangyan Island and Nansha Islands have always been a part of China's territory. The People's Republic of China has indisputable sovereignty over these islands and their adjacent waters. Claims to territorial sovereignty over Huangyan Island and Nansha Islands by any other country is illegal and invalid.[2]

On 6 May 2009 Malaysia and Vietnam filed a Joint Submission to the Commission on the Limits of the Continental Shelf, claiming the outer limits of their respective continental shelf beyond 200 nautical miles in the south of the South China Sea. In addition, on 7 May 2009, Vietnam filed another submission to the commission, claiming the outer limits of its continental shelf beyond 200 nautical miles in the north of the South China Sea. China's permanent mission to the United Nations in New York sent notes to the Secretary-General of the United Nations reiterating its position on the South China Sea: China has indisputable sovereignty over the islands in the South China Sea and the adjacent waters, and enjoys sovereign rights and jurisdiction over the relevant waters as well as the seabed and subsoil thereof. The above position is consistently held by the Chinese government, and is widely known by the international community. The continental shelves beyond 200 nautical miles as contained in the submissions by Malaysia and Vietnam have seriously infringed China's sovereignty, sovereign rights and jurisdiction in the South China Sea. In accordance with Article 5(a) of Annex I to the Rules of Procedure of the Commission on the Limits of the Continental Shelf, the Chinese government seriously requests the Commission not to consider the Submissions.[3]

In short, a host of historical facts have proved that it was the Chinese people who were the first to discover and develop the Nansha Islands and it was the Chinese government that has long exercised sovereignty and jurisdiction over these islands. The Nansha Islands have become an inalienable part of Chinese territory since ancient times.

International Recognition of China's Sovereignty over the Nansha Islands

Many countries, world public opinion, and publications of other countries recognize the Nansha Islands as Chinese territory.

1. The United Kingdom
   - *China Sea Pilot* compiled and printed by the Hydrography Department of the Royal Navy of the United Kingdom in 1912 has accounts of the activities of the Chinese people on the Nansha Islands in a number of places.
   - *The Far Eastern Economic Review* (Hong Kong) carried an article on 31 December 1973 which quotes the British High Commissioner to Singapore as having said in 1970: "Spratly Island was a Chinese dependency, part of Kwangtung Province ... and was returned to China after the war. We cannot find any indication of its having been acquired by any other country and so can only conclude it is still held by communist China."

2. France
   - *Le Monde Colonial Illustre* mentioned the Nansha Islands in its September 1933 issue. According to that issue, when a French gunboat named Malicieuse surveyed the Nanwei Island of the

Nansha Islands in 1930, they saw three Chinese on the island and when France invaded nine of the Nansha Islands by force in April 1933, they found all the people on the islands were Chinese, with 7 Chinese on the Nanzi Reef, 5 on the Zhongye Island, 4 on the Nanwei Island, thatched houses, water wells and holy statues left by Chinese on the Nanyue Island and a signboard with Chinese characters marking a grain storage on the Taiping Island.

- *Atlas International Larousse* published in 1965 in France marks the Xisha, Nansha and Dongsha Islands by their Chinese names and gives clear indication of their ownership by China in brackets.

3. Japan
   - *Yearbook of New China* published in Japan in 1966 describes the coastline of China as 11 thousand kilometres long from Liaodong Peninsula in the north to the Nansha Islands in the south, or 20 thousand kilometres if including the coastlines of all the islands along its coast.
   - *Yearbook of the World* published in Japan in 1972 says that Chinese territory includes not only the mainland, but also Hainan Island, Taiwan, Penghu Islands as well as the Dongsha, Xisha, Zhongsha, and Nansha Islands in the South China Sea.

4. The United States
   - *Columbia Lippincott World Toponymic Dictionary* published in the United States in 1961 states that the Nansha Islands on the South China Sea are part of Guangdong Province and belong to China.
   - *The World Mark Encyclopaedia of the Nations* published in the United States in 1963 says that the islands of the People's Republic extend southward to include those isles and coral reefs on the South China Sea at the north latitude 4°.
   - *World Administrative Divisions Encyclopaedia* published in 1971 says that the People's Republic has a number of archipelagos, including Hainan Island near the South China Sea, which is the largest, and a few others on the South China Sea extending to as far as the north latitude 4°, such as the Dongsha, Xisha, Zhongsha, and Nansha Islands.

5. Vietnam
   - Vice Foreign Minister Dung Van Chime of the Democratic Republic of Vietnam received Li Shimon, chargé d'affaires ad interim of

the Chinese Embassy in Vietnam and told him that "according to Vietnamese data, the Xisha and Nansha Islands are historically part of Chinese territory". Le Doc, Acting Director of the Asian Department of the Vietnamese Foreign Ministry, who was present then, added that "judging from history, these islands were already part of China at the time of the Song Dynasty".

- *Nhan Dan* of Vietnam reported in great detail on 6 September 1958 the Chinese government's declaration of 4 September 1958 that the breadth of the territorial sea of the People's Republic of China should be 12 nautical miles and that this provision should apply to all territories of the People's Republic of China, including all islands in the South China Sea. On 14 September the same year, Premier Pham Van Dong of the Vietnamese government solemnly stated in his note to Premier Zhou Enlai that Vietnam "recognises and supports the Declaration of the Government of the People's Republic of China on China's Territorial Sea".
- It is stated in the lesson "The People's Republic of China" of a standard Vietnamese school textbook on geography published in 1974 that the islands from the Nansha and Xisha Islands to Hainan Island and Taiwan constitute a great wall for the defence of the mainland of China.

Foreign Maps Indicating the South China Sea as part of Chinese territory include:

1. *The Welt-Atlas* published by the Federal Republic of Germany in 1954, 1961 and 1970 respectively;
2. *World Atlas* published by the Soviet Union in 1954 and 1967 respectively;
3. *World Atlas* published by Romania in 1957;
4. *Oxford Australian Atlas* and *Philips Record Atlas* published by Britain in 1957 and *Encyclopaedia Britannica World Atlas* published by Britain in 1958
5. *World Atlas* drawn and printed by the mapping unit of the Headquarters of the General Staff of the People's Army of Vietnam in 1960;
6. *Haack Welt Atlas* published by German Democratic in 1968;
7. *Daily Telegraph World Atlas* published by Britain in 1968;
8. *Atlas International Larousse* published by France in 1968 and 1969 respectively;

9. *World Map Ordinary* published by the Institut Geographique National (IGN) of France in 1968;
10. *World Atlas* published by the Surveying and Mapping Bureau of the Prime Minister's Office of Vietnam in 1972; and
11. *China Atlas* published by Neibonsya of Japan in 1973.

Instances of China's Sovereignty over the Nansha Islands being recognized in international conferences include:

1. The 1951 San Francisco Conference on Peace Treaty called on Japan to give up the Xisha and Nansha Islands. Andrei Gromyko, Head of the Delegation of the Soviet Union to the Conference, pointed out in his statement that the Xisha and Nansha Islands were an inalienable part of Chinese territory. It is true that the San Francisco Peace Treaty failed to unambiguously ask Japan to restore the Xisha and Nansha Islands to China. But the Xisha, Nansha, Dongsha, and Zhongsha Islands that Japan was asked to abandon were all clearly marked as Chinese territory in "A Map of Southeast Asia" of the *Standard World Atlas* published by Japan in 1952, the second year after the peace conference in San Francisco, which was recommended by the then Japanese Foreign Minister Katsuo Okazaki in his own handwriting.

2. The International Civil Aviation Organisation held its first conference on Asia-Pacific regional aviation in Manila on 27 October 1955. Sixteen countries or regions were represented at the conference, including South Vietnam and the Taiwan authorities, and Australia, Canada, Chile, Dominica, Japan, Laos, the Republic of Korea, the Philippines, Thailand, the United Kingdom, the United States, New Zealand, and France. The Chief Representative of the Philippines served as Chairman of the conference and the Chief Representative of France its first Vice Chairman. It was agreed at the conference that the Dongsha, Xisha, and Nansha Islands were located at the communication hub of the Pacific and therefore the meteorological reports of these islands were vital to world civil aviation services. In this context, the conference adopted Resolution No. 24, asking China's Taiwan authorities to improve meteorological observation on the Nansha Islands, four times a day. When this resolution was put to the vote, all the representatives, including those of the Philippines and South Vietnam, agreed to it. No representative at the conference made any objection to or reservation about it.[4]

CHINA'S BASIC STANCE AND POLICY IN SOLVING
THE SOUTH CHINA SEA ISSUE

Since the 1970s, countries such as Vietnam, the Philippines and Malaysia have sent troops to seize some uninhabited islands and reefs of the Nansha Islands, destroyed the marks of sovereignty erected by China there, and arrested, detained, or driven away by force Chinese fishermen. These countries develop oil and gas in the Nansha area, and claim most of the South China Sea as their territories, exclusive economic zones and continental shelves as mentioned above.

From the Chinese perspective, the South China Sea issue means: (1) Chinese territories in the South China Sea are illegally occupied and the resources exploited by foreign countries, which tends to escalate sometimes, (2) some parties concerned deny their former recognition of Chinese territories in the South China Sea before the mid-1970s, and (3) outsiders inappropriately interfere with the South China Sea affairs.

With regard to international disputes, China has always stood for peaceful settlement through negotiation and consultation between the parties concerned. In this spirit, China has solved a series of issues regarding territory and borders with some neighbouring countries through bilateral consultations and negotiations in an equitable and amicable manner. The South China Sea issue is not an exception. It is an issue between China and the other littoral states concerned. China and the states concerned are fully capable and confident of handling their disputes appropriately. Involvement by any external forces is undesirable and will only further complicate the situation.[5] On the other hand, outsiders' intervention is unlikely to change China's position on the major issues of the South China Sea.

China is committed to working with the countries concerned for the proper settlement of the disputes related to the South China Sea through peaceful negotiations and consultations in accordance with universally recognized international law, including the fundamental principles and legal regimes set forth in the 1982 UN Convention on the Law of the Sea (UNCLOS). This was explicitly written into the Joint Statement issued at the China-ASEAN informal summit in 1997 and the 2002 China-ASEAN Declaration on the Conduct of Parties in the South China Sea (DOC). This is not only what China stands for but also what China does. In recent years, China has had consultations and exchanged views on the South China Sea issue with the countries concerned, and a broad identity of views has been reached. The bilateral consultation mechanisms between China, the Philippines, Vietnam, and Malaysia respectively are in effective operation, and positive progress has been made in the dialogues. At the China-ASEAN Senior Officials Meetings (SOM) and China-ASEAN Post-Ministerial Conferences (PMC), the two sides have had candid exchanges of views on the South China Sea issue, and agreed to seek an appropriate solution to the problem by peaceful means and through friendly consultations. At the working group meeting on the implementation of the DOC, follow-up action was held in Kunming City of Yunnan Province in December 2010, the parties concerned reiterated commitment to the DOC, agreeing to devote themselves to safeguarding peace and stability in the South China Sea and making it a sea of peace, friendship and cooperation. Positive discussions were held on how to promote the follow-up action process. China and ASEAN countries maintain unimpeded communication on relevant issue. China hopes to strengthen dialogue and cooperation with other parties to jointly safeguard peace and stability in the South China Sea.[6]

China maintains that all the parties concerned should adopt a restrained, calm and constructive approach to the South China Sea issue. China has also put forward the proposition of "shelving disputes and going in for joint development". China is ready to shelve the disputes for the time being and conduct cooperation with the countries concerned pending settlement of the disputes.

CONCLUSION

China's stance on some major issues of the South China Sea can be summarized as follows:

1. China has indisputable territorial sovereignty over the islands and their adjacent waters in the South China Sea, which are supported by ample historical evidence and law.
2. China has always stood for peaceful settlement of the disputes of the South China Sea, particularly through bilateral negotiations and consultations between the parties concerned.
3. China has always advocated and promoted international cooperation in the South China Sea, including joint development of the resources and maintaining and safeguarding peace and security.

Notes

1. See <http://www.fmprc.gov.cn/eng/xwfw/2510/2535/t37152.htm>.
2. See <http://www.fmprc.gov.cn/eng/zxxx/t537810.htm>.
3. See <http://www.un.org/Depts/los/clcs_new/submissions_files/
    submission_mysvnm_33_2009.htm> and <http://www.un.org/Depts/los/
    clcs_new/submissions_files/submission_vnm_37_2009.htm>.
4. See, Ministry of Foreign Affairs of the People's Republic of China <www.
    fmprc.gov.cn>.
5. Ibid.
6. Foreign Ministry Spokesperson Jiang Yu's regular press conference on
    28 December 2010 <http://www.mfa.gov.cn/eng/xwfw/s2510/2511/t782317.
    htm>.

7

THE CHANGING CONTEXTS OF CHINA'S POLICY ON THE SOUTH CHINA SEA DISPUTE

Li Mingjiang[1]

China, since 1949, has not treated its territorial disputes with neighbouring countries as an isolated issue in its foreign and security policy. Rather, Beijing has always handled those territorial issues in the larger context of its strategic interests of the time. Chinese decision-makers made concessions on territorial contentions when they believed that those compromises served China's broader and longer-term strategic benefits. Conversely, China appeared to be quite stubborn when heavy-handedness and assertiveness served its other purposes, either domestic or international.

The South China Sea issue is no exception in China's foreign and security calculations. Over the decades, China's handling of the dispute has been affected by a wide range of factors, apart from territorial or sovereignty claims. There are many good examples to illustrate this point. For instance, it has been argued that the 1974 conflict between China and South Vietnam, which ended in China taking control of the whole Paracels, was partly motivated by Chinese anxiety of a Soviet security threat from the sea.[2] The 1988 Sino-Vietnamese conflict in the Spratlys had to do with the People's Liberation Army (PLA) Navy's interest in pushing for a greater budget when Beijing was reducing military expenditure in the 1980s.[3] The 1995 Mischief conflict was partly a result of internal elite political power struggles in China.[4] And the "calculated moderation" in China's approach to the South China Sea dispute in the past decade reflected China's attempt to balance its interests in domestic economic development, sovereignty claims, and regional strategic interests.[5] These cases sufficiently demonstrate that it is useful and highly necessary to take into consideration many other factors to better understand China's policy on the South China Sea dispute.

This chapter attempts to analyse some of the major factors that have helped to shape China's policy on the South China Sea in the past decade or so. I will then discuss whether the context of China's policy-making, both internal and external, has significantly changed and what impacts this changed context would have on China's future policy on the dispute.

STRATEGIC INTERESTS AND MODERATION

Throughout the 1990s, China made great efforts to normalize its relations with Southeast Asian states. Departing from its initial approach that favoured bilateral relations, China became more involved in multilateral and regional institutions,[6] especially in frameworks that allowed Beijing to enhance its dialogue with the Association of Southeast Asian Nations (ASEAN). When former president Jiang Zemin and all the ASEAN leaders organized the first ASEAN plus China Summit in December 1997, they issued a joint statement of establishing a relationship of good neighbourliness and mutual trust oriented towards the twenty-first century. As a consequence, economic and political relations between China and the ASEAN countries developed rapidly.[7] But security relations were tarnished by territorial disputes in the South China Sea. At the turn of the century, however, the tensions began to relax, thanks to a series of agreements: China and Vietnam signed a Treaty on the Land Border in December 1999, followed by an agreement demarcating maritime zones in the Gulf of Tonkin in 2000,[8] and in November 2002 China and ASEAN signed the Declaration on the Conduct of Parties in the South China Sea (DOC). Meanwhile, at the ASEAN-China summit in November 2001, ASEAN leaders accepted China's proposal to create a China-ASEAN Free Trade Area (CAFTA) that would include China, Brunei, Malaysia, Indonesia, the Philippines, Singapore and Thailand by the year 2010, followed by Cambodia, Laos, Myanmar and Vietnam by the year 2015.[9]

Generally speaking, China's approach to the South China Sea dispute in the first half of the past decade reflected the overall reorientation of Beijing's diplomacy in Southeast Asia, which many pundits characterize as "charm offensive" or "soft power". China has essentially attempted to seek some balance in pursuing its sovereign, economic, and strategic interests in the dispute. Given the political, economic, and strategic importance of the South China Sea for China, many people in China may have wished to use more assertive means to push for China's interests in the area. However, in the past decade there has been no major military conflict between China and other disputants.[10] The prediction that in the aftermath of the Asian financial crisis in 1997, ASEAN states would be unable to pressurize China into accepting multilateral negotiations turned out to be incorrect.[11] China, on one hand, held a strong position on its claim of sovereignty at all diplomatic occasions, took piecemeal actions to consolidate its presence in the South China Sea, and responded with stern warnings when other disputants acted against Chinese interests. But on the other hand, Beijing felt that it had to address other more important goals in its foreign policy towards Southeast Asia, entailing quite a few significant changes in the actual Chinese behaviour.

It is widely believed that China has only opted for a bilateral approach to the South China Sea dispute. In reality, this assertion is largely a myth. So far, there has been no serious discussion, either bilateral or multilateral, about the sovereignty issues of the islands or the demarcation of maritime zones. It makes little sense to say that China only favours a bilateral approach to the problem. So far, the positive things that have taken place in the South China Sea dispute are confidence-building measures and at the same time also measures to manage the dispute (with the exception of the joint China-Philippines-Vietnam seismic study being a small step towards joint development). And these things have been multilateral. In fact, the claims by different parties overlap so much that it is impossible for China to discuss with any single ASEAN claimant country if China is willing to solve this problem diplomatically at all in the future.

For all the existing confidence-building measures and dispute-management measures, China has been dealing with ASEAN as a collectivity over the dispute for many years. For instance, the 1997 Joint Statement of ASEAN and Chinese leaders discussed the possibility of adopting a code of conduct in the South China Sea. The DOC was signed by all ASEAN Foreign Ministers and Chinese Special Envoy Wang Yi in Phnom Penh on 4 November 2002. The 2003 Joint Declaration of the Heads

of State/Government of the Association of Southeast Asian Nations and
the People's Republic of China (PRC) on Strategic Partnership for Peace
and Prosperity mentions that the two sides will implement the DOC of
Parties in the South China Sea, and discuss and plan follow-up actions.
The Plan of Action to Implement the Joint Declaration on ASEAN-China
Strategic Partnership for Peace and Prosperity discussed in detail how the
two sides could implement the DOC.

The DOC has not proven to be very effective in managing the disputes
in the South China Sea. But one can perhaps get some sense of its positive
role by asking this question: Could the dispute have been worse if there
had been no DOC? Moreover, the DOC does seem to serve as a stepping
stone for further discussion and policy deliberation among the claimant
countries. The DOC, ineffective as it has been in regulating the actual
behaviours of relevant parties, does effect a certain moral restraint on the
parties concerned. This demonstrated to some extent China's acceptance of
norms to regulate issues concerning the South China Sea, no matter how
primitive and informal the norms are. Also, by joining the ASEAN Treaty
of Amity and Cooperation (TAC), China has legally committed itself to
not use force against members of ASEAN.

Why would China adopt these relatively more moderate policies? It
is an important question, not only to understand the history of the past
decade, but also to have some clue for future development. One factor that
most observers can agree upon is insufficient capability of the PLA Navy
(PLAN),[12] but this factor alone does not give us a satisfactory explanation:
after all, China did take forceful actions in 1974, 1988, and 1995 when its
navy was even more inferior. What essentially shaped China's policy on
the South China Sea dispute towards cooperation and moderation was the
strategic context that China found itself in and China's visionary response
to that context. There were various domestic factors that facilitated the
implementation of that moderate policy as well.

In the aftermath of the Tiananmen crackdown in 1989, China was
diplomatically isolated in the first half of the 1990s. In order to break
the isolation, Beijing began to engage with Southeast Asian nations
both bilaterally and multilaterally in the mid-1990s. In that process of
engagement, China learned that its engagement policy was welcomed
by regional states and was effective in broadening China's international
presence and participation. More importantly, China realized that
engagement was the best policy tool to counter the widespread "China

threat" discourse in the West and in China's neighbourhood. This policy line led to the Chinese decision not to devalue its currency during the Asian financial crisis in 1997–98, which won considerable praise from Southeast Asian countries.

In the past decade, two sets of strategic thinking have dominated the milieu of foreign policy making in China. One is the notion of "an important period of strategic opportunity" (*zhongyao zhanlue jiyu qi*), which was put forth in the political report of the 16th Party Congress and thereafter has been repeatedly emphasized by top Chinese leaders on numerous occasions. The basic idea of this concept is that the first twenty years of the new century would be China's strategic opportunity to develop itself. There are both good opportunities and serious challenges to China's development, but overall it is highly possible for China to experience another major leap forward in the two decades if China handles its domestic and international challenges properly. The implicit warning is that if this "important period of strategic importance" is missed, China may not have another opportunity to ensure another major take-off. The second notion that perhaps has operationalized the first strategic thinking is the Chinese leaders' dictum that China should constantly well coordinate its domestic and international situations (*tongchou guonei guowai liangge daju*). The basic idea is that China should do everything possible to create a conducive external environment for the sake of domestic socio-economic development.

Under these strategic thoughts, at the turn of the new century, China was even more cognizant and confident that further engagement with Southeast Asian countries served China's strategic interests. These strategic interests included the following aspects. First of all, Chinese decision-makers believed that China would need a stable and peaceful regional environment in order to concentrate on domestic economic development. Related to that consideration, China also needed the supply of raw materials and energy resources, the markets, and investment in regional states. There was the imperative of creating a positive image of China in East Asia in order to water down the "China threat" rhetoric.

But Beijing's strategic consideration became far more comprehensive. China also began to aim to establish a stronger strategic foothold in the region to compete with the United States' strategic influence. That was why we saw a dazzling series of amazing Chinese moves in proactively engaging with ASEAN: the Free Trade Area (FTA) initiative (including the early harvest scheme), the DOC, the signing of the TAC, the announcement for a strategic partnership, and the addition of many more official cooperation mechanisms, and many political documents proclaimed by Chinese and ASEAN leaders. The preponderant U.S. military presence in East Asia and its extensive security ties with many Southeast Asian countries were factors that Chinese policymakers had to contend with. Beijing understood that a heavy-handed Chinese approach could only push other claimant states much closer to Washington in the security arena.

China also believed that supporting ASEAN as a regional grouping served China's regional and even global strategic interests. Regionally, a more united and stronger ASEAN would help dilute American strategic supremacy and make members of ASEAN more confident in perceiving China's rise so that they did not have to side with the United States or any other major power to counterbalance China. Supporting ASEAN was also good for China's global strategy of encouraging the emergence of multipolarity.

Inside China, various conditions during much of the past decade were also conducive to a moderate policy in the South China Sea disputes. The military establishment, usually the more hawkish element in any country, continued to enjoy a significant budget allocation and was primarily occupied with various new programmes to modernize its warfare capabilities. The military leadership appeared to believe that China's military power still lagged far behind that of the United States and its allies in East Asia. A head-to-head confrontation with the United States or any other major power would not be a wise choice. The various Chinese maritime law enforcement agencies were also keen to beef up their capabilities rather than to use their inadequate capacity to prematurely challenge or provoke other disputant states in China's neighbourhood. Thus, maritime territorial disputes, to some extent, were put on the back burner.

It is often not fully recognized that the decade since the late 1990s were the most notable period of China starting to actively participate in various maritime cooperation projects in East Asia.[13] During this period, various Chinese maritime agencies engaged with Malaysia, the Philippines, Indonesia, Vietnam, and Thailand for maritime cooperation projects. During a visit to Southeast Asian countries by Wang Shuguang, the former head of China's State Oceanic Administration, he even proposed that maritime ministers of countries surrounding the South China Sea meet regularly to discuss multilateral cooperation in the maritime domain.[14] China has also participated in the United Nations Environment Programme's (UNEP) Global Meeting of Regional Seas and Global Programme of Action for the Protection of the Marine Environment from Land-based Activities, the Partnership in Environmental Management for the Seas of East Asia (PEMSEA), the Northwest Pacific Action Plan (NPAP), the North Pacific Coast Guard Forum (NPCGF), and the Container Security Initiative (CSI). Sun Zhihui, former chief of China's Oceanic Administration, noted at the Second East Asia Seas Congress meeting that China intends to deal with maritime issues in the region to promote peace and stability, so that China can concentrate on economic development in the next twenty-year "important period of strategic opportunity".[15] Clearly, China's maritime policy in the past decade was regarded as part of its larger strategic consideration.

NON-CONFRONTATIONAL ASSERTIVENESS: THE EMERGING NEW CONTEXT

The year 2010 was a significant one in China's foreign and security policy. It was probably the most complicated and turbulent year for China's international politics in the past decade. Beijing's unprecedented strong response to U.S. arms sales to Taiwan and President Obama's meeting with the Dalai Lama, China's political and security protection of North Korea in the wake of the Cheonan incident and the Yeonpyeong bombing, the reportedly assertive Chinese actions in the South China Sea, China's heavy-handed approach to U.S. naval exercises in the Yellow Sea, and Beijing's pressure tactics during the Sino-Japanese crisis over the Diaoyu/Senkaku Islands dispute can be seen as examples of China becoming more assertive in East Asia. It is widely believed that Beijing has jettisoned its erstwhile "low profile" international posture and has instead become more aggressive in pushing for its own narrowly defined national interests. Some analysts even believe that China is inclined to adopt a confrontational strategy in the region.

It is perhaps a crucial moment for the rest of the world, in particular regional states, to have an accurate assessment of China's strategic thinking with regard to East Asian security and the South China Sea dispute. While acknowledging the fact that China has become more assertive and is likely to remain so in the foreseeable future, we also have to be sober minded to note that China is unlikely to pursue any kind of confrontational strategy in its regional international politics. Non-confrontational assertiveness is likely to underpin China's foreign and security policy in the near future and it is the probable reality that ASEAN countries will have to grapple with.

What does China's non-confrontational assertiveness essentially mean? It means that at the strategic level, Beijing is not likely to pursue any conspicuous confrontation with other major powers or ASEAN. China is not likely to pursue an ostensibly coercive approach towards its smaller neighbours for fear that such coercion may adversely affect China's strategic position in the region and its relations with other major powers. But at the same time, China will be assertive in dealing with issues that are of crucial importance to its national interests. There may seem to be some contradictions between the strategic non-confrontation and tactical assertiveness, but it appears that China has been able to balance the two through dexterous diplomacy. In the past decade or more, for instance, China has arguably practiced non-confrontational assertiveness in its external policy with regard to human rights, maritime territorial and demarcation disputes, and even the Taiwan issue. Assertive actions were taken whenever China's core concerns on these issues were infringed upon. But at the same time, Beijing has always been careful not to escalate any dispute into a major long-term confrontation with any other major power. What is different from the past is that Beijing is likely to be willing to employ more assertive means in dealing with major disputed issues in its foreign relations.

In addition to this overall emerging context of non-confrontational assertiveness, the context of China's policy making in relation to the South China Sea is also subtly changing. First of all, there is widespread disappointment and frustration in China regarding the developments in the region. Similar to Vietnamese complaints of China's brutality against Vietnamese fishermen, China also complains that its traditional fishing ground in the Spratlys has been shrinking[16] and its fishermen have been badly treated. One Chinese report notes that since 1989, over 300 instances of Chinese fishing vessels being arrested, expelled and even fired upon have taken place in the Spratly area and over 80 Chinese fishing boats and over 1,800 Chinese fishermen have been arrested.[17] While most Chinese analysts agree with the government position that "shelving disputes and joint development" should still be the official position of China, some observers in China are increasingly critical of this policy. They argue that this policy has actually worked against Chinese interests in that it has allowed other claimant states to unilaterally exploit the resources in the South China Sea.[18]

Beijing is also unhappy with other states' attempts to rally under the ASEAN flag and use the ASEAN Regional Forum (ARF) to discuss the South China Sea issue to exert pressure on China.[19] China is particularly concerned about the involvement of other major powers, in particular the United States. In the understanding of Chinese scholars, Washington has been pursuing a policy of "active neutrality" in the South China Sea. It is a policy of "neutrality" in that the United States has openly stated that it does not support the territorial claim of any party and does not intend to get involved in the imbroglios. But it is active in the sense that it has repeatedly warned against any forceful means to solve the problem and any action that would impede the freedom and safety of navigation and the overall stability in the region. It is also an active policy in that the United States has quite strongly insisted on having the freedom of using the South China Sea, including China's exclusive economic zone (EEZ) areas, to conduct military surveillance activities.[20] The U.S. government has openly stated that it would protect the interests of American oil companies that have businesses and are assisting other claimant countries in energy exploitation in the South China Sea.[21] Various U.S.-led naval exercises in the South China Sea have reinforced Chinese analysts' negative views of Washington's role in the disputes.[22] Overall, many Chinese analysts conclude that the United States has continued to pursue a strategy of military preponderance in the South China Sea and has become more active in the disputes as part of a U.S. strategy to contain or constrain China's rise.[23]

In recent years, China has begun to pay more attention to the South China Sea, hoping to reap the potential energy resources. In 2005 the Chinese Ministry of Land and Resources identified the South China Sea as one of ten strategic energy zones and made plans to accelerate efforts to exploit the deep-water oil and gas in the region. China National Offshore Oil Corporation (CNOOC) and several scientific research institutes in China have stepped up efforts to further study the oil and gas reserves in the deep-water area in the South China Sea.[24] Despite doubts about the reported huge reserves of oil and gas in the South China Sea by various international experts, the Chinese seem to be quite certain about the prospect of energy resources in the area. Zhang Fengjiu, a senior engineer at CNOOC, reported that up to 2007 China had discovered 323.5 billion cubic metres of natural gas in the South China Sea. He also notes that

China has been extracting about 6 billion cubic metres of natural gas from the South China Sea annually.[25] Various research institutes in China have started a comprehensive study on methane gas hydrate (the so-called combustible ice) in the South China Sea.[26] In August 2006 China announced that it planned to invest RMB800 million in studying the exploration of combustible ice in the South China Sea and intended to trial extraction before 2015. It is estimated that the reserves of combustible ice in the northern part of the South China Sea would amount to 50 per cent of all the oil reserves in the land area of China.[27]

CNOOC plans to invest RMB200 billion (US$29 billion) before 2020 to set up 800 oil platforms in deep water areas. The company plans to produce 250 million tonnes of crude oil equivalent in deep water areas by 2015 and 500 million tonnes by 2020. CNOOC is now stepping up efforts, including developing the required technologies, equipment, and human resources, to meet these targets.[28] CNOOC has signed contracts with American, Canadian, and British oil companies to explore and exploit the oil and gas resources in the northern part of the South China Sea. In recent years, CNOOC, in cooperation with its partner Husky Energy, has discovered three areas of natural gas reserves on Block 29/26 in the Pearl River basin in the eastern part of the South China Sea. The latest discovery, the Liuhua 29-1 exploration well, announced by CNOOC on 9 February 2010, tested natural gas at an equipment-restricted rate of 57 million cubic feet per day.[29] According to Husky, "the three natural gas fields — Liwan 3-1, Liuhua 34-2 and Liuhua 29-1 — have confirmed the resource potential of a major gas development project in the South China Sea and support an earlier estimate of 4 to 6 trillion cubic feet of petroleum for the block."[30]

In addition to CNOOC, China National Petroleum Corporation (CNPC) and China Petrochemical Corporation (Sinopec) have also been granted areas in the South China Sea and have decided to make major investments in deep-water oil and gas projects.[31] Given the enormous Chinese interest in energy resources in the area, China may continue to emphasize its "shelving disputes and joint exploitation" policy. But at the same time, since many regional claimant states are not strongly interested in the Chinese proposal, it is quite likely that China may also step up efforts to unilaterally exploit the resources in the Spratlys area in the foreseeable future.[32]

Given all the changes that have taken place and the rapid rise in expectation for tangible material benefits, China is unmistakably poised to further assert its interests in the South China Sea, although these actions have other purposes that may not be relevant to the South China Sea disputes. In early 2009 the air force of the Guangzhou Military Region conducted a large-scale exercise in the far South China Sea. Many Chinese analysts regarded the exercise, in particular the airborne refuelling of China's indigenous J-10 jet fighters, as a deterrent signal that China sent to other claimant states. The exercise indicated that China is "gradually taking steps to adopt a more assertive strategy" towards the South China Sea disputes instead of simply issuing diplomatic protests as it had done in the past.[33]

In March 2009 China sent its fishery administration vessel 311, the largest fishery patrol vessel converted from a retired warship, to patrol the Paracels. In May another fishery administration fleet patrolled the Paracels. On 1 April 2010 two Chinese fishery administration vessels embarked to protect the activities of Chinese fishermen. Unlike similar patrols in the past, this time the Chinese government decided to conduct regular patrols in the Spratlys area. Liu Tianrong, a senior official at the Fishery Administration of the South Sea Area, said that at the sailing ceremony the crews of the two vessels were determined to counter piracy, resist the arrests of Chinese fishing boats by other states, oppose the actions of other states in expelling Chinese fishing boats, and highlight Chinese sovereignty in the South China Sea.[34] Four days later, the Chinese fishery administration fleet arrived at the southern end of the Spratly archipelago (N5'30) and began to provide protection for Chinese fishing boats. This is an area that the Chinese fishing community traditionally calls the "Southwest fishing area" because it is located in the Southwest of the Spratlys.[35] From late March to early April, a flotilla of the PLAN North Sea Fleet conducted long-distance excercises in the South China Sea.[36]

Over the last decade China has made progress in enhancing its maritime enforcement capabilities, including "unprecedented capability" of using satellites to monitor and conduct operations along its disputed maritime periphery,[37] although its enforcement capabilities still remain "balkanised and relatively weak" compared to other major powers.[38] China has though increasingly applied its capability to protect its interests in the South China Sea. During much of 2010, the outside world was concerned about the Chinese claim of treating the South China Sea issue as one of its "core national interests."[39] Although it is still unclear how, why, and under what context the Chinese officials made the remarks, the fact that

China has neither officially clarified nor refuted such rhetoric indicates that some segments in China intend to be serious about protecting the country's interests in the South China Sea.

IMPLICATIONS FOR CHINA-ASEAN INTERACTIONS IN THE SOUTH CHINA SEA

What does China's non-confrontational assertive policy posture in the South China Sea imply for ASEAN and its claimant countries in the disputes? Essentially, it means that in the coming years other claimant countries need to be prepared to deal with a China that is more likely to use pressure tactics on contentious issues between them. Beijing is less likely to make concessions on the South China Sea issue, for instance, its reluctance to reach a legally binding code of conduct or clear stance on the "my sovereignty" precondition for joint development schemes in the South China Sea. As China starts to be more active in protecting what it perceives as its own national interests in the South China Sea, disputes and skirmishes are possible. Unilateral actions by ASEAN claimant countries in the South China Sea would likely beget Chinese countermeasures and in fact might be used by China as an excuse to assert its own interests. If such a vicious circle of events came about it would have a significantly negative impact on China-ASEAN cooperation in many other areas; i.e., non-traditional security cooperation and regional economic integration.

At the same time, leaders in ASEAN countries may find it useful to note that China has little intention for any major confrontation with its Southeast Asian neighbours. Despite emerging signs of China becoming more assertive, there are significant constraints that could limit China flexing its muscles. China faces several dilemmas in the South China Sea disputes. First of all, the predicament is how to maintain the balance between the protection of its sovereign and other maritime interests in the South China Sea and at the same time to sustain peaceful and stable relations with Southeast Asian countries, particularly those nations that are direct claimant states. Southeast Asia has been often been dubbed as China's strategic backyard. Beijing needs to maintain good relations with its Southeast Asian neighbours in order to diffuse the "China threat" thesis, cultivate a positive China image on the international stage, and push for multipolarization in world politics. A heavy-handed approach could easily swing other claimant states to the security embrace of the United States and other external powers, for instance Japan and India. Secondly, Beijing has to constantly encounter the difficult maritime disputes with Japan in the East. The challenges in the East Sea are no less daunting than those in the South China Sea. In fact, in recent years, there have been numerous emerging crisis situations between China and Japan. Japan is a much stronger rival, both in terms of economic and military power, for China in the maritime domain. The challenge for Beijing is how to avoid the simultaneous occurrence and escalation of maritime conflicts in the East and in the South. In this sense, China will have to tread carefully in the South China Sea in order to avoid a two-front confrontation. Thirdly, and perhaps most importantly, the sober-minded view of China's political elite is that the essential task for China is to focus on domestic socio-economic development for decades to come. The Chinese elite firmly believe, perhaps rightly so, that a peaceful and stable environment, particularly in its East Asian neighbourhood, is indispensible for sustained domestic economic growth.

Given this context, China is likely to practice self-constraint so as to avoid a major confrontation with Southeast Asian countries. Beijing is also likely to reciprocate any regional states' goodwill to prevent any crisis from escalating. This essentially means that there is a good window of opportunity for the parties to maintain the status quo and manage the disputes well. It would be useful if the parties would endeavour to establish more effective mechanisms for crisis prevention and crisis management. The parties could also do a better job of explaining their strategic intentions to each other. Needless to say, such explanations will not completely clear the distrust between the disputants, but it might help in mitigating misunderstandings. In this sense, it is important to maintain regular high-level communications between the involved parties.

What ASEAN could further do is to continue to work on regional institutions and norms. The pace of regional institution building has been slow in recent years, but it is better than nothing. Regional institutions have always provided a suitable conduit for the leaders of China and ASEAN claimant states. One should also not play down the socialization effect of interactions in various regional institutions. Efforts to further develop norms in regulating regional international relations should continue and ASEAN could continue to play the driver's role.

The opportunity to push for joint development in the South China Sea may not be lost if ASEAN claimant countries are amenable to the idea. To push for win-win deals, one step that China could undertake is to further clarify its position on its claims in the South China Sea. For many years,

Beijing has pushed for a "joint development" scheme in the South China Sea. But at the same time, China has insisted that other claimant states have to recognize Chinese sovereignty in the South China Sea as a precondition. As one can imagine, regional states have categorically refused to accept the Chinese precondition. In light of the emerging consensus among Chinese scholars on the definition of the U-shaped line and bilateral and multilateral practices that have taken place in the South China Sea, it is possible for China to more clearly define the implications of its U-shaped line and practice significant flexibility in its "my sovereignty" precondition.

According to a Chinese maritime strategist, generally speaking, there are four views and interpretations of the U-shaped line.[40] The first view is that the islands and their adjacent waters within the line are areas of Chinese jurisdiction. This is also the official position: "China enjoys indisputable sovereignty over the islands and their adjacent waters in the Spratlys."[41] Still there is ambiguity over the extent of "adjacent waters". The second view is that the line is the boundary of China's historical rights, including sovereignty over the islands, islets, atolls and shoals and all the natural resources in the waters, while allowing other countries to have the freedom to navigate, overflight, and lay cables and pipelines under the water. The third view, largely held by some Taiwanese scholars, indicates that the South China Sea should be China's historical water, meaning that the area is China's internal water or territorial sea.[42] The fourth view is that the line represents the national territorial boundary; everything within the line is Chinese territory.

Some Chinese analysts believe that Beijing should provide a more clear-cut explanation for the U-shaped line sooner rather than later given the fact that other regional claimant states have stated their EEZ and continental shelf in the South China Sea and the fact that regional states have been aggressively exploiting oil and natural gas resources in the area.[43] The talks with Vietnam on the demarcation of maritime zones and resource development in the south of the Tonkin Gulf have added to the urgency for China to clarify its position on the U-shaped line.[44] China will need to promulgate its maritime baseline in the Spratlys and EEZ and continental shelf zones. All these measures are urgently needed because the Chinese patrol missions will have to be based on certain legal grounds. Without these legal measures, it is difficult for the Chinese patrol crews to determine the boundary of their patrols and actions appropriate to protect China's maritime interests in the Spratlys area.[45]

The debate in China has arrived at a point where China can now offer a clearer position on its claims in the South China Sea. Chinese analysts are aware that the possible Chinese claim of owning the South China Sea as its internal waters, territorial waters, or historical waters is weakened by the government's pronouncements regarding freedom and safety of foreign vessels and aircraft in and over the area. The fact that dotted lines are symbols typically used for undetermined state boundaries indicates that China may not be able to claim the area as part of its territory.[46] It is also argued that in the process of promulgating the South China Sea map and the dotted lines in the late 1940s, the explicit intention of the Chinese government (ROC) was to decide and publicize the boundaries and sovereignty of the Paracel and Spratly archipelagos. The Chinese government at that time did not intend to claim the whole water area of the South China Sea.[47]

There seems to be a widely held view that the nine dotted lines are not China's territorial boundary but support China's sovereign rights over the islands and islets and other relevant rights over the natural resources in the South China Sea.[48] Chinese maritime legal experts have taken note that the notion of "historical waters" has become less relevant in international maritime delimitations. Moreover, China had objected to the Vietnamese claim of historical waters in the Tonkin Gulf demarcation.[49] Many Chinese scholars believe that China enjoys "historical rights" in the South China Sea,[50] which are implied in Article 14 of the 1998 Chinese Law on the EEZ and Continental Shelf: "regulations in this law do not affect the historical rights that the PRC should enjoy". They argue that China has both legal rights that are derived from the UNCLOS and historical rights that are derived from the U-shaped line. All in all, these rights would include sovereignty over the islands and their adjacent waters and rights over the natural resources within the U-shaped line.[51]

In practice, China has shown considerable flexibility in its "my sovereignty" precondition in relation to joint development. In various official proclamations, Beijing has only claimed "sovereignty and sovereign rights over the islands and their adjacent waters" in the South China Sea. China has openly stated that it would allow the freedom of international communications in the South China Sea, including maritime navigation, flights in the airspace over the South China Sea, and the laying of cables and pipelines on the seabed. The China-Philippines-Vietnam joint seismic study, which was essentially part of "joint development", did not require any recognition of China's sovereignty in the area under study. China has already accepted "joint development" in its EEZ and continental shelf in the East China Sea with Japan and in the Tonkin Gulf with Vietnam; in neither case did China require the other party to accept Chinese sovereignty as a precondition. China also categorically rejected Vietnam's suggestion of treating the Tonkin Gulf as an area of historical waters during their demarcation negotiations. China is actively negotiating with Vietnam over "joint development" in the area south of the Tonkin Gulf, which is essentially part of the South China Sea.

For "joint development" to take place, China may consider some flexibility with regard to the "my sovereignty" precondition. In fact, all other claimant parties should also drop any position on sovereignty for any joint exploitation proposal because according to UNCLOS no country enjoys full sovereignty beyond its territorial sea. Insisting on "my sovereignty" contradicts with the notion of "shelving disputes". After all, the proposed "joint development" plan is not about the islands. If China could take the lead to further play down sovereignty claims in the South China Sea, it would significantly remove a barrier to "joint development".

A clearer Chinese position on its claims and willingness to push for benevolent objectives, i.e., truly win-win situations, would facilitate serious discussions of some of the grand proposals that have emerged. Xue Li, a senior strategic analyst at the Chinese Academy of Social Sciences, proposes a Spratly Energy Development Organisation to include all the seven claimant parties to jointly explore and exploit the energy resources in the Spratlys area.[52] Some Chinese scholars also believe that it would be a good idea to establish a South China Sea economic circle.[53] Further downplaying sovereignty in the waters of the South China Sea would certainly help the realization of the Pan-Beibu Gulf Economic Zone, which is now quite enthusiastically pushed by the Guangxi Ethnic Zhuang Autonomous Region in China.

Joint development and closer economic integration around the South China Sea could be the first major step towards a reasonable final solution to the disputes. The Chinese believe that the "shelving disputes and joint development" proposal has a benevolent intention. They feel that the proposal is not an end in itself, but rather a step towards the larger goal of finding a final solution to the disputes. They believe that joint development could help enhance understanding and gradually build consensus through cooperation so that one day the various parties could find realistic options to solve the problem once and for all.[54] It may even be possible to submit the disputes to international arbitration in the future.[55]

CONCLUSION

China's policy on the South China Sea issue has been shaped by many factors, which include domestic politics, public sentiment, domestic economic development, and most importantly China's own strategic calculations. The configuration of major factors that helped determine Beijing's approach to the dispute differed at different times, but obviously China's strategic thinking has had the most important impact on its decisions. This chapter has demonstrated how Beijing's strategic calculations in the decade since the late 1990s have entailed a more or less moderate approach to the South China Sea contention. China's strategic priority in striving to shape a stable and peaceful international environment, particularly in its neighbourhood, essentially limited China's choices in dealing with the dispute. "Calculated moderation" was perhaps the only logical option for China.

Starting in recent years, the context for China's strategic thinking has evolved somewhat. Beijing now understands that its strategic position has slightly changed in its favour, although the fundamentals of the geostrategic structure in East Asia may not have changed at all. China appears to be less worried about the possibility of any formal containment or policy to constrain it in the region that could be led by the United States. Beijing's perception of its own power and capability has also changed. Whereas in the past two decades it felt it was weak and vulnerable, now it has gained much confidence in handling tough regional issues. Together with this perception of power growth, no matter whether it is real, Chinese nationalism seems to be on the rise as well. Assertive nationalism in China has effectively become a double-edged sword for decision-makers when it comes to territorial and sovereignty disputes with neighbouring countries. Also, energy security has become an increasingly important component in China's strategic thinking. All these new trends mean that China is likely to be more assertive in handling regional disputes in the coming years.

But at the same time, there is little evidence to show that China intends to practice pure coercion or confrontation towards its maritime neighbours. Some of the fundamental elements and the context of China's previous strategic thinking still exist. China's actual behaviour in its management of territorial disputes in the region is likely to be characterized as non-confrontational assertiveness. Its assertiveness is likely to be manifested as intransigence, non-compromise, piecemeal reinforcements, and stern counter-measures in response to "intervention" by external powers.

In response to China's non-confrontational assertiveness, ASEAN (or some ASEAN countries) may attempt to play the balance of power game by getting external powers, i.e., the United States, involved in the dispute. This strategy might be effective to some extent in taming China's assertiveness. Overly playing this game may also result in China hardening its position and adopting countermeasures, which may further complicate the South China Sea disputes and damage the bilateral relations between individual ASEAN countries and China. ASEAN can play a proactive role in helping shape China's strategic thinking. It could continue attempts to convince China that properly managing the dispute serves China's strategic and long-term interests. It could continue to socialize China in various regional institutions and forums. And, most importantly, ASEAN (especially those claimant countries) could perhaps seriously consider the "joint development" option, as there is still fairly strong political and intellectual support for such initiatives in China.

Notes

1. Part of this chapter is adapted from the author's article, "Reconciling Assertiveness and Cooperation? China's Changing Approach to the South China Sea Dispute", *Security Challenges* 6, no. 2 (2010): 49–68.
2. Manvyn S. Samuels, *Contest for the South China Sea* (New York: Methuen, 1982). Chi-kin Lo, *China's Policy Towards Territorial Disputes: The Case of the South China Sea Islands* (New York: Routledge, 1989).
3. See John W. Garver, "China's Push through the South China Sea: The Interaction of Bureaucratic and National Interests", *China Quarterly*, no. 132 (December 1992): 999–1028.
4. Ian James Storey, "Creeping Assertiveness: China, the Philippines and the South China Sea Dispute", *Contemporary Southeast Asia* 21, no. 1 (1999).
5. Li Mingjiang, "Security in the South China Sea: China's Balancing Act and New Regional Dynamics", *RSIS Working Paper*, no. 149 (February 2008).
6. Christopher R. Hughes, "Nationalism and Multilateralism in Chinese Foreign Policy: Implications for Southeast Asia", *Pacific Review* 18, no. 1 (2005): 119–135; Ronald C. Keith, "China as a Rising World Power and its Response to 'Globalisation'", *Review of International Affairs* 3, no. 4 (2004): 507–23.
7. Saw Swee-Hock, Sheng Lijun, and Chin Kin-Wah, eds., *ASEAN-China Relations, Realities and Prospects* (Singapore: Institute of Southeast Asian Studies, 2005).

8. Zou Keyuan, "The Sino-Vietnamese Agreement on Maritime Boundary Delimitation in the Gulf of Tonkin", *Ocean Development and International Law*, no. 36 (2005): 13–24.

9. Sheng Lijun, "China-ASEAN Free Trade Area, Origins, Developments and Strategic Motivations", *ISEAS Working Paper*, International Politics and Security Issues Series no. 1 (Singapore: Institute of Southeast Asian Studies, 2003); Ian Storey, "China-ASEAN Summit: Beijing Charm Offensive Continues", *China Brief*, Jamestown Foundation 6, no. 23 (22 November 2006).

10. The territorial dispute in the SCS is often cited as evidence to support the doomsday scenario of security in East Asia; see, for example, Aaron L. Friedberg, "Ripe for Rivalry: Prospects for Peace in a Multipolar Asia", *International Security* 18, no. 3 (1993–94): 5–33.

11. For such a prediction, see Allan Collins, *The Security Dilemmas of Southeast Asia* (Basingstoke: Macmillan, 2000), p. 169.

12. Felix K. Chang, "Beijing's Reach in the South China Sea", *Orbis* 40, no. 3 (Summer 1996); Ralf Emmers, "The De-escalation of the Spratly Dispute in Sino-Southeast Asian Relations", *RSIS Working Paper*, no. 129 (6 June 2007).

13. Li Mingjiang, "China and Maritime Cooperation in East Asia: Recent Developments and Future Prospects", *Journal of Contemporary China* 19, no. 64 (2010): 291–310.

14. Yang Yan, "Zhongguo haiyang daibiaotuan fangwen dongnanya san guo" [Chinese marine delegation visits three Southeast Asian countries], *zhongguo haiyang bao* [China ocean newspaper], 24 December 2004.

15. Yu Jianbin, "Rang 'dongya hai jiayuan' geng meihao" [Making the East Asian Seas region a more beautiful home], *People's Daily*, 12 December 2006.

16. Xi Zhigang, "Zhongguo nanhai zhanlue xin siwei" [China's new thinking on the South China Sea issue], *moulue tiandi* [The strategic arena], no. 2 (2010): 56–60.

17. In <http://news.xinhuanet.com/mil/2010–04/06/content_13307981.htm> (accessed 5 April 2010).

18. Liu Zhongmin, "lengzhan hou dongnanya guojia nanhai zhengce de fazhan dongxiang yu zhongguo de duice sikao" [Developments and trends in Southeast Asian countries' South China Sea policies and China's responses], *nanyang wenti yanjiu* [Southeast Asian affairs], no. 2 (2008): 25–34; Wang Yongzhi et al., "Guanyu nanhai duan xu xian de zonghe taolun" [A comprehensive view of the South China Sea dotted line], *Journal of Ocean University of China* (Social Sciences Edition), no. 3 (2008): 1–5; Li Guoxuan, "nanhai gongtong kaifa zhiduhua: neihan, tiaojian yu Zhiyue yinsu" [The institutionalisation of joint development in the South China Sea: Scope, conditions, and constraints], *nanyang wenti yanjiu* [Southeast Asian affairs], no. 1 (2008): 61–68.

19. Liu, "lengzhan hou dongnanya guojia".

20. Cai Penghong, "meiguo nanhai zhengce pouxi" [Analysing American policy

towards the South China Sea issue], *xiandai guoji guanxi* [Contemporary international relations], no. 9 (2009): 1–7, 35.

21. Lu Fanghua, "shi xi nanhai wenti zhong de meiguo yinsu" [An examination of the U.S. factor in the South China Sea problem], *dongnanya nanya yanjiu* [Southeast Asia and South Asia studies], no. 4 (December 2009): 6–10.

22. Zhang Zuo, "mei jie 'kalate' yanxi, buju nan zhongguo hai" [The U.S. making plans in the South China Sea by staging the CARAT exercises], *huanqiu junshi* [Global military affairs], no. 202 (July 2009).

23. Lu, "shi xi nanhai wenti zhong"; Cai, "meiguo nanhai zhengce pouxi"; Wang Chuanjian, "meiguo de nan zhongguo hai zhengce: lishi yu xianshi" [American South China Sea policy: History and reality], *waijiao pinglun* [Diplomatic affairs], no. 6 (2009): 87–100.

24. *China Ocean Petroleum Newspaper*, 23 January 2009.

25. Zhang Fengjiu, "wo guo nanhai tianranqi kaifa qianjing zhanwang" [The prospect of natural gas exploitation in the South China Sea], *tianranqi gongye* [Natural gas industry] 29, no. 1 (January 2009): 17–20.

26. *China Land and Resources Newspaper*, 22 September 2008.

27. In <http://www.chinamining.com.cn/news/listnews.asp?classid=154&siteid=74942> (accessed 25 April 2010).

28. Zhou Shouwei, "nan zhongguo hai shenshui kaifa de tiaozhan yu jiyu" [Challenges and opportunities for deep water exploitation in the South China Sea], *gao keji yu canyehua* [Hi-technology and industrialization], December 2008, pp. 20–23.

29. <http://www.cnooc.com.cn/news.php?id=301091> (accessed 2 April 2010).

30. <http://www.huskyenergy.com/news/2010/husky-energy-announces-third-discovery-in-south-china-sea.asp> (accessed 3 April 2010).

31. <http://www.cs.com.cn/ssgs/02/200812/t20081229_1698907.htm> (accessed 22 March 2010).

32. Feng Yunfei, "Guanyu zhongguo nanhai kaifa zhanlue sixiang de tanjiu" [Thoughts on China's strategic approach to exploitation of the South China Sea], *canye yu keji luntan* [Industrial and science tribune] 7, no. 12 (2008): 35–37; Zhang, "wo guo nanhai tianranqi kaifa qianjing zhanwang".

33. Xi, "Zhongguo nanhai zhanlue xin siwei".

34. <http://news.xinhuanet.com/mil/2010–04/06/content_13307981.htm> (accessed 6 April 2010).

35. *Nanfang Ribao* [Southern daily], 7 April 2010.

36. <http://mil.huanqiu.com/china/2010–04/777498.html> (accessed 14 April 2010).

37. Peter J. Brown, "China's Navy Cruises into Pacific Ascendancy", *Asia Times*, 22 April 2010.

38. Lyle J. Goldstein, "Five Dragons Stirring up the Sea: Challenge and Opportunity in China's Improving Maritime Enforcement Capabilities", *Naval War College China Maritime Study*, 5 April 2010.

39. <http://www.nytimes.com/2010/04/24/world/asia/24navy.html?hp=&page wanted=all> (accessed 1 May 2010).
40. Jia Yu, "Nanhai 'duan xu xian' de falu diwei" [The legal status of the dotted line in the South China Sea], *China's Borderland History and Geography Studies*, no. 2 (2005).
41. <http://www.fmcoprc.gov.hk/chn/wj/fyrth/t310165.htm> (accessed 21 March 2010).
42. Cheng-yi Lin, "Taiwan's South China Sea Policy", *Asian Survey* 37, no.4 (1997): 323–24.
43. Wang et al., "Guanyu nanhai duan xu xian".
44. Li Linghua, "nanhai zhoubian guojia de haiyang huajie lifa yu shijian" [Regional states' legislation and practice in maritime demarcation in the South China Sea], *Journal of Guangdong Ocean University* 28 no. 2 (2008): 6–11.
45. Li Jinming, "nanhai jushi yu yingdui hanyangfa de xin fazhan" [The situation in the South China Sea and responses to the latest developments in the international law of the sea], *nanyang wenti yanjiu* [Southeast Asian affairs], no. 4 (2009): 12–19.
46. Yu, "Nanhai 'duan xu xian' de falu diwei".
47. Ibid.; Wu Jiahui et al., "zhong yue beibuwan huajie shuangying jieguo dui jiejue nanhai huajie wenti de qishi" [The win-win results in Sino-Vietnamese Tonkin Gulf demarcation and the implications for maritime delimitation in the South China Sea], *redai dili* [Tropical geography] 29, no. 6 (November 2009): 600–603.
48. Zhiguo Gao, "The South China Sea: From Conflict to Cooperation", *Ocean Development and International Law* 25 (1994): 346; Zhao Haili, *Haiyang fa wenti yanjiu* [Problems in the law of the sea] (Beijing: Peking University Press, 1996), p. 37; Li Linghua, "nanhai zhoubian guojia de haiyang huajie lifa yu shijian" [Regional states' legislation and practice in maritime demarcation in the South China Sea], *Journal of Guangdong Ocean University* 28 no. 2 (April 2008): 6–11; Zhao Xueqing and Cheng Lu, "Haiyang fa shiye xia de zhongguo nanhai dalujia huajie fenzheng", *Journal of Jinan University*, no. 6 (2009) 77–82.
49. Wang et al., "Guanyu nanhai duan xu xian".
50. Li Jinming, *nanhai zhengduan yu guoji haiyang fa* [South China Sea disputes and international law of the sea] (Beijing: Ocean Press, 2003), p. 59; Zou Keyuan, "Historic Rights in International Law and in China's Practice", *Ocean Development and International Law* 32, no. 2 (2001).
51. Yu, "Nanhai 'duan xu xian' de falu diwei".
52. Xue Li, "nansha nengyuan kaifa zuzhi: nanhai wenti de chulu" [Spratly energy development organization: A solution for the South China Sea issue], *shangwu zhoukan* [Business weekly] (20 June 2009), pp. 60–62.
53. Yu Wenjin et al., "nanhai jingji quan de tichu yu tantao" [A proposal and analysis of South China Sea economic circle], *diyu yanjiu yu kaifa* [Areal Research and Development] 27, no. 1 (2008): 6–10.

54. Li Guoxuan, "nanhai gongtong kaifa zhiduhua: neihan, tiaojian yu Zhiyue yinsu" [The institutionalization of joint development in the South China Sea: Scope, conditions, and constraints], *nanyang wenti yanjiu* [Southeast Asian affairs], no. 1 (2008): 61–68; Li Guoqiang, "dui jiejue nansha qundao zhuquan zhengyi jige fang'an de jiexi" [An analysis of the several proposals for the solution of the Spratly islands], *China's Borderland History and Geography Studies*, no. 3 (2000): 79–83.

55. Guo Yuan, "dui nanhai zhengduan de guoji haiyang fa fenxi" [An analysis of the application of international law of the sea on the South China Sea disputes], *beifang fa xue* [Legal studies in the north] 3, no. 14 (2009): 133–38.

Part Four
ASEAN Claimants' and Taiwan's Positions

8

SETTLEMENT OF THE SOUTH CHINA SEA DISPUTE
A Vietnamese View

Nguyen Thi Lan Anh[1]

The South China Sea is usually considered as having vital strategic and economic interest. It is a nexus of maritime routes, connecting the Indian and Pacific Oceans. It possesses a diverse marine environment with rich resources of fisheries and ideal conditions for marine research activities. In addition, the continental shelf in the South China Sea is believed to contain great oil and gas reserves. This gives rise to the existence of one of the most complicated and long-lasting sovereignty and maritime disputes. However, with its specific geographical characteristic of a semi-enclosed sea,[2] any exploration, exploitation, and management activities in the South China Sea must be conducted in a cooperative manner. In this regard, Article 123 of the United Nations Convention on the Law of the Sea (UNCLOS) is worthy of being quoted as a framework for cooperation of states bordering enclosed or semi-enclosed seas:

> States bordering an enclosed or semi-enclosed sea should cooperate with each other in the exercise of their rights and in the performance of their duties under this Convention. To this end they shall endeavour, directly or through an appropriate regional organisation: 1) to coordinate the

management, conservation, exploration and exploitation of the living resources of the sea; 2) to coordinate the implementation of their rights and duties with respect to the protection and preservation of the marine environment; 3) to coordinate their scientific research policies and undertake where appropriate joint programmes of scientific research in the area; and 4) to invite, as appropriate, other interested States or international organisations to cooperate with them in furtherance of the provisions of this article.

Such a framework must also be taken into account in settling the disputes in the South China Sea.

SOVEREIGNTY DISPUTES

The sovereignty disputes in the South China Sea mainly relate to some mid-ocean islands. The Paracels are disputed between Vietnam and China (including Taiwan). The Spratlys are disputed (as a whole or partly) between Vietnam, China (including Taiwan), Malaysia, Brunei, and the Philippines. The Scarborough Shoal is disputed between China (including Taiwan) and the Philippines.

With a long history and complicated claims from multiple parties, the sovereignty questions in the South China Sea disputes raise a number of issues of international law concerning territory acquisition. The international law concerning territory acquisition was well established in international customary law and consisted of five legal modes, namely occupation, prescription, cession, conquest, and accession. *Effectivités* was the vital condition in most of the modes and was developed through case law. In the *Eastern Greenland* case, two elements for effective occupation, the important element to establish title in territory acquisition, were laid down by the Permanent Court of International Justice, namely "the intention and will to exercise "sovereignty and the manifestation of state activity".[3] Intention can be inferred from official notifications and the display of sovereignty may be satisfied by concrete evidence of possession or control. *Effectivités* were also clarified by Arbitrator Huber in the *Island of Palmas* case as an actual and durable taking of possession within a reasonable time, i.e., the continuous and peaceful display of territorial sovereignty.[4] Furthermore, in the *Clipperton Island Arbitration*, the arbitrator held that effective occupation consists of a physical act or acts, the purpose of which is to exercise exclusive authority.[5] "Authority" according to Oppenheim means the establishment of proper state machinery, the actual display of state jurisdiction.[6] However, in a special case of uninhabited places, the requirements for *effectivités* are less strict. In the *Minquiers and Ecrehos* case, Judge Basdevant, in his separate opinion, emphasized that exercising effective military control did not necessarily mean garrisoning practically uninhabited or uninhabitable places, but that for this purpose, power to hold such areas at will and to prevent other states from occupying them was sufficient.[7] Also related to the special case of a very small island, in a more recent judgment of the *Qatar v. Bahrain* case, the Court held that certain activities such as the construction of navigational aids could be sufficient to support sovereignty claims.[8] In addition, acts of individuals by themselves are no substitution for the display of state authority. Unless authorized in advance or subsequently ratified, the activities of individuals can be neither attributed nor imputed to the state whose nationals they are.[9]

It is also important to mention that among five modes, cession is no longer a legitimate means of establishment of a title through the use of force or threat of force, and such will not create lawful title to territory under contemporary international law. In the early twentieth century, various efforts were made to prevent the use of force as a legal means under international law. Firstly, the second and the third Hague Conventions of 1907 limited the use of force to recover contract debt and required war to be preceded by a formal declaration.[10] Then, with the unprecedented suffering of World War I, the Covenant of the League of Nations required that war be used only as a last resort three months after the parties received a judicial settlement or report by the Council.[11] The Kellogg-Briand Pact of 1928 followed, in which the use of war was outlawed as an instrument of national policy. This marked the first general acceptance of the prohibition of the use of force, which was then codified in Article 2(4) of the United Nations Charter. Nowadays, war is no longer a legitimate instrument of national policy and all of the UN member states must refrain from the threat or use of force against the territorial integrity or political independence of any state. The use of force or threat of force will not create a lawful title to territory. In addition, although force can be used in self-defence under Article 51 of the UN Charter, it is not acceptable for acquiring new territory.[12] Therefore, all claimants in the South China Sea dispute must refrain from using force to create new title, strengthen the claim or to settle the dispute.

The law of the sea also plays an important role in identifying eligibility in sovereignty disputes. In general, seabed elevations are classified into three legal groups: islands, low-tide elevations and others which are always underwater even at low tide. Of the three groups, only islands allow states to generate title, thus are subject to sovereignty claims. Low-tide elevations cannot be fully assimilated with islands and other land territory.[13] The only significance of low-tide elevations are the possibility of them being used as base points if they are within the area of the territorial sea from islands according to Article 13(1), if they qualify as reefs under the provision of Article 6, or if some constructions are built upon them according to Article 7. However, such low tide elevations will not be used as base points if they are located within an overlapping area.[14] In addition to islands and low-tide elevations, other features in the Spratlys do not have any impact on questions concerning territorial sovereignty. However, the practice of the parties to the South China Sea disputes suggest that some elevations, although submerged at high tide or even low tide, are still objects of occupation and claims for both territorial issues and maritime zones. The parties have fortified these claims by constructing structures such as lighthouses, military structures, and weather stations in order to make the elevations stand above water at high tide. This is the case of some elevations such as Macclesfield Bank, Alexandra Bank, Prince Consort Bank, Prince of Wales Bank, Rifleman Bank, Vanguard Bank, and Mischief Reef. With activities by the states, these elevations lose their characteristic of being "naturally formed" and become artificial islands.[15] However, coastal states can only use low-tide or submerged elevations to build artificial islands if they have the sovereignty rights over the water area where the low-tide elevations are located.

With a large amount of features in the middle of the South China Sea, the sovereignty disputes may lead to maritime disputes and thus complicate the situation while producing challenges for dispute settlement.

MARITIME DISPUTES

The maritime disputes in the South China Sea may be generated from three sources, including the maritime zones of the mainland of littoral states, the maritime zones of the mid-ocean islands and the other maritime claims.

Regarding the first source, in line with the provisions of UNCLOS, all coastal states in the South China Sea, namely China (including Taiwan), Vietnam, Cambodia, Thailand, Indonesia, Malaysia, Brunei, and the

Philippines, have claimed maritime zones including 200 nautical miles of exclusive economic zone and continental shelf. Also, based on the stipulations of UNCLOS, China, the Philippines, Malaysia, and Vietnam have submitted their claims or preliminary information on the extended continental shelf to the Commission on the Extended Continental Shelf (CLCS).[16] Accordingly, Vietnam claimed its extended continental shelf independently in the eastern coast and jointly with Malaysia in the southern coast.[17] China, Brunei and the Philippines also have submitted preliminary information concerning their extended continental shelf to meet the deadline of the CLCS,[18] thus leaving the possibility of submitting their extended continental shelf claims later. These claims resulted in overlapping maritime claims between those generated from adjacent and opposite coasts of the littoral states.

In addition to maritime zones of the mainland, the second source of maritime dispute may be generated from the mid-ocean islands. The regime of islands is currently provided for under Article 121 of UNCLOS. Accordingly, an island is entitled to generate a full maritime zone if it can sustain human habitation or have economic life of its own.[19] The wording of this article is a topic of controversy[20] and even more controversial in trying to apply it to the case of the Paracels and Spratlys, where all features are very small in size, there is no habitation of ordinary people and there are limited natural resources in the islands themselves. Vietnam by its note verbal responding to the position of China and the Philippines on their extended continental shelves noted that its position is "without prejudice to the matters relating to the delimitation of the boundaries between states with opposite or adjacent coasts as well as positions of states that are parties to land and maritime disputes".[21] The phrase "without prejudice" implies that their extended continental shelves produce no overlapping territories, thus the Spratlys and Paracels produce no exclusive economic zone or continental shelf of their own.

The third source of maritime dispute comes from the maritime claims of China (including Taiwan). The claim first appeared with a map published in 1947 covering a large area of the South China Sea extending southward from 15 to 4 degrees north latitude to include the entire Spratlys and James Shoal.[22] No explanation was given by China or Taiwan for the purpose of the dotted lines drawn on the map.

Due to the ambiguity in explaining the significance of the dotted line, there are three different assumptions made as to the significance of the line. The first assumption is that the line shows the territorial claims of China to the islands within the line.[23] This means that the dotted line is only used to illustrate the territorial claims of China to islands in the South China Sea, including the Paracels and the Spratlys. The second assumption is that the waters within the line are the historic waters. The third assumption is that the water within the dotted line is the maritime spaces generated from the Paracels and Spratlys.

For the first basis, the legitimacy of the line will be dependent on the sovereignty issues which will be judged by international law concerning territorial acquisition and the nine dotted lines may not be relevant to maritime claims. On the second basis, the idea of the historic waters and historic bay, under international law of the sea, are a subject of controversy. Some scholars have tried to suggest a definition of historic waters. For example, Blum notes that "the term 'historic water' is applied nowadays in respect of maritime areas in general, with the reference to bodies of water which — in spite of their being situated beyond the normal limits of a State's maritime domain — are treated as if they were part of the maritime appurtenance of the littoral State" (1965, p. 261). Bouchez offers another definition that "[h]istoric waters are waters over which the coastal State, contrary to the generally applicable rules of international law, clearly, effectively, continuously, and over a substantial period of time, exercises sovereignty rights with the acquiescence of the community of States".[24] D.P. O'Connell also lays out three circumstances which could be considered as historic water: "1) bays claimed by states which are greater in extent, or less in configuration, than standard bays; 2) areas of claimed waters linked to a coast by offshore features but which are not enclosed under the standard rules; and 3) areas of claimed seas which would, but for the claim, be high seas because [they are] not covered by any rules specially concerned with bays or the delimitation of coastal waters (*maria clausa*)".[25]

In the *Fisheries* case, the court clarified that "historic waters are usually meant [sic] waters which are treated as internal waters but which would not have that character were it not for the existence of an historic title".[26] Furthermore, under the studies of the UN Secretariat in 1962, as requested by the UN International Law Commission, the common perception on historic water was described thus:

> The State which claims "historic waters" in effect claims a maritime area which, according to general international law, belongs to the high seas. As the high seas are *res communis omnium* and not *res nullius*, title to the area cannot be obtained by occupation. The acquisition by historic title is "adverse acquisition", akin to acquisition by prescription; in other

> words, title to "historic water" is obtained by a process through which the originally lawful owners, the community of states, are replaced by the coastal State. Title to "historic waters", therefore, has its origin in an illegal situation which was subsequently validated. This validation could not take place by the mere passage of time; it must be consummated by the acquiescence of the rightful owners.[27]

Despite all efforts to clarify the concept of historic waters, no definition of "historic waters" was given in the UNCLOS. The 1982 UNCLOS only refers to historic bays and historic title when it stipulates on the regime of bays, the delimitation of the territorial sea between states with opposite or adjacent coasts and limitation and exception in dispute settlement.[28] This may be deliberate because "historic waters" are treated as internal waters, thus by such a limited mention, the UNCLOS only allows the application of "historic waters" in the case of bays and within internal and territorial waters. Also, the International Law Commission suggested that states need to fulfil three conditions in order to claim historic water, namely (1) the actual exercise of coastal state authority over the area, (2) continuity over time of this exercise of authority and (3) the attitude of foreign states to the claim.[29] In a recent U.S. case, the U.S. Supreme Court also clarified that,

> [t]o make a historic waters claim, a State must show that the United States exercises authority over the area, has done so continuously, and has done so with the acquiescence of foreign nations. This exercise of sovereignty must have been, historically, an assertion of power to exclude all foreign vessels and navigation, including vessels engaged in "innocent passage," *i.e.*, passage that does not prejudice the coastal State's peace, good order, or security.[30]

In the current case, the area claimed by China is huge, covering almost all maritime space in the South China Sea. This area has never been the internal waters of China; other countries still have freedom of navigation and exercise sovereignty rights in the adjacent waters of the Spratlys. The publication of the map without an interpretation of the function of the dotted line will not be sufficient to prove that China has continuously exercised authority in the waters.

Furthermore, other states have never expressed their recognition of China's claim. A Vietnamese official said that the dotted line of China was exaggerated and legally groundless. "There is nothing in the international law of the sea that can justify this kind of claim."[31] Indonesia also expressed its concern over the publication of Chinese maps showing the unclear dotted lines. Hasjim Djalal, a senior Indonesian diplomat, commented that "the Chinese territorial claims are limited towards the islands and all rights related thereto, and not territorial claims over the South China Sea as a whole".[32] Dr Hamzah, the Director General of the Maritime Institute of Malaysia, also indicated that the line as a claim over the entire South China Sea was "frivolous, unreasonable and illogical".[33] Therefore, if the dotted line represents the maritime boundary of China in the South China Sea on the basis of historic waters, due to the lack of actually exercising authority and the objection of the states concerned, such a claim does not conform to the international law of the sea.

As for the final assumption regarding the regime of the Paracels and Spratlys, China, in recently opposing the extended continental shelf claims of Vietnam and Malaysia, said that "China has indisputable sovereignty over the islands in the South China Sea and the adjacent waters, and enjoys the sovereign rights and jurisdiction over the relevant waters as well as the seabed and subsoil thereof".[34] The phrases "sovereign rights and jurisdiction" and "relevant waters" indicated the exclusive economic zone and continental shelf of the islands, i.e., China supports the position that the Paracels and Spratlys have full maritime zones. In particular, the attachment of the nine dotted line map to such a declaration for the first time implied that the nine dotted line was claimed as the line covering the exclusive economic zone and continental shelf of the islands in the South China Sea instead of a line for the previous historic claim of China. This latest development may confirm that the last assumption is the current position of China on the meaning of the nine dotted lines. This, however, is subject to interpretation and application in good faith of Article 121 of UNCLOS.

TOWARDS DISPUTE SETTLEMENT

The South China Sea disputes only involve some of the littoral states in the sea; however, the management of the disputes may affect all of them. All states in the region share a common marine environment and benefit from natural resources of the ocean. Stability of the region is vital for the development of all these countries. Therefore, any approaches to dispute settlement must ensure that peace and security of the region are not endangered.

One of the basic principles emphasized in international dispute settlement is to use peaceful means. The most feasible prospect to end the

South China Sea disputes is to settle all disagreement through dialogue with the mutual respect of the interests of all parties concerned and on the basis of international law, especially the 1982 UNCLOS and the 2002 Declaration on the Code of conduct.

In order to have a comprehensive understanding of the interests and positions of each party, transparency plays a very important role. Transparency should apply to the limits of sovereignty and maritime claims, the legal basis for these, as well as the military activities conducted in the disputed areas in the South China Sea. Transparency shows the confidence of the parties in the legitimacy of their claims with the aim of providing better understanding for the other parties and the world community of their positions, thus narrowing the scope of the dispute and the questions of disagreement. Transparency also facilitates confidence building among parties, an element that is essential for any fruitful negotiation.

Notwithstanding sovereignty over some mid-ocean islands and maritime zones, the South China Sea disputes also relate to many issues that include natural resources, navigation, and maritime security. Some of these issues concern the sovereignty and sovereignty rights of parties to the disputes. Others may relate to all interested parties, even through they are not states of the region; e.g., navigation or maritime security. Also, taking into account that the South China Sea is a semi-enclosed sea, the settlement of some issues may not be limited to the parties of the sovereignty or maritime disputes. In this connection, some aspects of the disputes themselves contain international characteristic that cannot be fully solved without the participation of all parties concerned. The other aspects need to be settled directly by the claimants, as it is not appropriate to invite other states to participate in the negotiation if such participation is irrelevant to their claims or interests.

The negotiations must be based on the application of international law. However, reaching a common understanding and interpretation of the relevant provisions of the applicable laws is also a matter that requires good faith and effort from the parties concerned. One feasible measure to achieve common understanding is to promote transparent discussion of the dispute in different fora, either bilateral or multilateral, or by seeking advisory opinions from international courts and tribunals. In addition to international law, the fundamental principles that have been accepted in the Declaration of the Code of Conduct must be respected and serve as grounds for harmonizing the different interests of all claimants.

Finally, peace, security and stability are vital for all states in the region. Other states, even if not parties to the disputes, may facilitate the dispute settlement by providing initiatives, mediation or fora for discussion. In this regard, the initiative of Indonesia to organize a series of Workshops on Managing Potential Conflict in the South China Sea is valuable for confidence building and promoting cooperation in the region. The ASEAN framework is also a suitable forum for gathering all parties to the dispute as well as the littoral states of the South China Sea.

Notes

1. The opinions expressed in this paper are those of the author and do not necessarily represent any official position or policy of Vietnam.
2. As defined in Article 122 of UNCLOS: For the purposes of this Convention, "enclosed or semi-enclosed sea" means a gulf, basin or sea surrounded by two or more states and connected to another sea or the ocean by a narrow outlet or consisting entirely or primarily of the territorial seas and exclusive economic zones of two or more coastal states.
3. *Eastern Greenland Case (Denmark v. Norway)* (1933) PCIJ Series A/B no. 53, p. 22 at 63.
4. This requirement was illustrated in interpretation of terminology employed in the special agreement between the Netherlands and the United States in the award of the *Island of Palmas* case (1928) 2 RIAA, p. 829, reprinted in (1928) 22 *AJIL* 867, pp. 874–77.
5. *Clipperton Island Arbitration (France v. Mexico)* 2 RIAA 1105, also in (1932) 26 *AJIL* 390, p. 393.
6. Oppenheim, *International Law*, 8th edition, vol. 1 (London: Longman, 1955, p. 546.
7. *Minquiers and Ecrehos Case (France v. UK)* ICJ Reports (1953), p. 47; Individual opinion of Judge Basdevant, ICJ Report (1953), pp. 74, 78.
8. ICJ Report, 2001, p. 40 (para. 197).
9. Opinion of Judge Hsu Mo in the Fisheries case, ICJ Report, 1951 (para. 157).
10. Hague Convention II (Laws of War: The Limitation of Employment of Force for Recovery of Contract Debts) and Hague Convention III (Laws of War: The Opening of Hostilities). For full text, see website of Brigham Young University Library at <http://net.lib.byu.edu/~rdh7/wwi/hague.html> (accessed 20 May 2006).
11. Article 12(1) of the Covenant.
12. For further discussion on the legal development of international law on the rights of conquest, see Korman 1996, pp. 180–248.
13. ICJ Report 2001 (para. 202).

14. This restriction is in line with the judgment of the *Qatar v. Bahrain* case, ICJ Report, 2001 (para. 209).

15. In an attempt to define an artificial island, Johnson specified that an artificial island must be an island in the same sense that a natural island is an island, i.e., must be surrounded by water and permanently above water at high tide. However, it differs from a natural island as the natural element. For further discussion on the history of the legal regime of artificial islands, see Johnson 1951, p. 203.

16. Member states to the 1982 UNCLOS which generate a continental shelf to beyond 200 nautical miles must submit the information of the outer limit of their continental shelf to the CLCS as soon as possible but, in any case, within ten years of entry into force of the Convention for that state (Rules and Procedure of the Commission on the Limits of the Continental Shelf (hereafter Rules and Procedure, Doc. CLCS/40 of 2 July 2004.). Taking into account the difficulties that developing states are facing in preparing the information for submission, at the 11th meeting of member states to the Convention in 2001, the parties agreed that for state parties for which the Convention enters into force before 13 May 1999, the ten-year time shall be taken as commencing on that date. (Decision regarding the date of commencement of the ten-year period for making submissions to the Commission on the Limits of the Continental Shelf set out in Article 4 of Annex II to the LOSC, Doc, SPLOS/72 on 29 May 2001, para. [a].)

17. See the joint submission of Malaysia and Vietnam on 7 May 2009 <http://www.un.org/Depts/los/clcs_new/submissions_files/submission_mysvnm_33_2009.htm > and the submission of Vietnam on 8 May 2009 <http://www.un.org/Depts/los/clcs_new/submissions_files/submission_vnm_37_2009.htm>.

18. The submission of China was made on 11 May 2009, see <http://www.un.org/Depts/los/clcs_new/submissions_files/preliminary/chn2009preliminaryinformation_english.pdf>; The submission of Brunei was made on 12 May 2009, see <http://www.un.org/Depts/los/clcs_new/submissions_files/preliminary/brn2009preliminaryinformation.pdf>; The submission of the Philippines was made on 8 April 2009, see <http://www.un.org/Depts/los/clcs_new/submissions_files/submission_phl_22_2009.htm>.

19. Article 121 provided that:

    1. An island is a naturally formed area of land, surrounded by water, which is above water at high tide.

    2. Except as provided for in paragraph 3, the territorial sea, the contiguous zone, the exclusive economic zone and the continental shelf of an island are determined in accordance with the provisions of this Convention applicable to other land territory.

    3. Rocks which cannot sustain human habitation or economic life of their own shall have no exclusive economic zone or continental shelf.

20. For some discussion of the difficulty in interpreting this Article, see Charney, "Rocks Cannot Sustain Human Habitation" 93(1999) *AJIL*, pp. 863–77 and Kwiatkowska and Soons, "Entitlement to Maritime Areas of Rocks which Cannot Sustain Human Habitation or Economic Life of their Own" 21(1990) *NYIL*, 174, pp. 139–81. Brown commented on the wording of Article 121(3) that "in its present form, Article 121(3) appears to be [the] perfect recipe for confusion and conflict". For further details, see Brown E.D., "Rockall and the Limits of National Jurisdiction of the UK", Part I, *Marine Policy* (1978), p. 181 (para. 206).

21. Para. 3 of the Note Verbale dated 18 August 2009 of Vietnam. A similar position was shared by Malaysia in para. 3 of their Note Verbale dated 21 August 2009.

22. The earliest compiled map was found in 1914. For details of the origin and evolution of the map, see Li Jinming and Li Dexia, "The Dotted Line on the Chinese Map of the South China Sea: A Note", *ODIL*, vol. 34 (2003), p. 287 (para. 287–90).

23. This is the opinion of some Chinese scholars quoted in Lin 1997, p. 323 (para. 325).

24. Leo J. Bouchez, *Regime of Bays in International Law* (Leyden: Sijthoff, 1964), p. 281.

25. D.P. O'Connell, *The international Law of the Sea*, vol. 1 (Oxford, Clarendon Press, 1982), p. 417.

26. *Fisheries Jurisdiction, Judgment*, ICJ Reports (1951), p. 116 (para. 130).

27. UN Doc. A/CN.4/143, 9 March 1962, titled "Judicial Regime of Historic Waters, Including Historic Bays" (1962), *Yearbook of the International Law Commission*, p. 3 at 16, quoted in Zou Keyuan, "Historic Rights in International Law and in China's Practice", *ODIL*, vol. 32 (2001), p. 149 (para. 151).

28. For example, Article 10(6) says that "[t]he foregoing provisions do not apply to so-called 'historic bays'"; Article 15 mentions "by reason of historic title" as the exception in applying the meridian line in maritime delimitation, etc.

29. UN Doc. A/CN.4/143, 9 March 1962, titled "Judicial Regime of Historic Waters".

30. Alaska v. US, 545 US 75, 125 S.Ct. 2137 (2005) (para. 2141).

31. Huynh Minh Chinh, "Sovereignty of Vietnam over Hoang Sa (Paracels) and Truong Sa (Spratlys) and Peaceful Settlement of Disputes in the Bien Dong Sea (South China Sea)" in *ASEAN in the 21st Century: Opportunities and Challenges* (Hanoi: Institute for International Relations, 1996), pp. 98–99.

32. Hasjim Djalal, "Conflicting Territorial and Jurisdictional Claims in the South China Sea", *Indonesian Quarterly*, vol. 7 (1979), p. 3 (para. 42).

33. B.A. Hamzah, "Conflicting Jurisdiction Problems in the Spratlys: Scope for

Conflict Resolution", paper presented in the Second Workshop on Managing
Potential Conflicts in the South China Sea, Bandung, Indonesia, 15–18 July
1991, pp. 199–200, referred to in Keyuan, "Historic Rights in International
Law", p. 38.
34. Para. 2 of the Note Verbale of China dated on 7 May 2009.

References

Blum, Yehuda Z. *Historic Titles in International Law* (The Hague: Maritinus Nijhoff,
    1965).
Bouchez, Leo J. *Regime of Bays in International Law* (Leyden: Sijthoff, 1964).
Brown, E.D. "Rockall and the Limits of National Jurisdiction of the UK" (Part I).
    Marine Policy, 1978.
Charney. "Rocks Cannot Sustainable Human Habitation". *AJIL* 93 (1999).
Hague Convention II (Laws of War: The Limitation of Employment of Force for
    Recovery of Contract Debts) and Hague Convention III (Laws of War: The
    Opening of Hostilities). For full text, see website of Brigham Young University
    Library at <http://net.lib.byu.edu/~rdh7/wwi/hague.html> (accessed
    20 May 2006).
Hamzah. *Conflicting Jurisdiction Problems in the Spratlys: Scope for Conflict Resolution*.
    Paper presented in the Second Workshop on Managing Potential Conflicts in
    the South China Sea, Bandung, Indonesia, 15–18 July 1991.
Hasjim Djalal. "Conflicting Territorial and Jurisdictional Claims in the South China
    Sea". *Indonesian Quarterly* 7 (1979).
Huynh Minh Chinh. "Sovereignty of Vietnam over Hoang Sa (Paracels) and Truong
    Sa (Spratlys) and Peaceful Settlement of Disputes in the Bien Dong Sea (South
    China Sea)". In *ASEAN in the 21ˢᵗ Century: Opportunities and Challenges* (Hanoi:
    Institute for International Relations, 1996).
Johnson, D.N.H. "Artificial island". *ILQ* 4 (1951).
Korman, Sharon. *The Rights of Conquest: The Acquisition of Territory by Force in
    International Law and Practice* (Oxford: Clarendon Press, 1996).
Kwiatkowska and Soons. "Entitlement to Maritime Areas of Rocks which
    Cannot Sustain Human Habitation or Economic Life of their Own". *NYIL*
    21 (1990).
Li Jinming and Li Dexia. "The Dotted Line on the Chinese Map of the South China
    Sea: A Note". *ODIL* 34 (2003).
Lin, Cheng-yi. "Taiwan's South China Sea Policy". *Asian Survey* 37, no. 4 (1997).
O'Connell, D.P. *The International Law of the Sea*, vol. 1 (Oxford: Clarendon Press,
    1982).
Zou Keyuan. "Historic Rights in International Law and in China's Practice". *ODIL*
    32 (2001).

9

THE PHILIPPINES AND
THE SOUTH CHINA SEA

Rodolfo C. Severino

The Treaty of Peace with Japan, signed in San Francisco on 8 September 1951, states in its Article 2, "Japan renounces all right, title and claim to the Spratly Islands and to the Paracel Islands", which Japanese forces occupied just before and during World War II and from which they launched attacks on other countries in the region. However, the treaty does not say which nation is to have such right, title or claim to those islands, although the Vietnamese have asserted that, since those islands belong to Vietnam, it can be assumed that they reverted to Vietnam after Japan was divested of them.[1] The Chinese have made a similar claim on behalf of Chinese ownership.

The Philippines and Vietnam were among the forty-nine states that signed the treaty. Neither the People's Republic of China, which had taken control of the Chinese mainland almost two years earlier, nor the "Republic of China", which had fled to Taiwan but claimed to be the government of all of China, was invited to the San Francisco conference that produced the treaty. This was mainly because some of the participants in the conference recognized the People's Republic as the rightful government of China, while others continued to give recognition to the authorities on Taiwan as the government of all of China.

On 28 April 1952, the same day that the San Francisco Treaty entered into force, Japan and the "Republic of China", which Japan then considered as the Chinese government, signed a separate Treaty of Peace in Taipei. In it, the two parties "recognized" that, under the San Francisco Treaty, Japan had "renounced all right, title, and claim to Taiwan (Formosa) and Penghu (the Pescadores) as well as the Spratley Islands and the Paracel Islands", again without specifying which nation would have such right, title or claim. On 29 September 1972, Japan shifted its diplomatic relations from Taipei to Beijing by means of the Joint Communiqué issued during Prime Minister Kakuei Tanaka's visit to China. Without explicitly referring to the Paracels or the Spratlys, the communiqué stated that Japan "firmly maintains its stand under Article 8 of the Potsdam Proclamation" issued by the leaders of the Republic of China, the United Kingdom and the United States on 26 July 1945, which limited Japanese sovereignty "to the islands of Honshu, Hokkaido, Kyushu, Shikoku and such minor islands as we determine". Six years later, on 12 August 1978, Japan and the People's Republic signed a Treaty of Peace and Friendship, which reaffirmed the 1972 Joint Communiqué but was otherwise silent on territorial issues.

THE CLOMA CLAIM

Meanwhile, in 1947, fishing boats belonging to Tomás Cloma, a Filipino marine educator and entrepreneur, mainly in fishing-related ventures, started visiting the islands of the South China Sea that are closest to the Philippines. According to A.V.H. Hartendorp, Cloma "considered plans to establish an ice plant and cannery on Itu Aba and also to exploit the guano deposits on the islands."[2]

In 1956, after sending the training ship of his Philippine Maritime Institute on an expedition to the islands in early March, Cloma on 15 May proceeded, through a "Notice to the Whole World", to claim ownership of an area in the South China Sea of 64,976 square nautical miles. The coordinates indicated were roughly congruent with the area that the Philippine government was to claim as Kalayaan twenty-two years later.[3] On the same day, in a letter enclosing the "Notice" and its accompanying maps, Cloma wrote to the Secretary of Foreign Affairs, then Vice President Carlos P. García, informing the Philippine government that "about forty citizens of the Philippines were undertaking survey and occupation work 'in a territory in the China Sea outside of Philippine waters and not within the jurisdiction of any country', and that the territory being occupied was being claimed by him and his associates".[4]

Six days later, on 21 May, Cloma sent another letter to the Secretary of Foreign Affairs informing him that the territory that he was claiming had been named "Freedomland" and enclosing a list of the new names that he had given the individual islands and other features. Stressing that the claim to the territory had been made by citizens of the Philippines and not by the Philippine government or on its behalf, Cloma urged the government to support that claim rather than make one of its own lest a government claim invite "opposition from other countries".[5]

From July to September 1956, Cloma issued a flurry of documents, including a "Charter of the Free Territory of Freedomland" on 6 July providing for the country's territory, seal and flag. The territory included "all the islands, islets, isles, atolls, banks, reefs, shoals, fishing grounds and waters" within the set of coordinates laid down in the "Notice" and reiterated in the Charter, without specifying the nature or extent of the fishing grounds and waters. The Charter prescribed the structure of government and adopted all Philippine laws and judicial decisions. It incorporated the Universal Declaration of Human Rights and the Philippine Bill of Rights. An announcement signed by Cloma, a younger brother of his and three of his four sons on 7 July named him "Chairman, Supreme Council of State of Freedomland and Head of State" and two others as "Supreme Solon" and "Supreme Magistrate". A letter sent out by Cloma as "Head of State" on the same day announced the formation of the equivalent of a cabinet. In September, Cloma issued rules on citizenship and on coinage and currency.[6]

In a 6 July press statement, Cloma cited the strategic reasons behind his claim to "Freedomland" and his establishment of an independent state there. He warned that "Red China" could be recognized by the United Nations by the end of the year and thus could take over the claim of Nationalist China. He pointed to the resurgence of Japan, France and England and the rise of "the Vietnams" as other potential sources of threat to the Philippines. An independent "Freedomland", he said, would help avert these threats while sparing the Philippines the legal complications of annexing new territory.[7]

Although Cloma's activities had the whiff of farce — President Ramon Magsaysay has been quoted as calling them "comic opera" in asking Vice

President and Secretary of Foreign Affairs García to cut them short[8] — they were taken seriously enough to provoke protests, starting as early as May 1956, from Nationalist China on Taiwan, the Chinese Foreign Ministry in Beijing, *Guangming Daily* (a Hong Kong Chinese-language newspaper leaning towards the People's Republic of China), France, and South Vietnam (which called Cloma's endeavours a "burlesque adventure"[9]), all asserting opposing claims to all or parts of the area in question. Beyond protests, Nationalist Chinese forces took naval action against the activities of Cloma and his group.

After months of declining to do so, the Philippine government finally adopted a position on the "Freedomland" issue. This took the form of a letter, dated 8 February 1957, by Secretary of Foreign Affairs García in reply to a letter that Cloma had sent President Magsaysay, dated 14 December 1956. The Cloma letter had complained about Taiwanese activities, reported in the Taipei press, "trying to grab phosphate mining operation which is presently undertaken by us".[10] García carefully limited his response to the views of the Department of Foreign Affairs rather than the Philippine government itself. The Department of Foreign Affairs, he said, "regards the islands, islets, coral reefs, shoals, and sand cays, comprised within what you called 'Freedomland', with the exclusion of those belonging to the seven-island group known internationally as the Spratlys, as *res nullius*", that is, something that does not belong to anyone. This meant, he continued, "that they are open to economic exploitation and settlement by Filipino nationals,... so long as the exclusive sovereignty of any country over them has not been established". García added that "the Philippine Government considers (the Spratly) islands as under the de facto trusteeship of the Allied Powers of the Second World War,... there being no territorial settlement made by the Allied Powers ... with respect to their disposition". Finally, the Vice President invoked the Philippines' interest in the islands encompassed by "Freedomland" — their proximity to the Philippines, their historical and geological relations with the archipelago, their strategic value, and their economic potential. However, he took care to refrain from asserting a claim to sovereignty or ownership on the part of the Philippines itself.[11]

THE PHILIPPINE CLAIM

By 1971, the Philippine position seemed to have changed. A communiqué read by President Ferdinand Marcos at a press conference on 10 July 1971

announced the results of discussions at an emergency meeting of the
National Security Council on the security implications for the Philippines
of the occupation by Taiwanese forces of Itu Aba, referred to as Tai Ping
in Chinese and as Ligaw by the Philippines. Repeating the view that
"Freedomland" was not part of the Spratlys,[12] the announcement reaffirmed
the Philippine position that the Spratlys were "under the *de facto* trusteeship
of the allied powers", by virtue of which "no one may introduce troops
on any of these islands without the permission and consent of the allied
powers". It revealed that the Philippine government had asked Taipei
to remove its troops from Itu Aba, since their deployment there did not
have the consent of the allies. The Marcos statement reiterated that, on
the other hand, "Freedomland" was *res nullius* that could be acquired by
"occupation and effective administration". It concluded by announcing
that "we are in effective occupation and control of Pagasa (Thitu), Lawak
(Nanshan Island) and Patag (Flat Island)".[13] Both Taipei and Beijing
immediately issued protests.

On 17 November 1971, Secretary of Foreign Affairs Carlos P. Romulo
submitted a memorandum to Marcos recommending, in the light of
increasingly dangerous encounters between Philippine and Nationalist
Chinese forces in "Freedomland", that the Philippine military presence
in the area be augmented. The memorandum urged that the islands be
developed and populated, the place used as a penal colony, the Philippine
flag kept hoisted in the territory, and Philippine governmental processes
extended there. Romulo asserted that these measures would reinforce the
Philippine position that "these islands are part of Philippine territory".[14]
The Philippines' Undersecretary of Foreign Affairs, José D. Ingles, was to
recall that in March 1972 he had asserted at the UN Seabed Committee
"the effective occupation by the Philippines of the Kalayaan Islands".[15]

In a letter to Marcos on 22 March 1972, a former Philippine diplomat,
Juan Arreglado, signing himself as "Chairman Advisory Council of the Free
Territory of Freedomland", complained that "the claims now put forward
by the Philippine government run counter to its formal commitments
as expressly stated in the letter" of Secretary García of 8 February 1957.
Arreglado claimed that the exchange of letters between Cloma and García
made clear the Philippines' "recognition of the existence of the Free
Territory of Freedomland as a 'Protected State'" of the Philippines. Quoting
Ingles as saying at the UN that "Freedomland ... has been and is now
under effective occupation and control of the Philippine Government",

Arreglado stated that the undersecretary had indicated a change in the official position of the Philippines "by laying claim directly to ownership and occupation of Freedomland".[16]

This internal Philippine dispute seems to have been resolved by the "Deed of Assignment and Waiver of Rights" that Cloma, on behalf of Tomás Cloma & Associates, signed on 4 December 1974 transferring to the Philippine government "all rights and interests they might have acquired" over "Freedomland" on the strength of "discovery and occupation" and by virtue of "exploration, development, exploitation, and utilization". The deed reproduced the coordinates laid down in the original proclamation and charter, both dated 6 July 1956.[17]

However, the deed was apparently executed under duress. In their biography of Cloma, José V. Abueva, Arnold P. Alamon and Oliva Z. Domingo write:

> The Philippines' subsequent claim to Freedomland since 1974 is based on Cloma's involuntary cession of his rights to the Government under the martial law regime of President Marcos.... In December 1974, the Government forcibly took over Freedomland from Cloma and Associates while Cloma was still under house arrest after spending 57 days in prison at Camp Crame, the headquarters of the Philippine Constabulary in Quezon City.... Under extreme duress, (Cloma, then 70) had to cede all the rights over Freedomland acquired by Cloma and Associates to the Philippine Government.... His daughter, Celia, convinced him to finally cede his rights over Freedomland/Kalayaan Islands in exchange for his freedom.[18]

In a 15 July 1987 memorandum addressed to President Corazon C. Aquino, Arreglado and Pedro Vargas, writing for Tomás Cloma & Associates, asked for the reimbursement of "expenses" incurred from 1947 to 1974 in the "exploration, occupation, development, administration, organization and settlement of Freedomland". The memorandum charged that "the arrest and detention of Atty. Tomas Cloma, Sr. was motivated solely by the overwhelming desire of the Martial Law Regime ... to induce and compel Tomas Cloma & Associates to accept and sign the ... Deed of Assignment and Waiver of Rights". It claimed that, "in view of the fact that Atty. Tomas Cloma, Sr. was already more than seventy years of age at that time, with frail physical constitution and whose health required then medical care and attention, and the threat hanging over his head that he would be rearrested and detained again in the stockade for an indefinite period of time, Tomas Cloma & Associates had no other alternative but to agree and sign the aforesaid DEED."[19]

Then, Tomás Cloma & Associates stated that, "despite all the acts of injustice, compulsion and abuse of power inflicted on the person of Atty. Tomas Cloma, Sr. by the ruling authorities of the Martial Law Regime, we are in perfect accord with the issuance on June 11, 1978 of Presidential Decree No. 1596" claiming possession of and sovereignty over "Freedomland". After setting forth the bases and reasons for its claim to "Freedomland" and describing its background, Tomás Cloma & Associates requested 50 million Philippine pesos from the Philippine government as "just, equitable and reasonable" compensation for laying the basis for "the eventual acquisition of ownership and sovereignty over Freedomland by the Philippines".[20] Thus, despite the charge that Cloma had signed under duress the transfer of all rights to and interests in "Freedomland" to the Philippine government in 1974, Tomás Cloma & Associates was now, in 1987, freely affirming that transfer.

On 11 June 1978, under his martial-law powers, Marcos had issued a decree formalizing the Philippine claim, declaring that an area off Palawan outside the Treaty of Paris limits, "including the seabed, subsoil, continental margin and air space", was to "belong and be subject to the sovereignty of the Philippines". To be known as "Kalayaan", meaning freedom, the area was almost entirely congruent with but slightly larger than Cloma's "Freedomland". The decree, numbered PD 1596, designated, both in the preamble and in the operative part, the coordinates bounding the claimed area:

> From a point [on the Philippine Treaty Limits] at latitude 7°40' North and longitude 116°00 East of Greenwich, thence, due West along the parallel of 7°40' N to its intersection with the meridian of longitude 112°10' E, thence, due north along the meridian of 112°10' E to its intersection with the parallel of 9°00' N, thence northeastward to the intersection of parallel of 12°00' N with the meridian of longitude 114°30' E, thence, due East along the parallel of 12°00' N to its intersection with the meridian of 118°00' E, thence, due South along the meridian of longitude 118°00' E to its intersection with the parallel of 10°00' N, thence Southwestwards to the point of beginning at 7°40' N, latitude and 116°00' E longitude.

The area thus claimed covered 70,150 square nautical miles.

The decree constituted Kalayaan "as a distinct and separate municipality of the Province of Palawan". It asserted that "much of the … area is part of the continental margin of the Philippine archipelago" and that "by virtue of their proximity" the island group was "vital to the security and economic survival of the Philippines". It invoked "history, indispensable need, and effective occupation and control established in accordance with international law" in supporting the Philippine claim, affirming that other states' "claims to some of these areas … have lapsed by abandonment". Since then, the residents of the islands occupied by the Philippines, including the troops there, have taken part in Philippine elections. By June 1978, Philippine forces had occupied four more islands or other land features, in addition to the three whose occupation Marcos had announced in July 1971. Afterwards, the Philippines is reported to have taken possession of two more land features in the Spratlys.

Although it is outside the limits set by the Treaty of Paris and other international agreements governing Philippine territory, the Philippines considers Scarborough Shoal, a group of islands, reefs and rocks in the South China Sea about 200 kilometres west of Subic Bay in Luzon, as part of the main Philippine archipelago. It has been the scene of much Philippine activity. For centuries, Filipino fishermen have used its waters for fishing and its lagoon for shelter. When the United States was still in control of large military bases in the Philippines, the United States, as well as the Philippine, Air Force used Scarborough for target practice. Media reports state that the Philippines constructed a lighthouse and raised its flag on the shoal in the 1960s. The Philippine Navy has operated in the area and occasionally arrested or chased away foreign fishermen, particularly those engaged in illegal fishing methods. Scarborough's official Philippine name, Bajo de Masinloc, meaning "below Masinloc" in Spanish, refers to Masinloc, a town in Zambales province, the Spanish-language name of Scarborough obviously dating it back to Spanish times.

In November 2007, Representative Antonio V. Cuenco of Cebu filed a bill in the House of Representatives seeking further to amend the baselines act of 1961, as amended in 1968. In doing so, the bill would extend the Philippines' baselines to connect the outermost points of the area in the South China Sea claimed in the 1978 Marcos decree and in the Scarborough Shoal area. There would be twelve such points in the Kalayaan Island Group and six at Scarborough Shoal. The bill prescribed that, in the case of each of two base points in Kalayaan, Iroquois Reef and Sabina Shoal, a "permanent structure such as a lighthouse should be established on its low-tide elevation".[21] This suggestion was obviously motivated by the need to have the proposed base points conform to the UNCLOS requirements on such base points and the baselines that connect them.

Evidently with the UNCLOS requirements and foreign policy and tactical considerations in mind, however, the Department of Foreign Affairs opposed the move to draw the baselines to encompass the entire Kalayaan claim and Scarborough Shoal. President Gloria Macapagal-Arroyo, in January 2009, endorsed a version introduced in the Senate by three of its committees and six individual senators, including Miriam Defensor-Santiago. Supported by the Department of Foreign Affairs, the Senate bill would *not* extend the baselines to the Kalayaan Island Group or Scarborough Shoal. Instead, it would declare a "regime of islands", as envisioned in Article 121 of the UNCLOS, for the land features in the Kalayaan Island Group as defined in the Marcos decree and Bajo de Masinloc, that is, Scarborough Shoal.[22] The Senate version substantially prevailed in the bill that the Congress finally passed and President Arroyo signed into law on 10 March 2009.[23]

The new act invokes Article 121 of the UNCLOS in declaring a "regime of islands" for the land features in the Philippine-claimed Kalayaan Island Group and Scarborough Shoal. According to that article, an island may have its own territorial sea, contiguous zone, exclusive economic zone and continental shelf as determined in the same way as other land territory. However, "[r]ocks which cannot sustain human habitation or economic life of their own shall have no exclusive economic zone or continental shelf". The Philippines has refrained from designating which of the South China Sea land features that it claims are islands and which are mere "rocks" in the UNCLOS sense, apparently preferring to reserve for itself a measure of ambiguity. Moreover, the Philippines retains the option of amending the new law in the future so as to draw baselines around the Kalayaan islands or Scarborough Shoal or both. Nevertheless, by maintaining its baselines only around its main archipelago, instead of using Scarborough shoal and other land features in the South China Sea as base points, and declaring a regime of islands for those features, the new law brings the Philippine claim closer to conformity with the UNCLOS as far as the maritime regimes in these areas are concerned. This is something that still cannot be said of the Chinese or Vietnamese claim. China and Vietnam promptly lodged protests against the enactment of the new law, asserting their claims to both the Spratlys and Scarborough Shoal. Unfortunately, some commentators confuse the original Cuenco bill, which would have extended the Philippines' archipelagic baselines to the Spratlys and Scarborough Shoal, with the act as finally passed and signed into law, which does not.

CHINA'S CLAIM

Partly in response to the Cloma group's activities, Taiwanese forces, in July 1956, returned to re-establish a permanent presence on Itu Aba. After the Japanese defeat in the Pacific War, those forces had planted Nationalist Chinese flags and stone markers on Itu Aba, Spratly Island and West York Island and set up a garrison on Itu Aba in December 1946, mainly to forestall apparent French attempts to return to the area. Moreover, the Allies had designated the (Nationalist) Chinese as recipients of the surrender of the Japanese forces in the area north of 16° North latitude. However, the Nationalists abandoned Itu Aba in June 1950, evidently for two reasons. One was the fall of the southern Chinese island of Hainan to the Communist Chinese, which made it difficult for the Nationalists to supply the garrison on Itu Aba. The other reason was that all Nationalist forces were deemed necessary for the defence of Taiwan itself.

On 7 July 1956, Cloma and several Philippine Maritime Institute cadets delivered to the (Nationalist) Chinese embassy in Manila a Nationalist Chinese flag that Cloma said they had removed from Itu Aba. The removal of the flag had evoked a protest from the Nationalist Chinese government. At the beginning of October, as the institute's training ship lay at anchor in the northwest corner of the area claimed by Cloma, it was approached by two Nationalist Chinese naval vessels. Filemon Cloma, Tomás Cloma's younger brother, who was in command of the Philippine ship, was invited to board one of the Nationalist Chinese vessels, where a heated four-hour discussion of the islands' ownership took place. During this time, a "Chinese boarding party" searched the PMI ship and confiscated arms, maps and documents. Hartendorp's citation of Tomás Cloma's account continues:

> The next day, the Captain was again invited aboard the Chinese ship, and this time he took two of his officers with him and was treated "more formally." But "even under grave threats to their lives, Captain Cloma refused to sign a statement that they will leave Freedomland and will

not come back. He also refused to recognize that Freedomland is Chinese territory. However, he was forced to accede to surrender the arms against receipt."[24]

Lu Ning, a Chinese academic who used to be an official at the Chinese Foreign Ministry, cites a different version of those events. Quoting Taiwan's "An Account of Naval Patrol in the Spratly Sea Frontiers", he states that the (Nationalist) Chinese "obtained" from Captain Cloma the following note, which the Chinese had evidently written for him:

> We assure that we received your friendly visit and check with no disturbance or anything lost on board of our ship. In order to keep up sincere friendship between the Republic of China and the Republic of the Philippines, we will not make further training voyages or landings in the territorial waters of your country and will accept your proper disposal after investigations in conformity with national laws of the Republic of China and international law in case we break our promise.[25]

China claims that it has long considered the Spratlys, as well as the Paracels, as its own, calling the Spratlys and environs Nansha and the Paracels area Xisha. The Chinese claim, espoused by both Beijing and Taipei, which basically have the same outlook on territorial issues, goes all the way back to the Han Dynasty (BC 206 to AD 220) and invokes sporadic contacts by Chinese people with the islands of the South China Sea, as reflected in travel reports, classical literature and local chronicles. Also cited have been the maps drawn in the Tang Dynasty (618–907) and the standardization of the islands' names and descriptions of currents in the Song (960–1279). So have been the establishment of an astronomical observation point in the Spratlys by the Yuan Dynasty (1271–1368) and the identification of the South China Sea islands in records of the Zheng He voyages during the Ming period (1368–1644). The more or less permanent presence of Hainanese fishermen in the South China Sea islands from as early as the Jin Dynasty (265–420) to the twentieth century has been noted.

As international acceptance of the Western concept of jurisdiction over fixed territories gained momentum, China — imperial, Nationalist and the People's Republic — took actions to assert its claim to the South China Sea islands in contemporary ways, like official statements, protests, the reaffirmation of claims, maps, agreements and conventions, laws, and various other acts of sovereignty. These often took the form of protests against the claims and encroachments of others while asserting Chinese ownership of and sovereignty over the islands and, ambiguously, the seas around them. In 1883, the Chinese protested against German surveys of the Paracels and the Spratlys. As a result of China's defeat by France in a war over French designs on Vietnam, the Chinese were compelled in 1887 to sign a treaty that, among other provisions, apparently assigned the Paracels and the Spratlys to China. To pre-empt further French moves and thwart French ambitions, China sent in 1902 a naval task force to inspect the South China Sea islands, planting flags and markers there. In 1907, as an outcome of another inspection tour, detailed plans were drawn up for the exploration of resources in and around the islands. In 1911, the new republic that had replaced the Qing Dynasty (1644–1911) placed the Paracels and the Spratlys under a county on Hainan. In December 1947, even as the Chinese civil war was going on, the Chinese communists incorporated the two groups of islands into Guangdong province.[26]

In 1947, the Nationalist government of China published a map, the Location Map of the South China Sea Islands, in which nine bars or an "interrupted line" enclosed the South China Sea. The U-shaped series of bars starts, on the north, between Luzon and Taiwan, skirts the western coast of Luzon and Palawan and East Malaysia, and, from 4°N latitude, rises northwards along the eastern coast of Vietnam. It remains unclear what those nine bars signify — whether they represent a Chinese claim to all the waters within them, a claim that would contravene the UNCLOS, which does not recognize "historical" claims to open seas, or merely to the land features that they encompass and the maritime regimes that those features generate.

Sam Bateman, a Senior Fellow at the S. Rajaratnam School of International Studies of the Nanyang Technological University in Singapore and a former Australian naval officer, asserts that it cannot be the former, since the bars are merely drawn on a map without the coordinates required for establishing jurisdictional boundaries.[27] B.A. Hamzah of the University of Malaya, formerly with the Maritime Institute of Malaysia and Malaysia's Institute of Strategic and International Studies, agrees that "without the coordinates the line is not legal", only showing China's "dominion or suzerainty" in the South China Sea. He points out that, the nine bars having antedated the UNCLOS's coming into force, no Chinese political leaders would be willing to drop the line lest they be accused of abandoning China's historical claim to the South China Sea. "Nevertheless," Hamzah stresses, "it will indeed be a gesture of goodwill to take steps to make the line consistent with UNCLOS."[28] In any case, ASEAN delegations have asked Chinese officials directly what the nine bars indicate, but have not elicited a definitive response. It is interesting to note that Indonesia, concerned over a possible Chinese claim to its gas-rich Natuna archipelago, has put the query down in writing.

Although China was not a participant in the 1951 San Francisco conference, Zhou Enlai, then Foreign Minister of the People's Republic of China, issued a statement before the treaty of peace with Japan was signed asserting Chinese sovereignty over the Spratlys and the Paracels. The new government in Beijing had hit out at a U.S.-UK draft for the treaty. The draft, eventually adopted in substance, declared that Japan was renouncing all claims to the Paracels and the Spratlys but did not specify which party would have sovereignty over them. (A Soviet attempt to declare Chinese ownership of and sovereignty over the islands had been soundly voted down.) A similar provision was included in the 1952 Japan–(Nationalist) China treaty of peace. Although the provision also failed to state to which party the Paracels and Spratlys belonged, Lu Ning argues:

> The Sino-Japanese Treaty is different from the San Francisco Treaty in two ways. The former is a bilateral treaty, dealing with only bilateral issues. The intended recipient for the territories, though not mentioned, is obvious. Secondly, unlike the San Francisco Treaty which treats the Paracels and the Spratlys in a separate paragraph from the one dealing with Taiwan and the Pescadores, the Sino-Japanese Treaty includes them in one single paragraph, thus indicating that Japan considers the legal status of the South China Sea archipelagos the same as those of Taiwan and the Pescadores.[29]

In September 1958, the People's Republic of China issued a Declaration on the Territorial Sea. That document extended the breadth of China's territorial sea to 12 nautical miles, a concept that had been gaining currency in international discussions on maritime issues and was to be finally enshrined in the 1982 UNCLOS. The declaration, at that time still using the Wade-Giles system of English orthography, applied the extension "to all territories of the People's Republic of China, including the Chinese mainland and its coastal islands, as well as Taiwan and its surrounding islands, the Penghu (Pescadores) Islands, the Tungsha Islands, the Hsisha Islands (Paracels), the Chungsha Islands (Macclesfield Bank), the Nansha Islands (Spratlys) and all other islands belonging to China which are separated from the mainland and its coastal islands by the high seas".[30] The designation of the waters between the mainland and the claimed island possessions as "the high seas" could be interpreted as ruling out the notion that the Chinese considered the entire South China Sea as territorial or internal waters.

In 1988 China created a new province, called Hainan, out of Hainan island, the Paracels, Macclesfield Bank and the Spratlys, all of which, according to Chinese law, had belonged to Guangdong Province. In February 1992 the Standing Committee of China's National People's Congress passed a law proclaiming the country's 12-nautical-mile territorial sea and a contiguous zone with a breadth of 12 nautical miles beyond the territorial sea, as UNCLOS prescribes. Its Article 2 states, using Pinyin in the English translation, "The PRC's territorial sea refers to the waters adjacent to its territorial land. The PRC's territorial land includes the mainland and its offshore islands, Taiwan and the various affiliated islands including Diaoyu Island, Penghu Islands, Dongsha Islands, Xisha Islands, Nansha (Spratly) Islands and other islands that belong to the People's Republic of China."[31] Although the law reaffirms China's claim to the land features in the South China Sea as its "territorial land", it does not make the distinction between islands, which, under UNCLOS, can generate their own territorial sea, contiguous zone and exclusive economic zone, and mere rocks, which cannot. The nature of the maritime regimes around those land features thus remains unclear and ambiguous.

VIETNAM'S CLAIM

From the late 1920s to shortly after World War II, the French, too, actively maintained a claim to the Spratlys, a claim that Vietnam was to press as its own in its capacity as successor state to France. A June 1929 letter from the governor of Cochinchina, in today's Vietnam, indicated that Spratly Island had been "administratively joined" to Baria province. In April 1930 the French raised their flag on Spratly Island, and their Indochinese authorities announced the island's annexation. Three years later they sent vessels to the Spratlys and occupied six islands there, publishing in July 1933 an official notice of their annexation and, later in the year, declaring them part of Baria province, an act that the Republic of Vietnam confirmed in 1956. Claiming the islands as theirs, the Chinese protested the 1933 French actions. So did the Japanese, who started in late 1937 to occupy some of the islands in the Spratlys. In 1939 the Japanese declared their occupation of the Pratas, the Paracels and the Spratlys, placed the

Spratlys, which they named Shinnan Gunto (New Southern Archipelago), under the administration of Kaohsiung on Taiwan, then a Japanese colony, and later used them to launch attacks on Southeast Asia. The British, too, who were also claiming Spratly Island and Amboyna Cay, had protested against the French claims and actions in the Spratlys.

Like the Chinese, the Vietnamese date their presence in the Paracels and the Spratlys to centuries past and lay claim to them on the basis of discovery, use and occupation. At the 1951 San Francisco Peace Conference, the Vietnamese representative, Tran Van Huu, Prime Minister and Minister of Foreign Affairs, asserted Vietnam's right to the Paracels and the Spratlys, without anyone challenging him. As recalled above, South Vietnam protested against Cloma's announcement of his "discovery" of "Freedomland". It affirmed Vietnam's ownership of the Spratlys as successor state to France, which, however, having annexed the islands in the 1930s, claimed continued sovereignty over the archipelago.

After the 1954 Geneva agreements resulted in the temporary partition of Vietnam, South Vietnam took over about half of the Paracels from the French, who had laid claim to them, as they did to the Spratlys, in the early 1930s. The forces of the People's Republic of China, on the other hand, had maintained their hold on Woody Island and other parts of the eastern portion of the Paracels, having taken them from the Nationalists. Nationalist forces had gone to that part of the Paracels to receive the surrender of Japanese troops in pursuance of the 1945 Potsdam Proclamation. In September 1973, South Vietnam, after awarding offshore oil-exploration contracts to leading multinational companies, announced the annexation of eleven land features in the Spratlys.

Within about four months, in January 1974, Chinese and South Vietnamese naval and commando forces clashed in the Paracels as they pursued their countries' conflicting claims to the entire area. In the end, the Chinese troops evicted the South Vietnamese from the Paracels. The Chinese thus avoided the necessity of seizing the islands from a reunified Vietnam ruled by China's then allies in Hanoi, which was closely linked to the power of the Soviet Union, a source of threat to Beijing. With the Paris negotiations on a political settlement of the Vietnam conflict going on, the United States, for its part, refrained from going to the aid of its South Vietnamese allies.

The retreating South Vietnamese forces repaired to the Spratlys. In April 1975, even before the fall of Saigon, North Vietnamese forces forcibly took the land features occupied by the South Vietnamese in the Spratlys.

By 1987, Vietnam had occupied fifteen land features in the Spratlys. With the Chinese attack on Vietnam towards the end of 1978 having brought the animosity between the two countries out into the open, and with Soviet military support for Vietnam now unlikely, Chinese forces engaged those of Vietnam near Johnson Reef in the Spratlys area in March 1988. The brief naval battle resulted in more than seventy Vietnamese dead and one Vietnamese vessel sunk and two damaged. In geopolitical terms, the more serious outcome was that their victory in that battle enabled the Chinese to firm up and expand their military presence in the Spratlys. In June 1988 they set up their first permanent military post there, and two months later conducted military exercises around the islands, reefs and atolls. In April and May 1989, they occupied two more atolls in the Spratlys previously held by Vietnam.[32] At the same time, Vietnam increased the number of land features under its control to twenty-one in 1988 and to twenty-four in 1989. On the other hand, by 2000, China had occupied seven land features in the Spratlys, not including the Taiwanese-occupied Itu Aba.

MALAYSIA AND BRUNEI DARUSSALAM

In October 1977, Malaysia placed sovereignty markers on eleven land features in the Spratlys and, in December 1979, published a new map depicting its territorial waters and continental shelf. The continental shelf and exclusive economic zone projected from East Malaysia, that is, from Sabah and Sarawak, encompassed the southern portion of the Spratlys, which is part of the areas claimed by China, Vietnam and the Philippines, and covered the continental shelf and "exclusive fishing zone" of Brunei Darussalam. Notably, the Malaysian claim includes Amboyna Cay, where Vietnam is present by virtue of a previous French claim, and Commodore Reef (Terumbu Laksamana), which the Philippines occupies (and calls Rizal Reef). In 1983 Malaysia proceeded to establish a permanent presence on Terumbu Layang-Layang (Swallow Reef), which it opened for tourism in 1991. The Malaysians have also occupied Terumbu Ubi (Ardasier and Dallas Reefs), Terumbu Mantanani (Mariveles Reef), and Terumbu Peninjau (Investigator Reef). Malaysia bases its claim on the features' locations on its continental shelf and has invoked national security and their proximity to the Malaysian mainland in making the claim.

Since 1984, Brunei Darussalam has claimed an "exclusive fishing zone" and a continental shelf projected from its coastline into the South China Sea. Brunei Darussalam and Malaysia have been holding talks, at least since 2003, on their conflicting claims. At the end of the visit to Brunei Darussalam of Malaysia's then–Prime Minister Abdullah Ahmad Badawi on 15–16 March 2009, the Malaysian leader and Brunei's Sultan Hassanal Bolkiah issued a joint press statement announcing, among other things:

> Both Leaders noted the agreement of their respective Governments on the key elements contained in the Exchange of Letters, which included the final delimitation of maritime boundaries between Brunei Darussalam and Malaysia, the establishment of Commercial Arrangement Area (CAA) in oil and gas, the modalities for the final demarcation of the land boundary between Brunei Darussalam and Malaysia and unsuspendable rights of maritime access for nationals and residents of Malaysia across Brunei's maritime zones en route to and from their destination in Sarawak, Malaysia provided that Brunei's laws and regulations are observed.[33]

The texts of the letters exchanged have not been made public, but on 3 May 2010 Malaysia's Ministry of Foreign Affairs issued a statement on the 16 March 2009 agreement. The statement read in part:

> The key elements are the final delimitation of maritime boundaries between Malaysia and Brunei Darussalam, the establishment of a Commercial Arrangement Area (CAA) for oil and gas, the modalities for the final demarcation of the land boundary between Malaysia and Brunei Darussalam, and unsuspendable rights of maritime access for nationals and residents of Malaysia across Brunei Darussalam's maritime zones.
>
> With regard to the maritime areas, the Exchange of Letters established the final delimitation of territorial sea, continental shelf and exclusive economic zone of both States. Malaysia's oil concession Blocks L and M which coincided with Brunei Darussalam's Blocks J and K are recognised under the Exchange of Letters as being situated within Brunei Darussalam's maritime areas, over which Brunei Darussalam is entitled to exercise sovereign rights under the relevant provisions of the United Nations Convention on the Law of the Sea 1982 (UNCLOS 1982). The establishment of the CAA incorporating these Blocks provides for a sharing of revenues from the exploitation of oil and gas in the CAA between the two States.[34]

The statement said that the Malaysian Cabinet had approved the contents of the agreement. The land boundary mentioned by both the March 2009 joint statement and the May 2010 foreign ministry statement refers to Limbang, a part of Malaysia's Sarawak that separates the two parts of Brunei Darussalam.

After he stepped down from Malaysia's political leadership, Abdullah Badawi, on 30 April 2010, had explained on the Malaysian foreign ministry's website:

> Regarding the maritime area, Malaysia and Brunei also agreed to establish a final and permanent sea boundary. This agreement serves to settle certain overlapping claims which existed in the past, which included the area of the concession blocks known before as Block L and Block M. Sovereign rights to the resources in this area now belongs to Brunei. However for this area, the agreement includes a commercial arrangement under which Malaysia will be allowed to participate on a commercial basis to jointly develop the oil and gas resources in this area for a period of 40 years. The financial and operational modalities for giving effect to this arrangement will be further discussed by the two sides. This means that in so far as the oil and gas resources are concerned, the agreement is not a loss for Malaysia.[35]

UNCLOS AS WATERSHED

One way of considering the conflicting claims to the waters of the South China Sea would be to use the effectivity of the UNCLOS as a kind of historical watershed, with agreed rules governing such claims after the UNCLOS entered into force for its signatories. All claimants to the South China Sea are parties to the convention. The Philippines was the eleventh party to ratify it, in 1984. Vietnam followed ten years later. China, Malaysia and Brunei Darussalam did so in 1996. Before the UNCLOS's entry into force on 16 November 1994, the nature of the maritime regimes that China, Vietnam and the Philippines were claiming was vague at best. Lu Ning has pointed out that, up to at least the Ming Dynasty (1368–1644), the Chinese concept of jurisdiction was based on the "nationality principle" rather than on "well-defined geographical territory". China seems to have begun accepting, in some measure, Western concepts of geographic international boundaries by the late seventeenth century and, specifically, maritime boundaries by the late nineteenth century. Lu Ning goes on:

> Furthermore, the concept of geographically-based sovereignty with rigidly delineated territorial land and waters in which the state exercises exclusive jurisdiction was alien to China and much of the rest of Asia. For centuries China had maintained an elaborate hierarchical system of a universal state in which the central empire oversaw a hierarchy of

tributary states. Jurisdiction was based on social organization, history, degree of sinicization and the loyalty of subjects. Consequently, Chinese boundaries in the periphery were never carefully delineated in accordance with contemporary international law and tended to be ill-defined and vague. What are regarded as official acts of territorial acquisition in contemporary international law, such as raising the flag and making official proclamations of incorporation, were neither known to nor necessary for China which regarded itself as the centre of a universal state that answered to no one.[36]

The Chinese concept of a "hierarchical system of a universal state" has, of course, become obsolete, even, it seems, in the Chinese view, as it has become accepted that international relations are based on well-defined territorial jurisdictions. With respect to maritime jurisdictions, the UNCLOS and previous maritime agreements lay down specific rules and criteria for determining the nature and extent of regimes on the sea and on the seabed, although, even after the ratification and entry into force of the UNCLOS, some claims continue to be vague and sea-related rules continue to be the subject of conflicting interpretations. Almost all countries of the world have ratified UNCLOS, the most egregious exception being the United States. They include most, if not all, of Asia, counting even such landlocked countries as Laos and Mongolia. Thus, without going into the legal niceties and nuances of this matter, one could say that all claimants to waters of the South China Sea have to ensure that their claims are based on and consistent with the provisions of UNCLOS, to which they are all parties, notwithstanding the fact that some of those provisions remain open to different interpretations. At the same time, one must remember that UNCLOS does not deal with the substance of claims to land features or their bases, in the South China Sea or elsewhere. As a Taiwanese scholar has been quoted as pointing out, "it is not the waters which give title to islands but islands which confer rights to waters".[37]

With the Philippines in early 2009 declaring a regime of islands for Scarborough Shoal and the other land features in the South China Sea that it claims, it has moved in the direction of making its claims more consistent with UNCLOS. Malaysia and Vietnam seem to have done so, too. On 6 May 2009, Malaysia and Vietnam filed, as required by UNCLOS, a "joint submission" to the UN Commission on the Limits of the Continental Shelf, which, according to Robert Beckman, Director of the Centre for International Law and associate professor of law at the National University of Singapore, "suggests that they have taken the position that sovereign rights to the resources of the South China Sea should be determined by principles governing the continental shelf as measured from the mainland coast". Beckman continues, "By not measuring their continental shelves or EEZs from any of the islands which they claim in the South China Sea, they have in effect taken the position that no islands in the South China Sea should be entitled to more than a 12nm territorial sea — the maximum permitted by UNCLOS."[38]

Thus, with Malaysia and Brunei Darussalam appearing to have negotiated a settlement of their overlapping maritime claims, the Southeast Asian claimants seem to have made their respective claims more closely aligned with the pertinent UNCLOS provisions. China, on the other hand, while maintaining the official character of the nine bars, has not defined the nature of the waters that they encompass.

The Southeast Asian claimants' moves have, of course, not completely clarified the kinds of maritime regime envisioned in their claims. Much less have the basic conflicts among the various claims to land features been resolved. As long as the claims to the land features, to the islands, reefs, shoals and atolls, remain in conflict, the claims to the waters around them cannot be reconciled. In this situation, the most that the claimants can do is to reassure one another that they will not resort to military force to assert their claims and not occupy hitherto unoccupied features. They can adopt other confidence building measures and carry out cooperative activities, including joint development. One step towards mutual confidence could be to clarify the nature of one's maritime claims in the South China Sea and to align those claims, as far as possible, with the provisions of UNCLOS.

DEALING WITH CHINA

China, of course, is uppermost in the concerns of the Philippines, as well as of other Southeast Asian countries, with respect to the South China Sea. The Philippines has regarded China, among the rival claimants to the Spratlys, as the only source of military threat and as the only potential hegemon in the region. It certainly cannot match China in military power. The Philippines has also known that it cannot depend on its 1951 mutual defence treaty with the United States or, until 1992, when the Philippine-U.S. military bases agreement expired, on the presence of those bases as a deterrent to any Chinese threat in the South China Sea. After all, the United States has repeatedly made it known that it does not consider the mutual defence treaty to apply to the disputed territories in the South China Sea, although the United States has expressed its opposition to the use of force in asserting claims there and to attempts to exercise hegemony in the region. At the same time, the Chinese have made repeated assurances that they would respect freedom of navigation in the South China Sea, a matter of primary concern to the United States. In this light, Manila has relied on strengthening relations with China and, after the discovery of Chinese facilities on Mischief Reef, on raising the political and diplomatic cost of any change, Chinese-induced or otherwise, to the status quo in the South China Sea. Its hold on those land features that it claims and occupies has been made more tenacious. Part of this has been the putative strengthening of the legal basis for the Philippine claim to Scarborough Shoal and the Kalayaan Island Group.

The need to deal with the jurisdictional disputes in the South China Sea and their strategic implications was one of the three principal motives for Manila's decision, in the early 1970s, to extend recognition to the People's Republic as the government of all of China, transfer diplomatic relations from Taipei to Beijing, and otherwise establish good relations with the communist regime. (The other two were to seal Beijing's commitment to cease its support for the communist insurgency in the Philippines and to seek assurances, in a period of energy insecurity, of the supply of Chinese crude oil, at "friendship prices", at a time when China was still an exporter of oil.)

In the talks during the breakthrough visit of President Ferdinand Marcos to China in June 1975, the last year of the Great Proletarian Cultural Revolution, Deng Xiaoping, newly rehabilitated (only to be sacked again ten months later) and subbing as Vice Premier for the ailing Premier Zhou Enlai, proposed that the issue of sovereignty pertaining to the South China Sea be "shelved" and that the two countries embark on "joint development" in the area, a proposal that Deng and his successors have repeated to Vice President Salvador Laurel, President Corazon Aquino and other Philippine leaders and, at every opportunity, to others in the world ever since.

Five months after the publication in February 1992 of China's law on its territorial sea and contiguous zone, referred to above, which reaffirmed Beijing's claim to the land features of the South China Sea, the Philippines chaired and hosted the ASEAN Ministerial Meeting and Post-Ministerial

Conferences, the annual gatherings of the Foreign Ministers of ASEAN and its Dialogue Partners. Manila took the opportunity to lead ASEAN in issuing, on 22 July, the ASEAN Declaration on the South China Sea. The declaration affirmed that "sovereignty and jurisdictional issues" were to be resolved "by peaceful means, without resort to force". It urged "all parties concerned to exercise restraint". The Ministers would "explore the possibility of cooperation" on the safety of maritime navigation and communication, the protection of the marine environment, search-and-rescue operations, combating piracy and armed robbery at sea, and the campaign against illicit trafficking in drugs. Finally, the declaration called for the application of the principles of the Treaty of Amity and Cooperation in Southeast Asia as a basis for a "code of international conduct over the South China Sea".[39]

The Foreign Ministers of China and Russia, ASEAN's "consultative partners", attended the public sessions as guests of the ASEAN Chairman. Raul Manglapus, the Philippines' Secretary of Foreign Affairs, and Romualdo Ong, the country's representative to the ASEAN Senior Officials Meeting, sought to get China to associate itself with the declaration. After hurried telephone consultations with Beijing, Qian Qichen, the Chinese Foreign Minister, declined the proposal on the ground that China had not been involved in the drafting of the resolution. Perhaps a deeper and more genuine reason was the Chinese preference for bilateral discussions on the South China Sea issues to dealing with ASEAN as a group. However, he said, China associated itself with the declaration's "principles".

In February 1995, the atmosphere of sweetness and light generated by the steadily strengthening relationship of China with ASEAN and its members was rudely disturbed by the discovery of Chinese structures on Mischief Reef, a mostly underwater reef in the South China Sea just a little over 200 kilometres west of the Philippine island of Palawan. (Its English name is attributed to Heribert Mischief, a German member of the crew of Henry Spratly, who is said to have discovered the reef in 1791. China calls it Meiji Jiao, and the Philippines Panganiban Reef.) The Philippine government apparently learned about the Chinese occupation when several Filipino fishermen reported that Chinese on the reef had detained them for over a week. Photographed by the Philippine Air Force, the structures appeared to be made of steel, flew the Chinese flag, and displayed quite clearly parabolic antennas on their roofs. The Chinese initially claimed, however, that these were intended as shelters for Chinese fishermen. It took all of two weeks for the Chinese Foreign Ministry to react to the Philippines' announcement of its discovery. As for ASEAN, on 18 March 1995, a few weeks after the announcement, the Foreign Ministers issued a statement entitled "Recent Developments in the South China Sea (1995)" and saying, in full:

> We, the ASEAN Foreign Ministers, express our serious concern over recent developments which affect peace and stability in the South China Sea.
>
> We urge all concerned to remain faithful to the letter and spirit of the Manila Declaration on the South China Sea which we issued in July 1992 and which has been endorsed by other countries and the Non-Aligned Movement. The Manila Declaration urges all concerned to resolve differences in the South China Sea by peaceful means and to refrain from taking actions that destabilize the situation.
>
> We call upon all parties to refrain from taking actions that destabilize the region and further threaten the peace and security of the South China Sea. We specifically call for the early resolution of the problems caused by recent developments in Mischief Reef.
>
> We urge countries in the region to undertake cooperative activities which increase trust and confidence and promote stability in the area.
>
> We encourage all claimants and other countries in Southeast Asia to address the issue in various fora, including the Indonesia-sponsored Workshop Series on Managing Potential Conflicts in the South China Sea.[40]

The strong, if non-hostile, tone of this statement reflected the alarm with which the ASEAN senior officials viewed the Mischief Reef developments. Although the statement did not mention China by name, the reference was clear. Indeed, in the process of discussing these developments and drafting the ASEAN statement on them, the senior officials were clearly concerned by China's possible intention and its temerity in extending its sway all the way to Mischief Reef.

At the first meeting of the ASEAN and Chinese senior Foreign Ministry officials, in April 1995 in Hangzhou, a forum that I had proposed the year before, the ASEAN delegations raised pointed questions about the Chinese position on the South China Sea and particularly about the developments on Mischief Reef. The ASEAN officials, including those whose countries laid no claims to any part of the South China Sea, also asked the Chinese directly about the significance of the nine bars enclosing the entire South China Sea on Chinese maps without eliciting a response. (The Chinese have not responded either to the same, but more formal, query that Indonesia had addressed to them, although they are said to have assured Indonesia that there was "no problem" between the two countries concerning territorial or maritime claims.) Nevertheless, the discussions were significant, being the first time that China dealt with the South China Sea question in a multilateral setting, as opposed to its preference for discussing it only bilaterally.

In the same month, Secretary of Foreign Affairs Roberto R. Romulo, testifying before a joint hearing by the House Committees on Foreign Affairs and Defense on the developments on Mischief Reef, laid down the elements of the Philippine position on the issue:

- The Panganiban Reef is part of Philippine territory. As sovereign owners, we will enforce our laws....
- The actions taken by elements identified with the People's Republic of China are violative of international law and the norms of friendly relations between nations.
- The Philippines will exhaust all peaceful means in resolving this issue....
- While the use of self-defense is our inherent right, the aggressive use of force is not an option.
- This matter is not just a bilateral concern for the Philippines, but a multilateral concern for all claimants and all other parties interested in the peace and stability of the region.[41]

At their annual meeting in July, the ASEAN Foreign Ministers stated in their joint communiqué:

> The Foreign Ministers expressed their concern over recent events in the South China Sea. They encouraged all parties concerned to reaffirm their commitment to the principles contained in the 1992 ASEAN Declaration on the South China Sea, which urges all claimants to resolve their differences by peaceful means and to exercise self-restraint. They also called on them to refrain from taking actions that could destabilise the region, including possibly undermining the freedom of navigation and aviation in the affected areas. They also encouraged the claimants to address the issue in various bilateral and multilateral fora.[42]

In August, as Undersecretary of Foreign Affairs of the Philippines, I held talks in Manila with Wang Yingfan, then the Director-General of the Department of Asian Affairs of China's Ministry of Foreign Affairs, in which we discussed the Mischief Reef issue. We agreed that, pending the resolution of the dispute, the two sides would refrain from using force and instead seek to settle their disputes peacefully through consultations, "in accordance with the recognized principles of international law, including the UN Convention on the Law of the Sea", and "without prejudice to the freedom of navigation in the South China Sea". We also agreed that our countries would promote cooperation in a wide range of areas, including "the protection and conservation of the marine resources of the South China Sea".[43]

The next year, in March, I had another round of consultations with China, also in Manila, this time with Tang Jiaxuan, Vice Minister of Foreign Affairs and later Foreign Minister and then State Councilor. Re-affirming the provisions of the August 1995 joint statement, we agreed to set up "a bilateral consultative mechanism to explore ways of cooperation in the South China Sea".[44]

In May 1996 China announced the baselines along its southeastern coast and around the Paracels. These are straight baselines connecting forty-nine base points, identified by coordinates, along the coast and linking twenty-eight base points, also defined by precise coordinates, around the Paracels. A number of scholars have pointed out that China could not legally draw straight baselines around the Paracels, as that group of islands cannot be considered as an archipelago under UNCLOS. Some have even questioned the way the baselines were drawn. The Chinese declaration also stated, "The Government of the People's Republic of China will announce the remaining baselines of the territorial sea of the People's Republic of China at another time."[45] Significantly, no baselines have been announced since then for the Spratlys or for any other area in the South China Sea outside the Paracels.

THE DECLARATION ON THE CONDUCT OF PARTIES

At every opportunity, the Philippines and ASEAN as a whole have sought to "internationalize" the South China Sea issue so as to subject the Chinese to greater international pressure. ASEAN has endeavoured to draw international attention to the South China Sea as a flashpoint for regional tension and conflict and a possible threat to maritime shipping, including at the United Nations, forums like the ASEAN-EU Ministerial Meeting, and, starting at the 1992 NAM summit chaired and hosted by Indonesia, the meetings of the Non-Aligned Movement (NAM). (All ASEAN members belong to NAM, which China attends, although it is not a member.) The Philippines has also emphasized the environmentally destructive — and illegal — methods of fishing, like dynamite and cyanide, used by Chinese, and Taiwanese, as well as other, fishermen in waters under Philippine jurisdiction, disputed or not.

At the first ministerial meeting of the ASEAN Regional Forum (ARF), in July 1994, the South China Sea issue had, in deference to Chinese sensitivities, been discussed not in a plenary but over dinner. At the very next meeting, in August 1995, after the revelation of China's occupation of Mischief Reef, the subject moved to the regular session. According to the chairman's statement of that meeting, the Ministers "expressed concern on overlapping sovereignty claims in the region. They encouraged all claimants to reaffirm their commitment to the principles contained in relevant international laws and conventions, and the ASEAN's 1992 Declaration on the South China Sea".[46] Discussions on the subject, however, became more and more perfunctory, as ASEAN and China undertook negotiations on a code of conduct for the South China Sea and as the realization dawned on the participants that the ARF was not built to resolve questions of territorial jurisdiction or otherwise do anything concrete about them.

Following the discovery of the Chinese installations on Mischief Reef, the Philippines sought to engage China in the development of an agreed code of conduct for the South China Sea in order to reduce the sense of threat and uncertainty among countries and peoples concerned with the area. The process involved the rest of ASEAN as a group. While ASEAN gained by the apparent willingness of China to speak to ASEAN as an entity, it lost in terms of the waning interest on the part of the rest of the international community in the issue.

In the joint communiqué issued at the end of their annual meeting in July 1996, the ASEAN Foreign Ministers stated:

> The Foreign Ministers expressed their concern over the situation in the South China Sea, and stressed that several outstanding issues remain a major concern for ASEAN. In the spirit of the Manila Declaration on the South China Sea, the Ministers called for the peaceful resolution of the dispute and self-restraint by parties concerned. The Ministers were pleased to observe, however, that the parties concerned have expressed their willingness to resolve the problem by peaceful means in accordance with recognized international law in general and the UNCLOS of 1982 in

particular. The Ministers also reiterated the significance of the ongoing informal workshop series on Managing Potential Conflict in the South China Sea, and welcomed the continuing bilateral cooperation and discussions among the claimant countries. They endorsed the idea of concluding a regional code of conduct in the South China Sea which will lay the foundation for long-term stability in the area and foster understanding among claimant countries. (Typographical errors have been corrected.)[47]

In the negotiations on a code of conduct that followed, China adamantly refused to include the Paracels in the scope of the code. As expected, Vietnam was the strongest advocate of their inclusion. The failure to agree on the area of coverage of the instrument led to the refusal of some of the negotiators to call it a "code", which, it was argued, would imply its legally binding character, something impossible to do without a clear definition of where it would apply. Thus, the document finally adopted was called the "Declaration on the Conduct of Parties in the South China Sea". The ASEAN Foreign Ministers and Wang Yi, China's Vice Foreign Minister designated as Special Envoy for the event, signed the declaration in Phnom Penh on 4 November 2002 on the occasion of the annual ASEAN-China Summit.

The declaration committed the ASEAN countries and China to freedom of navigation and overflight in the South China Sea, the peaceful settlement of disputes there, and the exercise of "self-restraint", specifically refraining from inhabiting "presently uninhabited" land features. They undertook to promote mutual confidence through, among other means, dialogues between defence and military officials, the "just and humane treatment" of persons in danger or in distress, the voluntary prior notification of joint or combined military exercises, and the voluntary exchange of "relevant information". They agreed to cooperate in a wide range of areas, including marine environmental protection, marine scientific research, the safety of navigation and communication at sea, search and rescue, and combating transnational crime. However, the declaration did not specify the deployment of military forces or the reinforcement of structures in already occupied land features among the activities to be covered by self-restraint.[48]

In September 2004, during a hurried visit by President Arroyo to China, among the agreements signed in her presence was an "Agreement for Seismic Undertaking for Certain Areas in the South China Sea By and

Between China National Offshore Oil Corporation and Philippine National Oil Company". Although the text of the agreement was not made public, the Philippine government did explain in a press release that PNOC and CNOOC would do a joint seismic study in the South China Sea for three years, denying, to rather universal disbelief, that the agreement had any "reference to petroleum exploration and production" and adding that "the national *oil* (italics mine) company of a third country" could take part. The agreement surprised and upset other ASEAN countries, primarily Vietnam. In March 2005, however, Vietnam, probably seeing the futility of opposing it, joined in the arrangement, which was duly modified. The Chinese, who conducted most of the survey, are reported not to have shared all of their findings with the Philippines or Vietnam. Barry Wain, writer-in-residence at the Institute of Southeast Asian Studies in Singapore and formerly of the *Wall Street Journal Asia*, wrote in early 2008:

> For a start, the Philippine government has broken ranks with the Association of Southeast Asian Nations, which was dealing with China as a bloc on the South China Sea issue. The Philippines has also made breathtaking concessions in agreeing to the area for study, including parts of its own continental shelf not even claimed by China and Vietnam. Through its actions, Manila has given a certain legitimacy to China's legally spurious "historic claim" to most of the South China Sea....
>
> Ironically, it was Manila that first sought a united front and rallied Asean to confront China over its intrusion into Mischief Reef a decade earlier. Sold the idea by politicians with business links who have other deals going with the Chinese, Ms. Arroyo did not seek the view of her foreign ministry, Philippine officials say.[49]

The article raised an uproar in political circles and in the mass media in the Philippines, although the agreement in question had been concluded more than three years before. The agreement was allowed to expire in June 2008.

While the Philippines-China deal marked, as an unintended consequence, a departure from the multilateral approach that Manila had sought to foster in dealing with China with respect to the South China Sea, the Philippines apparently did not enter into the agreement within a broad strategic context. After all, neither the Department of Foreign Affairs nor the National Security Council had been involved in, much less consulted on, it; only the national oil company ostensibly took part. In any case, the agreement's expiration seems to have laid the matter to rest, except that

Manila's willingness to conclude it may have raised doubts about the Philippines' dependability on this and other issues.

Although the Chinese have retreated in some measure and resigned themselves to dealing with ASEAN as a group, they seem to have maintained their old position of insisting on holding bilateral discussions with individual Southeast Asian claimants. In a lecture at the Institute of Southeast Asian Studies organized by ISEAS' ASEAN Studies Centre in November 2009, China's ambassador to ASEAN, Xue Hanqin, declared:

> In the follow-up negotiations on the draft guidelines for the implementation of the DOC (Declaration on the Conduct of Parties in the South China Sea), the work got stuck mainly because of the difference over the modality of their (ASEAN member-states') consultations. The key issue is whether ASEAN Member States should consult among themselves first before they consult with China. ASEAN members insist on such a consensual approach towards China, while the Chinese side does not think this is in line with the understanding of DOC.... The whole issue of South China Sea is not a matter between ASEAN as an organization and China, but among the relevant countries. ASEAN could serve as a valuable facilitator to promote mutual trust among the Parties, but not turn itself into a party to the dispute.[50]

In this regard, one must make the distinction between the negotiation or adjudication of the legal jurisdictional disputes and the interim measures that must be taken in managing the situation created by the disputes. In negotiating a territorial dispute or submitting it for adjudication, only the parties to the dispute are and should be involved. Even here, in the case of the Spratlys, the process of negotiation or adjudication is made extremely complicated by the fact that more than two parties are involved. On the other hand, in terms of the measures for managing the situation pending a settlement of the jurisdictional issues, clearly all ASEAN member countries, and others affected, have an interest in them. All have a stake in regional peace, in the relaxation of regional tensions, in the promotion of stability in the area, in cooperation in ensuring the cleanliness and productivity of a shared body of water, and in keeping trade routes and transportation links open and free. The DOC was negotiated between ASEAN and China. The declaration was issued on the occasion of the ASEAN-China summit. All ASEAN member states participated in its negotiation and are parties to it. At bottom, no outside party can or should tell ASEAN on what issues its members are to take coordinated or common positions.

Recently, however, the Chinese seem to have come around to emphasizing the need to distinguish between negotiating or adjudicating the jurisdictional or sovereignty disputes, in which only the parties concerned should be involved, and what they call "confidence building" measures, in which a much larger number of countries have an interest.

THE U.S. INVOLVEMENT

The United States created a stir in July 2010, when, at the annual ministerial meeting of the ASEAN Regional Forum (ARF), Secretary of State Hillary Rodham Clinton reiterated, in unusually clear and strong terms, the American position on the South China Sea disputes and its interest in that body of water. What she actually said at the meeting has apparently not been made public. However, the U.S. Department of State has released the transcript of the media conference that Secretary Clinton gave immediately after the ARF meeting. The transcript quotes her as saying:

> The United States supports a collaborative diplomatic process by all claimants for resolving the various territorial disputes without coercion. We oppose the use or threat of force by any claimant. While the United States does not take sides on the competing territorial disputes over land features in the South China Sea, we believe claimants should pursue their territorial claims … and rights to maritime space in accordance with the UN convention on the law of the sea. Consistent with customary international law, legitimate claims to maritime space in the South China Sea should be derived solely from legitimate claims to land features.
>
> The US supports the 2002 ASEAN-China declaration on the conduct of parties in the South China Sea. We encourage the parties to reach agreement on a full code of conduct. The US is prepared to facilitate initiatives and confidence building measures consistent with the declaration because it is in the interest of all claimants and the broader international community for unimpeded commerce to proceed under lawful conditions. Respect for the interests of the international community and responsible efforts to address these unresolved claims and (sic) help create the conditions for resolution of the disputes and a lowering of regional tensions.[51]

At the ARF ministerial meeting, China's Foreign Minister, Yang Jiechi, almost immediately responded to Secretary Clinton's statement. The text of his remarks has not been made public either, but the website of China's Ministry of Foreign Affairs gives a detailed account of what he said:

Yang said, the first question is what is the situation in the South China
Sea. Is it peaceful and stable? Or is it tense? From today's discussion, most
people say the situation is peaceful. And in my bilateral discussions with
both ASEAN colleagues and others, they all say that there is no threat to
regional peace and stability.

Second, is it an issue between China and ASEAN as a whole?
Obviously not. We do have some territorial or maritime rights disputes
with certain members of ASEAN. It is because we are neighbors. And
those disputes shouldn't be viewed as ones between China and ASEAN
as a whole just because the countries involved are ASEAN members. The
non-claimant ASEAN countries tell the Chinese side that they are not
part of the disputes, they don't take sides and they hope these disputes
will be settled through bilateral consultations between the countries
concerned.

Third, what is the consensus of countries in the region with regard
to the South China Sea issue? The consensus is to have these disputes
solved peacefully through friendly consultations in the interest of peace
and stability in the South China Sea and good-neighborly relations.
According to the *Declaration on the Conduct of Parties in the South China
Sea* (DOC), it is to exercise restraint, and not to make it an international
issue or multilateral issue. Channels of discussion are there, and they are
open and smooth. Everybody admit this.

Fourth, what is the function of the DOC? Its function is to enhance
mutual trust among the countries concerned and to create favorable
conditions and good atmosphere for final solution to the disputes. China
and ASEAN countries issued this DOC. There have been joint working
group consultations. And when the conditions are ripe, senior officials'
meeting can also be held.

Fifth, has navigation freedom and safety been hindered in the South
China Sea? Obviously not. Trade has been growing rapidly in this region
and China has become the number one trading partner of many countries
in the region. Some countries have not been able to export more to China,
not because the navigation freedom has been hindered, but because they
set high barriers for high-tech exports.

Sixth, what is the purpose of talking about coercion on the South
China Sea issue? China all along believes that all countries, big or small,
are equal. China, being a big country, also has its legitimate concerns. Is
the expression of one's legitimate concerns coercion? That is not logical.
The non-claimant countries hate it that some try to coerce them into taking
sides on the South China Sea issue.

Seventh, what will be the consequences to if this issue is turned into
an international or multilateral one? It will only make matters worse and

the resolution more difficult. International practices show that the best way to resolve such disputes is for countries concerned to have direct bilateral negotiations. Asia has already stood up and gained its dignity. Asian countries can properly address each other's concerns on the basis of equality and mutual respect.[52]

THE POSSIBILITY OF RESOLUTION

It is highly unlikely that the jurisdictional disputes in the South China Sea will be resolved anytime soon, if ever. If only bilateral issues were involved, they could in theory be resolved by recourse to the International Court of Justice in The Hague, by arbitration, or by other peaceful means of settling international disputes. Even so, the litigation would be fraught with difficulty and uncertainty. In the case of the Spratlys, the multilateral character of the disputes and the varied natures of the claims make the conflicting claims immensely more complex. There is, of course, the possibility of the use of armed force. A successful resort to force could entrench the dominance of the power wielding it, but, under present and foreseeable circumstances, would not resolve the disputes themselves to the satisfaction of all. It could result only from a particularly unfortunate concatenation of massive political and strategic miscalculations and only make things worse. Hence, neither armed conflict nor a definitive legal resolution is likely or plausible in the South China Sea in the foreseeable future.

Most fundamentally, the resolution of the jurisdictional disputes is possible only as a result of a combination of compromises worked out by the claimant states. However, such compromises are made extremely difficult, if not impossible, first, by the nationalist emotions — and the tendency of politicians to exploit or be swayed by them — inevitably aroused by territorial issues. Related to this is the aversion of political leaders to appearing to be giving up national territory or other areas of jurisdiction.

Secondly, and perhaps more importantly, the claimants consider their positions on and in the South China Sea as vital to their strategic interests. Malaysia has to have some degree of control over the vast expanse of sea that separates — and connects — East and West Malaysia. Brunei Darussalam seeks to secure for itself jurisdiction over its exclusive economic zone and continental shelf, which cuts right across Malaysia's claimed EEZ, and the right to exploit the resources in them. The Philippines would feel threatened from the west if it did not push out the frontiers of its jurisdiction to its claimed Kalayaan Island Group and Scarborough Shoal. China seeks control of the South China Sea in order to avoid being "contained", pressured or even attacked from the southeast, as it was in the past, and to increase Beijing's influence on an important passageway for international trade. When they were in authority over China, the Nationalists were driven by the same motives. Today, although now confined to the islands that they control, Taiwan politicians cannot be seen as being weaker than Beijing in asserting territorial claims. Refusing to leave China in control of what it calls the East Sea, Vietnam would be hemmed in by Chinese power if it did not have a foothold in the South China Sea.

Non-claimants, too, have a deep interest in peace and stability in the region of the South China Sea and in freedom of navigation on and overflight over that body of water. Included in these are countries whose international trade traverses the South China Sea in large volumes, countries like those of ASEAN, Japan, South Korea, Taiwan, Hong Kong, Europe's leading trading nations, the United States and China itself. The exporters of crude oil, much of their products destined for East Asia, also have a stake in what happens in the South China Sea. The United States professes an interest in the right to ferret out information on military developments in China on the grounds of the alleged lack of transparency in those developments, a right that Beijing, of course, contests.

On a global scale, the clash of interests that seems to have the greatest impact on the world in general and on Southeast Asia in particular is the one between the interests of China, which considers the South China Sea issue as primarily for the claimants to deal with, and those of the United States, which insists on its role as vital to Asia-Pacific peace and stability and on its interest in freedom of navigation on and overflight over the world's oceans. Yet, the interests of China and the United States are so intertwined politically and economically in Asia and around the world that both have a stake in good and stable relations between them. Southeast Asia, too, including the Philippines, has an interest in the well-being and stability of those bilateral, great-power relations. At the same time, there seems to be a contradiction between, on the one hand, the desirability of the United States lending its powerful voice to the rule of international law and to free and open sea and air lanes and, on the other, the proposition that public pressure can only harden Chinese disregard for UNCLOS strictures on maritime claims. It was probably with the latter in mind that the Philippines' Foreign Secretary, Alberto Romulo, declined, as reported by Agence France-Presse, to support publicly Hillary Clinton's ARF intervention.

Meanwhile, there remain problems that can be dealt with and opportunities that can be seized only through international cooperation, primarily among the claimants. Sam Bateman observes:

> Most regional analysts agree that conflict between the parties is most unlikely. However, there is a need to acknowledge that sovereignty claims, and hence maritime boundaries, will not be resolved in the foreseeable future. We must get away from the notion that the South China Sea can be managed effectively on the basis of unilateral jurisdiction and sole ownership of the resources. A cooperative management regime is the only solution.
>
> The only acceptable framework for such a regime would appear to be a web of provisional arrangements covering cooperation for different functions and perhaps even with different geographical areas for each function. The functions to be considered might include development of oil and gas resources, fisheries management, marine safety, law and order at sea, marine scientific research, and preservation and protection of the marine environment. However, such an approach requires a lot of talking, bargaining and some "give and take". This is not occurring at present.[53]

Despite the reasonableness of his proposition, Bateman himself acknowledges that "negotiating a joint arrangement between three or more parties can prove extremely difficult".[54] One difficulty is the lack of confidence and mutual suspicion between the claimants, a condition exacerbated by the very existence of the conflicting claims. Another is that many attempts at or proposals for cooperation would run into questions of sovereign jurisdiction.

In the case of the Philippines, its current constitution provides, "The State shall protect the nation's marine wealth in its archipelagic waters, territorial sea, and exclusive economic zone, and reserve its use and enjoyment exclusively to Filipino citizens."[55] Unless some way is found to get around this constitutional constraint, it would be difficult for the Philippines to conduct "joint development" of the resources in its maritime jurisdiction, particularly since Manila has refrained from identifying which of the land features that it claims are islands and which are mere rocks; thus, its maritime jurisdiction in the Spratlys and the area of application of the constitutional constraint cited above remain murky.

Much has been made and written about the energy resources beneath the South China Sea and the fish that abound in it as critical reasons, in an era of concern over energy and food scarcity, for the scramble for jurisdiction over the land features and seas of that body of water. The recent history of the Spratlys has been marked by claimants granting to international companies oil and/or gas concessions in areas of the South China Sea that they claim, which then provokes protests from other claimants. However, just as fundamental, and often related to the need for secure access to the food and energy resources of the South China Sea, are the claimants' strategic considerations, described above.

Driven by such considerations, none of the claimants can afford to back down from its claims to the land features of the South China Sea. In the interest of regional peace and stability, the most that one can expect in the foreseeable future is far from a definitive resolution of the conflicting claims — a "grand solution", in the words of Mark Valencia, a leading authority on maritime issues. Even attempts to adjust the maritime claims to the requirements of UNCLOS, as the Philippines, Vietnam, Malaysia and Brunei Darussalam seem to have made in early 2009, can be considered as endeavours to strengthen the legal foundations of the claims. Nevertheless, declaring a regime of islands for the claimed land features in the South China Sea on the part of China and Vietnam could make the maritime regimes around those features less ambiguous and thus constitute a step towards a further relaxation of tensions in the area.

Meanwhile, in order to reduce the chances of territorial disputes developing into armed conflict, measures could be taken to increase the claimants' stakes in good relations with one another and in cooperation for common purposes and to raise the political cost of any resort to violent action. In this light, one can place one's hopes on the reluctance of any of the claimants, at this point, to upset the regional stability from which all of them have benefited so much, provided that no one is given cause to perceive any immediate threat to its core interests. The same holds true for the United States as well as China.

THE INFORMAL WORKSHOPS

It is to build mutual confidence, overcome mutual suspicions and work out mutually beneficial cooperative activities, while promoting the principle of non-recourse to force or other unilateral action, that Hashim

Djalal, Indonesia's foremost authority on maritime law, has spearheaded the series of "Workshops on Managing Potential Conflict in the South China Sea". Convened by Indonesia's Department of Foreign Affairs and Centre for Southeast Asian Studies, the annual workshops, all held in one place or another in Indonesia, started in 1990 and, until 2001, were supported by the Canadian International Development Agency through the University of British Columbia. Participants in the workshops include officials, in their "personal capacity", from all ASEAN countries, claimants or not, and, significantly, since 1991, from both the Chinese mainland and Taiwan, as well as Vietnam (which was to become an ASEAN member only in 1995).

In the pursuit of confidence building, "joint development" and networking, the workshops promote peaceful cooperative activities. Specifically, these activities cover assessments of living and non-living resources, marine environmental protection, navigational safety, search and rescue, and marine scientific research. For these purposes, a working group on marine scientific research deals with the development of a database and the exchange of information, the monitoring of the sea level and tides, and biodiversity. There is a technical working group on the environment. The technical working group on legal matters stays away from questions of jurisdiction but addresses less controversial issues like drug trafficking, piracy, armed robbery at sea, environmental legislation, the interpretation of UNCLOS, and legal issues arising from the work of other groups.[56]

Although the workshops are not meant to resolve or even discuss jurisdictional issues, they do build confidence, promote the exercise of self-restraint, uphold the principle of the non-use of force in dealing with territorial questions, provide a venue for dialogue, consultation and the clarification of issues, and foster cooperation. It was at the workshops that the Philippines and China first discussed the elements of a code to govern conduct in the South China Sea.

The 2001 workshop was the last one that Canada supported. The participants, nevertheless, decided to convene the workshop the next year and to contribute to the series' funding on a voluntary basis. The workshop has taken place every year since then.

To skirt the problem of jurisdiction, Hashim Djalal for a while pushed the idea of cooperation in an area in the middle of the South China Sea where no exclusive economic zone, legitimately measured and projected from mainland or archipelagic baselines, overlaps with another (dubbed the "doughnut" scheme). The proposal, however, apparently has not gained traction, although a Chinese scholar seems to have revived it recently even if Beijing had initially opposed it.

CONCLUSION

In the conclusion to their paper on the South China Sea, Clive Schofield and Ian Storey point out that, in the end, it will take a political settlement to resolve the South China Sea disputes, the prospects of which are exceedingly slight:

> Diplomacy is still the favored option by all parties concerned, and there remains a general commitment to cooperative approaches aimed at reducing the chances of conflict, joint development, and protecting the marine environment. Yet the political will to translate rhetoric into reality is lacking as demonstrated by the failure of ASEAN and China to conclude a more robust Code of Conduct for the South China Sea. All the while, the claimants continue to build up their presence in the Paracel and Spratly Islands, fortify their occupied atolls, and enhance their military capabilities.
>
> In the end, for all the merits of exhaustive analyses of the relative virtues (or otherwise) of each claimant state's territorial and maritime claims in international legal terms, it has to be recognized that this would only really be relevant were the disputes to be resolved through international adjudication and this remains a remote possibility. This is not to argue that the legal positions of the parties are not important and will not influence negotiating positions or be subject to lively debate and contention among the parties, but it is nonetheless clear that if the South China Sea disputes are to be settled, such resolution will derive from a political rather than essentially legal process. Unfortunately, the prospects of such a political settlement seem vanishingly small.[57]

While Schofield and Storey are right in their assessment, policymakers in the claimant countries need to move towards improving the situation, even if such moves are short of a definitive settlement of their conflicting claims, the prospects of which, in any case, are, in the words of Schofield and Storey, "vanishingly small".

One such move would be to improve on the current Declaration of Conduct. Schofield and Storey call for a "more robust" code of conduct, Hillary Clinton for a "full" code of conduct. Others have been more specific, envisioning a code of conduct that is "legally binding". In such visions, it is unclear who would enforce the code and how. This means that there would really be no substantive difference between a legal code and a political declaration. Moreover, until the question of whether it would cover the Paracels is resolved, no "legally binding" code is possible, unless the parties change their positions, the irreconcilable nature of which made the adoption of a "legally binding" code impossible in the first place. Instead, ASEAN and China would do well to build and put flesh on the current declaration by carrying out its provisions, elaborating on them or taking measures not foreseen in it but consistent with its spirit.

The first principle of the declaration is the peaceful settlement of disputes. This means that not only must the settlement of disputes be peaceful, that is, not by force, but moves have to be made towards a settlement. For one thing, China has to stop proclaiming that it has "indisputable sovereignty" over the South China Sea, when there are, in fact, disputes, which are the source of the problem to begin with. The claimants should begin to distinguish among the land features that they claim which are islands and which are rocks, as defined by Article 121 of UNCLOS. This distinction is critical to the kinds of maritime jurisdiction that one can claim. Making it can bring a measure of clarity to the claimants' maritime claims and to the rights of others and thus, particularly if done simultaneously, improve stability in the region.

The declaration enjoins the exercise of "self-restraint" on the parties, specifically committing them to "refraining from action of inhabiting on (*sic*) the presently uninhabited islands, reefs, shoals, cays, and other features". The parties could agree to specify that the deployment of military forces or the reinforcement of structures in already occupied land features is among the activities covered by self-restraint.

The declaration calls for dialogues and exchanges of views between their defence and military officials as a confidence building measure. In October 2010, the Defence Ministers of ASEAN's ten members and eight other countries, including China, Japan and the United States, met for the first time in Hanoi. As reported in the media, among the wide range of subjects discussed — among the eighteen and in bilateral talks — was the situation in the South China Sea. In this sense, one of the measures that the declaration calls for is already being carried out. Subsequent meetings, too, could offer opportunities for the Ministers of China and other claimant-countries to hold confidence building talks.

The parties to the declaration might enter into specific agreements committing them to carrying out the measures specified in it, including "ensuring just and humane treatment" of persons "in danger or in distress", notifying "other Parties concerned" of impending joint or combined military exercises, and exchanging "relevant information". They could undertake the cooperative activities that the declaration suggests in the areas of the marine environment, marine scientific research, safety of navigation, search and rescue, and combating transnational crime.

Above all, aligning claims with the provisions and requirements of UNCLOS would go a long way towards reducing mutual suspicions, stabilizing things in East Asia, ensuring open and free sea lanes and aviation paths, helping to improve relations all around, and, for the Philippines, the diminution of a sense of threat to national security.

Notes

This chapter was first published as "The South China Sea", in *Where in the World is the Philippines? Debating Its National Territory*, by Rodolfo C. Severino (Singapore: Institute of Southeast Asian Studies, 2010).

1. Republic of Vietnam Ministry of Foreign Affairs, *White Paper on the Hoang Sa (Paracel) and Truong Sa (Spratly) Islands* (Saigon, 1975), p. 75.
2. A.V.H. Hartendorp, *History of Industry and Trade of the Philippines: The Magsaysay Administration* (Manila: Philippine Education Company, 1961), p. 212.
3. The text of the Notice is in Appendix D to Juan M. Arreglado, *Kalayaan: Historical, Legal, Political Background* (Manila: Foreign Service Institute, 1982), p. 21.
4. Quoted in Hartendorp, *History of Industry and Trade*, p. 212.
5. Quoted in ibid., p. 213.
6. These documents are reproduced as Appendices E, F, G, H, I, K and L to Arreglado, *Kalayaan*, pp. 22–34.
7. Quoted in Hartendorp, *History of Industry and Trade*, pp. 223–24.
8. Ibid., p. 225.
9. Republic of Vietnam Ministry of Foreign Affairs, *White Paper*, p. 75.
10. Ibid., p. 231.
11. Quoted in full in Hartendorp, *History of Industry and Trade*, pp. 232–33.
12. The Spratlys take their name from Richard Spratly, a British whaler of the nineteenth century.
13. Appendix S to Arreglado, *Kalayaan*, pp. 45–46.
14. Appendix R to Arreglado, *Kalayaan*, pp. 43–44.

15. José D. Ingles, *Philippine Foreign Policy* (Manila: Lyceum of the Philippines, 1982), p. 229.
16. Appendix P to Arreglado, *Kalayaan*, pp. 39–41.
17. Appendix Z to Arreglado, *Kalayaan*, pp. 83–84.
18. José V. Abueva, Arnold P. Alamon and Oliva Z. Domingo, *Admiral Tomas Cloma* (Quezon City, Philippines, University of the Philippines, 1999), pp. 33–34, 51 and 151.
19. Tomás Cloma & Associates, *Memorandum for Her Excellency Corazon C. Aquino, President of the Philippines, Malacañang Palace, Manila* (15 July 1987), document in author's possession.
20. Ibid.
21. Text of House bill in author's possession.
22. Text of Senate bill in author's possession.
23. Rodolfo C. Severino, *Clarifying the New Philippine Baselines Law*, online discussion forum, ASEAN Studies Centre, Institute of Southeast Asian Studies, 2009 <http://www.iseas.edu.sg/aseanstudiescentre>.
24. Hartendorp, *History of Industry and Trade*, pp. 224–27.
25. Lu Ning, *Flashpoint Spratlys!* (Singapore: Dolphin Trade Press Pte Ltd, 1995), p. 32.
26. The Chinese claim is summarized in ibid., pp. 5–30.
27. Sam Bateman, *Commentary on "Energy and Geopolitics in the South China Sea" by Michael Richardson* (Singapore: Online Discussion Forum, ASEAN Studies Centre, Institute of Southeast Asian Studies, <www.iseas.edu,sg/aseanstudiescentre>, 2009), pp. 7–8.
28. B.A. Hamzah, *Pax Sinica and Regional Maritime Order in the Spratlys*, online discussion forum, ASEAN Studies Centre, Institute of Southeast Asian Studies, 2009 <http://www.iseas.edu.sg/aseanstudiescentre>, p. 4.
29. Lu Ning, *Flashpoint Spratlys!*, p. 30.
30. An English translation of the declaration is appended to Jeanette Greenfield, *China and the Law of the Sea, Air, and Environment* (Germantown, MD: Sijthoff and Noordhoff, 1979), p. 243.
31. http://huwu.org/Depts/los/LEGISLATIONANDTREATIES/PDFFILES/CHN_1992_Law.pdf.
32. This narrative is taken from Bob Catley and Makmur Keliat, *Spratlys: The Dispute in the South China Sea* (Aldershot, England, and Brookfield, VT: Ashgate, 1997), p. 82. That account, in turn, is based on contemporary media reports.
33. <http://www.fmprc.gov.cn/ce/cebn/eng/wlxw/t542877.htm>, para. 3.
34. <http://www.kln.gov.my/web/guest/pr2010/-/asset_publisher/X9Nx/content/press-release-:-the-exchange-of-letters-between-yab-dato'-seri-abdullah-haji-ahmad-badawi-prime-minister-of-malaysia-and-his-majesty-sultan-haji-hassanal-bolkiah-mu'izzaddin-waddaulah-english-version-only;j

sessionid=868CDC421965796C4269F388022C0C81?redirect=%2Fweb%2Fgue
st%2Fpr2010>.

35. Statement by Tun Abdullah Ahmad Badawi on the Exchange of Letters Between
    Malaysia and Brunei Darussalam, dated 16 March 2009 (<http://www.kln.
    gov.my/web/guest/>).

36. Lu Ning, *Flashpoint Spratlys!*, p. 16.

37. Steven Yu Kuan-tsyh, "Who Owns the Paracels and Spratlys? An Evaluation
    of the Nature and Legal Basis of the Conflicting Territorial Claims", paper
    presented at the second Workshop on Managing Potential Conflicts in the
    South China Sea, Bandung, Indonesia, 15–18 July 1991, p. 27, as quoted in
    Catley and Keliat, *Spratlys*, pp. 38–39.

38. Robert Beckman, "South China Sea: Worsening Dispute or Growing Clarity
    in Claims?", in *RSIS Commentaries* (Singapore: S. Rajaratnam School of
    International Studies, 16 August 2010), p. 2.

39. <http://www.asean.org/3634.htm>.

40. <http://www.asean.org/5232.htm>.

41. Roberto R. Romulo, *The Tasks Before Us: Territorial Integrity and Regional Peace
    and Stability* (Manila, 10 April 1995).

42. Joint Communique of the Twenty-Eighth Asean Ministerial Meeting,
    Bandar Seri Begawan, 29–30 July 1995 <http://www.aseansec.org/2087.
    htm>, para. 9.

43. Joint Statement: RP-PRC Consultations on the South China Sea and on Other
    Areas of Cooperation, 9–10 August 1995.

44. Joint Press Communiqué on Philippines-China Consultations, 15 March
    1996.

45. Declaration of the Government of the People's Republic of China on the
    baselines of the territorial sea, 15 May 1996 <http://www.un.org/Depts/
    los/LEGISLATIONANDTREATIES/PDFFILES/ CHN_1996_Declaration.
    pdf>.

46. <http://www.aseanregionalforum.org/PublicLibrary/ARFChairmans
    StatementsandReports/ChairmansStatementofthe2ndMeetingoftheASE/
    tabid/199/Default.aspx>.

47. Joint Communique of The 29th ASEAN Ministerial Meeting (AMM) Jakarta,
    20–21 July 1996 <http://www.asean.org/3663.htm>, para. 11.

48. <http://www.aseansec.org/13163.htm>.

49. Barry Wain, "Manila's Bungle in the South China Sea", *Far Eastern Economic
    Review*, January/February 2008.

50. Xue Hanqin: *China-ASEAN Cooperation: A Model of Good Neighbourliness and
    Friendly Cooperation*, Singapore, 19 November 2009 <http://www.iseas.edu.
    sg/aseanstudiescentre/Speech-Xue-Hanqin-19-9-09.pdf>, pp. 24–25.

51. Remarks at Press Availability by Secretary Hillary Rodham Clinton in Hanoi,

Vietnam, 23 July 2010, in <http://www.state.gov/secretary/rm/2010/07/145095.htm>.

52. Foreign Minister Yang Jiechi Refutes Fallacies on the South China Sea Issue <http://www.mfa.gov.cn/eng/zxxx/t719460.htm>.

53. Sam Bateman, *Commentary*, p. 8.

54. Ibid., p. 8.

55. Section 2, Article XII, of the 1987 Philippine Constitution.

56. The statements issued at the end of the 1991 to 2002 workshops are reproduced in Hasjim Djalal, *Preventive Diplomacy in Southeast Asia: Lessons Learned* (Jakarta: The Habibie Center, 2003), pp. 229–78.

57. Clive Schofield and Ian Storey, *The South China Sea Dispute: Increasing Stakes and Rising Tensions* (Washington, DC: Jamestown Foundation, November 2009), p. 42.

10

MALAYSIA'S MARITIME CLAIMS IN THE SOUTH CHINA SEA
Security and Military Dimensions

Dzirhan Mahadzir

Malaysia's maritime boundaries border those of six other countries, namely, Brunei, Indonesia, the Philippines, Singapore, Thailand, and Vietnam. Because of the number of littoral countries around the South China Sea, these boundaries are more apparent there compared to the rest of Malaysia's maritime space. Malaysia's maritime territory in the South China Sea is basically divided into two parts, separated in-between by Indonesia's Exclusive Economic Zone. Of Malaysia's two areas of the South China Sea, one borders the East Coast of Peninsular Malaysia and the other borders the Malaysian states of Sabah and Sarawak (collectively referred to as East Malaysia) on the island of Borneo. It is the East Malaysian part of the South China Sea that is the most contentious area, particularly given the various overlapping claims over the Spratly Islands.

Malaysia's maritime territory in the South China Sea encompasses twelve features, be they islands, rocks, reefs, shoals and atolls in the Spratly Islands. Malaysia maintains a physical presence on five of the features.

These are Pulau Layang-Layang (Swallow Reef), Terumbu Mantanani (Mariveles Reef), Terumbu Ubi (Ardasier Reef), Terumbu Siput (Erica Reef), and Terumbu Peninjau (Investigator Reef). Two other features, though lying within Malaysia's claims, are occupied by the Philippines and Vietnam, with the Philippines occupying Terumbu Laksamana (Commodore Reef) and the Vietnamese occupying Pulau Amboyna Kecil (Amboyna Cay). Malaysian special forces actually landed on Pulau Amboyna in 1978 and placed markers, but the Vietnamese who subsequently occupied the feature destroyed them. Malaysia then began a series of gradual claims of several positions in the area beginning in May 1983 when special forces personnel occupied Pulau Layang-Layang (Swallow Reef). The full details of the developments of these military outposts will be discussed later in the chapter.

The current official position of the Malaysian government towards its claims can be seen in the replies of the Malaysian government to Senator Tunku Abdul Aziz on issues regarding the Spratly Islands and the South China Sea. The two transcripts below dated 6 May 2010 and 28 July 2010 were originally provided in Bahasa Malaysia by the Senator's office to the media and obtained by the author. I have translated the transcript and edited out the routine salutation and greetings in the response to the Senator's question.

Here follows the transcript of Deputy Foreign Minister Kohilan Pillay's response to Senator Tunku Abdul Aziz's question in regard to the Spratlys on 6 May 2010. It begins with the Senator's question:

> Senator Tunku Abdul Aziz asks the Foreign Minister to state the government's views in regard to the statements of then Deputy Foreign Minister, Dato' Lee Chee Leong in an interview with online media KL Security on 22 September 2009 that supports joint development of the South China Sea.

Response by Deputy Foreign Minister Kohilan Pillay:

> As mentioned in the past in this august house, there exist overlapping maritime claims and conflicting claims on geographical features such as islands, reefs and such in the South China Sea. The conflicting claims in the South China Sea involve Malaysia, Vietnam, Brunei Darussalam, the Philippines and the People's Republic of China.
>
> The People's Republic of China claims the entire South China Sea, including the Spratly Islands. However, claims by the People's Republic

of China are disputed because they are inconsistent with international law, including the provisions of the Convention on the Organisation of the United Nations Law of the Sea of 1982 (United Nations Convention on the Law of the Sea 1982 — UNCLOS 1982). Malaysia is of the view that islands and reefs in the continental shelf area of Malaysia are owned by Malaysia.

Currently, Malaysia does not undertake any joint development with any countries in the South China Sea area offshore of Sabah and Sarawak. This is consistent with the stance that the area of the continental shelf claimed by Malaysia belongs to Malaysia and any proposed actions with other countries need to be in accord with that stance.

For the further information of your Excellency, issues relating to claims on the islands and reefs are addressed based on the spirit and aspirations contained in the Declaration on the Conduct of Parties in the South China Sea (DOC) signed by ASEAN and the People's Republic of China on 4 November 2002. Through this Declaration, the parties that have overlapping claims in the South China Sea are committed to resolve such disputes and find an amicable settlement through negotiations without using force or the threat of force. Confidence-building efforts are also being undertaken by the states involved.

Malaysia is always sensitive to issues involving overlapping claims to the islands of Malaysia and the region. Efforts are constantly undertaken to strengthen Malaysia's claims on the geographical features of the maritime areas concerned. Malaysia has always encouraged bilateral talks with neighbouring countries to define maritime boundaries in areas where no boundary agreements exists. Malaysia believes that the overlapping claims should be resolved at the negotiating table, with reference to third parties such as the International Court of Justice (ICJ) or the Arbitration Tribunal being the last option to obtain a solution.

And this is the transcript of Senate Parliamentary Hansard on 28 July 2010 on the reply of Deputy Foreign Minister Pillay to the Senator's question:

Senator Tunku Abdul Aziz requests the Foreign Minister to state the government's position towards a proposal for all ASEAN claimants on the Spratlys to use a single entity to negotiate with China over sovereignty issues there. Have Royal Malaysian Navy (RMN) ships come across Chinese warships/enforcement entering Malaysia's exclusive economic zone (EEZ) without notice?

Answer by Deputy Foreign Minister Kohilan Pillay:

As mentioned in the past in this august house, there exist the issue of overlapping claims and demands on the geographic features in the South China Sea. The overlapping claims in the South China Sea involve Malaysia, Vietnam, Brunei Darussalam, the Philippines and the People's Republic of China. For the information of this august house, the People's Republic of China claims the entire South China Sea including the Spratly Islands.

As mentioned in the past in this house, the issue in respect of claims on the islands, reefs and maritime areas are handled based on the spirit and aspirations contained in the DOC signed by ASEAN and the People's Republic of China on 4 November 2002. Through this declaration, the parties with overlapping claims in the South China Sea are committed to resolving conflicts and disputes in respect of the overlapping claims in a peaceful manner without the use of violence or intimidation and to pursue a path of negotiation. Meanwhile, efforts are being undertaken to build confidence between the countries involved. In this case, I am pleased to announce that discussions are under way to implement cooperation activities under the framework of the DOC to heighten confidence and avoid tension in the South China Sea.

Malaysia is always sensitive to issues involving overlapping claims on the islands of Malaysia and the region. Efforts are always undertaken to strengthen Malaysia's claims over geographic features in the maritime area concerned. We believe a solution to the issue of overlapping claims can be achieved through peaceful discussion without using force. In this case, Malaysia is establishing bilateral talks with neighbouring countries to define the boundaries of the areas in which no maritime boundary agreements exist. Malaysia believes that the overlapping claims should be resolved in bilateral negotiations, and that reference to a third party such as the ICJ or Tribunal of Arbitration would be the last option for achieving a solution.

At the same time, Malaysia has always taken into account current developments. Malaysia views that the issue of overlapping claims in the South China Sea should be resolved on a bilateral or multilateral basis and involve only countries who have overlapping claims. At this time, there is no proposal from any ASEAN country that has an overlapping claim for a merger as one entity to negotiate with the People's Republic of China.

On the issue of whether RMN warships are tracking and preventing Chinese ships from entering the exclusive economic zone without notice,

I would like to inform you that patrols and surveillance are carried out continuously in the maritime area claimed in the South China Sea. At the same time, the provisions of international law allows ships to sail the seas under the principle of freedom of navigation without having to seek approval of a coastal nation. However, in regard to ships that carry out activities contrary to the principles of navigation, such as conducting marine scientific research within the exclusive economic zone, among others, Malaysia can and will take appropriate action. I am happy to declare that the navy is constantly monitoring the activities of foreign warships in the South China Sea.

Both answers clearly illustrates Malaysia's stance on a peaceful resolution to the issue, though it would consider obtaining a judgment from a third party as a last resort. The answers also stress the importance of building upon the DOC in resolving such claims. Noticeably Malaysia has stated that negotiations on the claims should only involve the countries which have overlapping claims with each other and not involve countries who do not have claims in the region. This appears also to indicate that where negotiating on specific areas and zones, only countries which have overlapping claims in those specific areas should be involved in negotiations and such negotiations should not include countries that have claims in the Spratlys but not on the specific area that is the focus of the negotiation.

Despite its commitment to peaceful resolutions to claims on the Spratlys and the South China Sea, Malaysia has not neglected its ability to protect its claims by force if necessary. However, it should be noted that the Malaysian posture to the use of military force to protect such claims is purely defensive in nature and based on the fact that Malaysia would be responding to aggression. To further understand the Malaysian military position on the Spratlys, there follows a timeline of how the country developed its claims with regard to the activities of its military and the establishment of bases and outposts there.

TIMELINE OF MALAYSIAN ESTABLISHMENT OF BASES/OUTPOSTS IN THE SOUTH CHINA SEA

- 1978: Malaysian Navy special forces land on the various features and place markers. The marker on Amboyna Kecil (Amboyna Cay) is subsequently destroyed by Vietnam who then occupied the feature.

- May 1983: Malaysian Navy special forces land on the then Terumbu Layang-Layang (Swallow Reef) and establish a basecamp. Subsequent construction and enlargement of the reef leads Malaysia to call it Pulau Layang-Layang (Layang-Layang Island).
- April 1986: Naval station "Lima" constructed on Layang-Layang. The work was conducted by the Army's Royal Engineers regiment with both army and naval special forces providing a security detachment. This was a continuing process in which the island was extended in size and additional facilities built upon it, including a runway capable of use by C-130 Hercules aircraft. Layang-Layang is currently about 7.3 km long and 2.2 km wide with a land space of around 6 hectares. Aside from naval personnel, the Royal Malaysian Air Force are said to have an air defence missile detachment with MANPADs and personnel to support incoming flights stationed there. The army is also said to periodically rotate in special forces personnel there.
- 1986: Naval station "Uniform" constructed on Terumbu Ubi (Ardasier Reef). Originally a module built on a barge, this was enlarged over the following years and a channel built in 2000 to allow RMN CB-90 combat boats to operate from the lagoon.
- November 1986: Naval station "Mike" constructed on Terumbu Mantanani (Mariveles Reef). This was a purpose-built habitat module anchored on the reef. Amboyna Cay lies 40 nautical miles away from it.
- 1991: Resort constructed on Pulau Layang-Layang.
- April 1999: Naval station "Sierra" constructed on Terumbu Siput (Erica Reef). Sierra was a specially designed module built by PSC Naval Dockyard and designed as a floating vessel to allow it to be towed to its location. The entire towing and stationing operation was conducted with the RMN disguising the movement through the use of several ships in an operation known as Ops Sri Petaling. Initially the station was also declared as being used for scientific and marine research to prevent any adverse reaction and pressure from the claimants in the area.
- April 1999: Naval Station "Papa" constructed on Terumbu Peninjau (Investigator Reef). Station Papa was also a module built on top of a barge and constructed by PSC Naval Dockyard. The module was towed together with the Station Sierra module under Ops Sri

Petaling. Station Papa was likewise declared a maritime scientific
research station to avoid complaints from other claimants.
- July 2004: Marine Research Station Pulau Layang-Layang opened.

From the timeline above it can clearly be seen that Malaysia has not
established further outposts or stations since the installations of Station
Sierra and Papa in 1999, though work to upgrade its existing positions have
been carried out. With the Code of Conduct declaration, it is highly unlikely
that Malaysia will build further structures in the area. The establishment of
a resort and research station facilities on Layang-Layang has been part of
a subtle Malaysian strategy to promote the area for international visitors
from the West and thus constrain aggression towards Malaysia's claim by
virtue of the presence of third-party nationals.

Much has been made of public visits by Malaysian national leaders
to the island in recent years, particularly the visit of Prime Minister
Abdullah Badawi in March 2009, with some saying of the visit that
Malaysia was mounting a strong media campaign towards promoting its
claims. However, the context of these media tours should be understood.
The author has personal knowledge of the tours, which were organized
by the Public Relations Department of the Ministry of Defence, as he
was invited as a member of the media covering the military to follow the
media tours in 2007, 2008 and 2009, but had to decline on each occasion
due to conflicting schedules.

The three tours formed part of an established pattern of annual
media tours organized by the Defence Ministry, which would normally
see the Defence Minister along with either the Chief of Defence Force
(CDF) or a service chief in attendance. For 2007 to 2009 it was decided
to take the media to visit East Malaysia and observe the armed forces
operations there, with a visit to Layang-Layang forming only part of the
itinerary rather than the whole purpose of the tour. Due to scheduling
conflicts, neither the Minister, CDF, or service chief were able to attend
the 2007 tour which was carried out in December. Instead, Dr Jasbil Singh,
Principle Assistant Secretary at the Ministry of Defence, led the media
tour. In August 2008 Defence Minister Najib led the tour. But it was the
visit of Prime Minister Abdullah Badawi in March 2009 that prompted
speculation as to Malaysia's intent in the region and that the visit was
orchestrated to assert Malaysia's claims in the Spratlys. This is actually
baseless, as the reason Prime Minister Badawi was there was due to him

being Defence Minister. The author was informed about the 2009 tour as early as September 2008, prior to Abdullah making a portfolio swap with Najib in which Abdullah exchanged his position as Finance Minister to become Defence Minister and Najib became Finance Minister in turn. The author had been told by MOD PR prior to this swap that Defence Minister Najib would be taking the media again to East Malaysia in 2009, thus disproving that the Prime Minister's visit there in 2009 was strongly connected to asserting Malaysia's claim. Furthermore the extensive media coverage on Badawi's visit was actually due to the make-up of the media contingent. In 2007 and 2008, the journalists who went on the tours were those who covered the defence beat and generally not high ranking in the media hierarchy. However, the 2009 tour, with the Prime Minister on board, prompted many requests from senior media figures and editors to join the tour. The requests were granted and thus resulted in excessive media coverage. The media-blitz in 2009 was more coincidence than a direct strategy to assert Malaysia's claims via use of the media in conjunction with the visit of the Prime Minister. In 2010 a media tour was again taken to East Malaysia, this time with current Defence Minister Dr Ahmad Zahid Hamidi, though no visit to Layang-Layang was organized due to budgetary cutbacks and the costs involved in bringing the media via C-130 to the island, though the author understands from his sources that concerns over the reaction of other countries towards the media reports on the 2009 tour also formed part of the reason that no media tours since then included a visit to Layang-Layang.

MALAYSIAN MILITARY AND DEFENCE DEVELOPMENTS IN THE SPRATLYS

As much of the specifics of Malaysia's military plans and policies are not publicly available, much of the following is based on the author's own personal assessment and experience of the issue, though, where appropriate, reference will be made to the 2010 National Defence Policy that was released in December of that year by the Ministry of Defence.

The National Defence Policy defines the three vital areas of Malaysia to be defended as (1) the Main Area, (2) the Offshore Economic Area, and (3) the Strategic Maritime and Aerospace Routes. "The Main Area covers the Peninsular Malaysia, Sabah and Sarawak land-space along with its territorial waters and airspace. These areas are to be protected to the utmost from any form of external threat", states the National Defence policy. It should be noted that the exclusion of the mention of defending against internal threats is due to the fact that dealing with internal threats are the province of the Home Ministry and the Royal Malaysian Police.

The Offshore Economic Area is the Economic Exclusion Zone and the nation's continental shelf. This area, which lies in the South China Sea, is rich with fishery resources and hydrocarbons and forms one of the main contributions to the country's economy. This clearly outlines that the protection of the South China Sea due to its importance to the economy is of priority. Finally, the Strategic Maritime and Aerospace Routes of Malaysia are as follows: (1) Air and Sea routes that connect Peninsular Malaysia and Sabah/Sarawak, (2) the Strait of Malacca and entry/exit routes, and (3) the Singapore Strait and entry/exit routes.

Moreover, the National Defence Policy booklet outlines the strategic dilemma faced by Malaysia in defence of the nation and its interests. It states, "The physical separation of Peninsular Malaysia with Sabah and Sarawak by the South China Sea requires the nation to give attention to the air and sea routes between the two areas. Any threat or disruption to the sea and air routes there can threaten the stability of the two areas and as a whole, Malaysia."

This in essence sums up the problem faced by Malaysia, in that Peninsular and East Malaysia are basically two separate territorial entities physically separated by a vast maritime body, over much of which Malaysia does not have territorial sovereignty or control. As such Malaysian defence planning and deployments focus on the necessity to divide its forces into two and maintain a sufficient military force in each area that would not be heavily dependent upon swift reinforcements, assistance or support from the military assets and forces in the other area. This is very much reflected in the organizational structure of the Royal Malaysian Navy and Royal Malaysian Air Force who bear the responsibility of securing the routes between Peninsular and East Malaysia and also the territorial waters, EEZ and continental shelf areas. The Royal Malaysian Navy maintains three areas of commands: (1) COMNAV I whose area of responsibility is from the South China Sea side of Peninsular Malaysia and the EEZ there to the lower end of the Strait of Malacca, (2) COMNAV II which is responsible for the waters around East Malaysia and the EEZ there, and (3) COMNAV III which is responsible for the upper half of the Strait of Malacca and Malaysian waters in the northwest of the peninsular. Meanwhile the

Royal Malaysian Air Force divides its operational commands into two: No. 1 Air Division for Peninsular Malaysia and No. 2 Air Division for East Malaysia.

However, the deployment and maintenance of sufficient military forces in both parts of the nation has been difficult for both the RMN and Royal Malaysian Air Force (RMAF), owing to the small size of both forces. The RMN has less than forty vessels in its inventory capable of carrying out operational patrols, while the RMAF's frontline combat aircraft fleet consists of eighteen Su-30MKM, eight F/A-18 Hornets and six MiG-29s, with around two to three dozen secondary combat aircraft in the form of F-5Es, Bae Hawks and MB-339s, the latter two primarily used for training and ground-attack roles. This has resulted in the RMAF rotating one or more flight detachments of four combat aircraft from the fighter squadrons in and out East Malaysia, rather than permanently stationing a squadron there, such as is the case with its helicopter and fixed-wing transports. The RMAF's long-term strategic plan calls for the service to reach a targeted strength of six multirole aircraft fighter squadrons, two of which will then be stationed permanently in East Malaysia. However, the budgetary constraints facing Malaysia that limit defence funding means that the six-squadron target is unlikely to be achieved in the near future, and that the rotations of flight detachments of combat aircraft to East Malaysia will continue for a while.

The RMN's operational target is to ensure that a minimum of six ships are on patrol at any given time: three around Peninsular Malaysia and three around East Malaysia. This was stated by RMN chief, Admiral Aziz Jaafar, and reported in *Janes Defence Weekly* on 30 April 2010. The RMN chief also stated in that report that the RMN would be able to maintain such an operational tempo in the near term, but not in the long term unless it acquired additional surface ships. The RMN's six Kedah class offshore patrol vessels (OPVs) are divided and stationed equally between three naval bases, two at RMN Kuantan to patrol the Peninsular Malaysian side of the South China Sea, two at RMN Lumut to patrol the Strait of Malacca and two at RMN Sepanggar in East Malaysia to patrol the South China Sea area there. The Navy maintains much of the responsibility for the security and defence of the Spratlys, and the five naval stations there are all operationally controlled by the RMN and largely manned by RMN personnel. The Spratlys and the South China Sea area around them are known to the RMN as the GSP operational area, which roughly translates to "Frontier Reconnaissance Island Chain". The area is under the control of COMNAV II, based at RMN Sepanggar base near Kota Kinabalu in Sabah.

The further importance of the GSP area is illustrated by the basing of the RMN's two recently acquired French-built Scorpene class submarines at RMN Sepanggar. The submarines recently completed their weapons-firing trial and initial operational capability training stage. The first fleet exercise involving the submarine KD Tunku Abdul Rahman took place from 29 July to 6 August 2010 in the South China Sea. The exercise known as Operation Sea Training Exercise/Fleet Integration Training with Submarine 2010 (OSTEX/SUB FIT 2010) involved ten other RMN ships, including the frigates KD Lekiu and KD Lekir and the Patrol Vessels KD Perak, KD Terengganu, KD Pahang, KD Kedah and 1,000 personnel from the RMN and RMAF. Also participating were elements of the RMN's special forces, diving and air defence teams. The RMAF fielded two Bae Hawks, a Beechcraft 200T Maritime Patrol Aircraft and an S-61 helicopter for the exercise. The exercise was staged from the RMN's COMNAV II HQ at RMN. An RMN official press release on the exercise stated that the purpose of the exercise was to assess the RMN's fleet readiness, develop the capabilities of the RMN and RMAF in operations with submarines, to highlight the RMN's presence in the South China Sea and to test contingency plans for the defence of the RMN posts located in the Spratly Islands. The RMN though has held much of the training and firing exercises involving submarines well clear of the Spratlys so as not to inflame claimants there. Still of interest was the need to highlight the RMN's presence in the South China Sea and to test contingency plans to defend the RMN stations. While it is only natural that the RMN prepares contingency plans and test its readiness over the South China Sea and the Spratlys, the author notes with interests that in recent years there has been a greater focus on such scenarios, something illustrated later in the same year when the joint RMN/RMAF exercise ANGSA 2010 was carried out in the Strait of Malacca from 23 September to 6 October.

Both the RMN and RMAF have a strong cooperative partnership based on years of working together in Malaysia's maritime domain. The two services hold an annual exercise called ANGSA, an acronym for "ANGkasa SAmudera", Angkasa meaning aerospace and Samudera meaning maritime in Bahasa. The ANGSA exercises are actually in a two-year format, with a command post exercise (CPX) in the first year and a field training exercise (FTX) held the following year based on the scenario of the previous year's CPX. Although originally beginning as an RMN/RMAF exercise, recent years have seen Army elements also taking part, particularly the Army's Air Defence Group and special forces. The author has been told that Army participation will now be standard for such exercises. The ANGSA 2010 exercise, held as an FTX, gave further indication that the threat scenario that both the RMN and RMAF expected to face conventionally would be in relation to the South China Sea and the Spratlys. While the exercise — involving nine RMN ships and two helicopters and twenty-eight RMAF aircraft, including the Su-30MKMs and F/a-18s — took place around the island of Langkawi and the Strait of Malacca, some of the activities carried out in the exercise point specifically to a Spratlys concern. Some of the activities that took place in the exercise included the involvement of Army airborne and amphibious operations specialists who provided input on the tasks of reinforcing or deploying troops by sea and air to islands. It should be noted that other than the islands of Penang and Langkawi, the only islands that Malaysia has a military presence in lie in the Spratlys. The RMAF Su-30MKMs participating in the exercise successfully carried out aerial refuelling to other aircraft, including the F/A-18s, using buddy store tanks, allowing the RMAF to carry out missions at greater range and endurance. Although the RMAF has KC-130 tankers capable of conducting aerial refuelling, it would seem that the RMAF is looking to even further increase the striking range of its frontline aircraft. Currently the F/A-18s are the only aircraft in the RMAF inventory with a dedicated maritime strike capability in the form of the Boeing Harpoon anti-ship missiles. Clearly, the ability to conduct long-range strikes in the maritime domain for the RMAF is tied to the Spratlys situation.

Further illustration of the military's concern in regard to the South China Sea and the Spratly's was illustrated by a joint press conference held after the exercise on 6 October 2010 by RMN chief Admiral Aziz and his RMAF counterpart General Rodzali at which the author was present. Both stated that the security of the South China Sea is the priority of the two services and stressed the need for Malaysia to improve its Maritime Domain Awareness capabilities in the South China Sea to ensure security in the area. Neither chief would specify the nature of the threats to security faced by Malaysia in the area, though General Rodzali stated, "since a significant portion of the country's economy is tied to that region, such as resources and trade routes, it is only natural that we have to prepare for any threats in that region and we have to enhance our MDA capabilities there". Admiral Aziz stated that the RMN and RMAF have agreed that the next Angsa field exercise, scheduled in 2012, will be held in the South China Sea with a preliminary command post exercise held in 2011. "We already hold exercises in that area but we need to do more joint exercises there to enhance our capabilities to respond to any threats there" he said. The RMN chief added though that the planners were still studying the matter of whether the exercise in 2012 will be held in the Peninsular or East Malaysian side of the South China Sea.

The Malaysian military's concern over the Spratlys is well founded as there have been numerous incursions, into what Malaysia considers Malaysian waters in both the EEZ and its claims in the Spratlys, by foreign vessels whose activities are deemed more than innocent passage. The RMN and RMAF have had to chase such ships out of the area. A significant number of these ships are said to be from the People's Republic of China, with a U.S. military officer telling the author that some of the ships, although bearing markings of Chinese maritime enforcement agencies, are in reality Chinese military ships or manned by the People's Liberation Army Navy (PLAN). Most of these incidents go unreported and are not publicised by Malaysia as the government does not want to inflame tensions or provoke a media confrontation over the incidents. However, two incidents in 2010 — on 19 April and 29–30 April — have come to light. Interestingly though, the reasons both these incidents became known is not because Malaysia released information about them but instead because they were reported in various Chinese newspapers and blogs (with one blogger on board one of the Chinese vessels during the 19 April incident[1]), all of whom were incensed at the Malaysians chasing Chinese ships out of what China considers its territorial waters. The Malaysia-based defence/security blog, ASEAN Security (AS) Observer, compiled an account of these two incidents in Bahasa Malaysia on 30 July 2010, based on the Chinese reports. The AS Observer blog also obtained confirmation from RMN chief Admiral Aziz of the occurrence of the 29–30 April incident. The two incidents are summarized below:

- On 19 April at 0800 hrs, two patrol vessels of China's maritime enforcement department bearing the pennant numbers 83 and 81 were said to have entered the waters near Layang-Layang. The

Malaysian military responded by dispatching the missile boat KD Serang and an RMAF C-130 to the scene. The RMAF uses some of its C-130 for maritime patrol duties along with the dedicated Beechcraft 200T. Both the KD Serang and the C-130 shadowed the Chinese ships with the C-130 making several passes towards the ships until they left the area at 1500 hrs.

- On 29 April at 1000 hrs, three patrol ships from China's Fishery Department, bearing the pennant numbers 311, 301 and 302 entered Malaysia's EEZ and were 22 km off Layang-Layang when the RMN missile boat KD Ganas arrived at the scene and ordered the ships out of the area, stating it was part of the Malaysian EEZ, with KD Ganas said to be only 300 m away from ship no. 311. Chinese media reports claim that the three ships declared to KD Ganas that the EEZ waters of the South China Sea belong to China and Malaysia had no right to evict the ships. At 1150 hrs an RMAF Beechcraft 200T arrived to support the KD Ganas with a fifteen-minute overflight while the KD Ganas continued to shadow the three ships and prevented them from coming closer to Layang-Layang. At 1500 hrs the Chinese ships split up, with 311 heading in one direction while 302 and 301 headed in another. Ganas shadowed 302 and 301 until 2300 hrs when both ships were deemed to be out of Malaysian waters, while a second RMN ship picked up the trail of the 311, coming across it at 2000 hrs and shadowing it until 0300 hrs on 30 April.

These two incidents, the author believes, are likely a small portion of what is a larger number of incursions by foreign ships in the area deemed to be Malaysian waters. However, such incidents are likely unreported by Malaysia due to Malaysia not wanting to jeopardize its relations with the offending country or to draw unnecessary attention to the Spratlys issue which it hopes to resolve peacefully.

CONCLUSION

In conclusion from the above, it can be seen that Malaysia is firm on its claims in the Spratlys, though it hopes for a peaceful resolution to the situation with an emphasis that only those with claims should be the ones negotiating and outsiders should not be involved in the process. However, despite Malaysia's stated view of a peaceful resolution to the issue, it is prepared for a situation where its claims may have to be defended by military force. So the Malaysian military continues to prepare and improve its abilities to face any military threats towards its claims.

Note

1   At <http://blog.sina.com.cn/s/blog_485f35ff0100kjmw.html>.

11

TAIWAN'S SOUTH CHINA SEA POLICY REVIVAL

Fu-Kuo Liu

Since the beginning of exploration in the South China Sea, the Republic of China (ROC or Taiwan) has controlled the Xisha Islands (Paracel Islands), Zhongsha (Macclesfield Bank), Nansha (Spratly Islands) and Dongsha (Pratas Islands). Inherited from recorded history, the ROC has undeniably claimed sovereignty over the large part of the South China Sea within a "U-shaped line" for many decades. Over the last few decades or so, although the ROC's claim has not changed at all, its ambiguous political status in the international community weakens its position in the disputes of the South China Sea (SCS). As a result, diplomatic setbacks in the international community have discouraged the government in Taipei from any new efforts to activate its South China Sea policy. The typical focus of the political agenda in Taipei has been very much on an inward-looking approach of democratization. Political inability and a lack of political will to cope with the challenges in the SCS seem inevitable for Taipei.

For political reasons Taiwan has over the last decades been neglected in the process of negotiating the code of conduct in the South China Sea. Taiwan remains the only claimant to not have diplomatic relations with any country in the region. Further, political confrontation in the Taiwan

Strait continues to be critical to Taiwan's survival. As a result, not only have neighbouring countries been very cautious of the Chinese attitude in dealing with Taiwan, but Taiwan has also contradicted itself on its position in the SCS.

When cross-strait relations were antagonistic, Taiwan stood almost no chance to engage in any discussion of international affairs on the official level in the region. For decades hostility was the nature of the cross-strait relationship. Nevertheless, President Ma Ying-jeou came to power in May 2008 and has since shifted the negative course in the relationship with Mainland China. Up to the end of 2010, fifteen formal agreements were signed to facilitate mutual cooperation across the Taiwan Strait. The Economic Cooperation Framework Agreement (ECFA) has proven to have made the most important progress made so far, as it has led to broader institutional cooperation. It has opened new opportunities and demands for China and Taiwan to cooperate in the context of the South China Sea. How has Taiwan extended efforts to cooperate with China in SCS affairs? Are there internal or external political obstacles to cross-strait cooperation? Would further cooperation between China and Taiwan help facilitate Taiwan's participation in regional discussions of dispute settlement? This seems more likely judging from the trend of cross-strait cooperation.

The greatest challenge to a role for Taiwan in the SCS is whether China and ASEAN would accept it, followed by how exactly the negotiation process would begin. Although Taiwan is not yet in the process of negotiating a peaceful settlement in the South China Sea, it does not mean that Taiwan has been denied engagement or is even out of the game. The purpose of this chapter is to interpret and clarify Taiwan's South China Sea policy and its new efforts at reviving appropriate policy. It will also look into the political difficulty and dilemma that Taiwan faces today. As the big power competition develops in the SCS and as the cross-strait relationship develops, Taiwan is under mounting pressure, both internally and externally, to refine its SCS policy. The big challenge for Taipei now, of course, is how to rationalize its SCS policy and gain recognition in the region.

HISTORIC PROGRESS OF THE CLAIM

What practical efforts has Taiwan made to the claim of sovereignty in the South China Sea? During the era of President Chiang Kai-shek (in power

Figure 11.1
The 1947 Original 11-Dotted Line

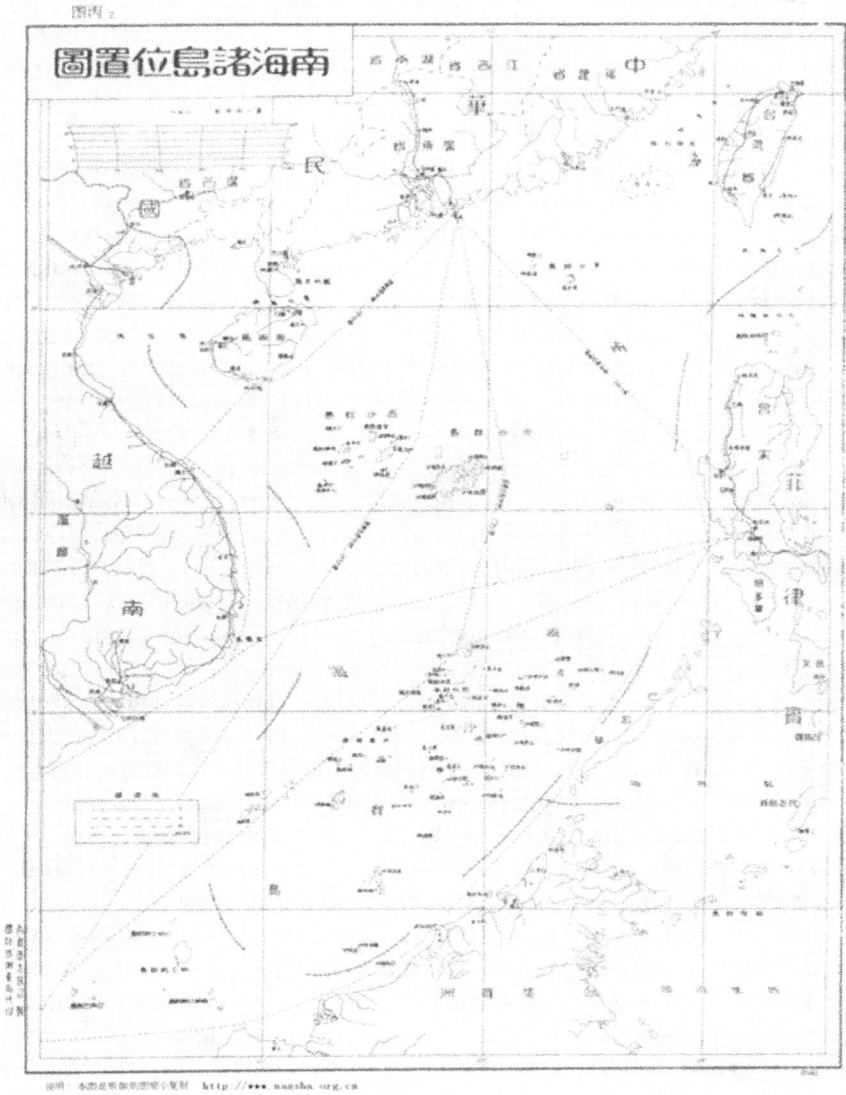

Source: Ministry of Interior, ROC <http://www.land.moi.gov.tw/filelink/uploadlink-1045.pdf>.

1948–75), Taiwan effectively controlled the entire area within the U-shaped line, which was drawn and published by the Ministry of Interior of the Republic of China in 1947. At the time it was published the international community recorded no objection. During the following decades Taiwan's claim of sovereignty has not changed at all, but the competing claims of sovereignty began to appear.

Taiwanese President Lee Teng-hui established a "South China Sea Task Force" in 1992 that coordinated inter-agency work and regularly assigned missions to different agencies. The following year Taiwan issued the "Policy Guidelines for the South China Sea", re-emphasizing the legal claims. The guidelines became the basic structure of its SCS decision-making mechanism. During the second half of the 1990s, Taiwan appeared to be more active in terms of the SCS policy. In order to strengthen the claims, a comprehensive exploration programme was proposed and implemented. This programme covered environmental protection, search and rescue, the deployment of undersea cables to Dongsha and Nansha Islands, construction of a meteorology station, and energy exploration.

In April 1995 the Taiwan marine police announced they would send three patrol boats to Nansha Islands to protect fishermen and to reiterate sovereignty claims. A Philippines military officer publicly threatened to attack any ship entering its waters. Lacking inter-agency coordination in Taiwan, the mission suddenly turned into a diplomatic gaffe. The mishandling of the mission saw the government publicly floundering and it was a setback for the sovereignty claim.[1] The incident showed that Taipei's various government agencies were not prepared to launch such a complicated military-diplomatic mission in the SCS. However, a positive result was that it created public awareness of the complicated reality of the situation. Since then Taipei has been very cautious in dealing on SCS issues. A year later the ROC Navy quietly conducted a mission to the Taiping Islands and reinforced the military presence there.

During the term of President Chen Shui-bian, Taiwan's sovereignty claims were reiterated. Because political hostility had intensified across the Taiwan Strait, the DPP government's position on the issue of political independence heightened Taiwan's diplomatic isolation. In November 2002 China and ASEAN signed the Declaration on the Conducts of Parties in the South China Sea (DOC). Taiwan was completely left out of the

Figure 11.2
The 1947 *U*-Shaped Line

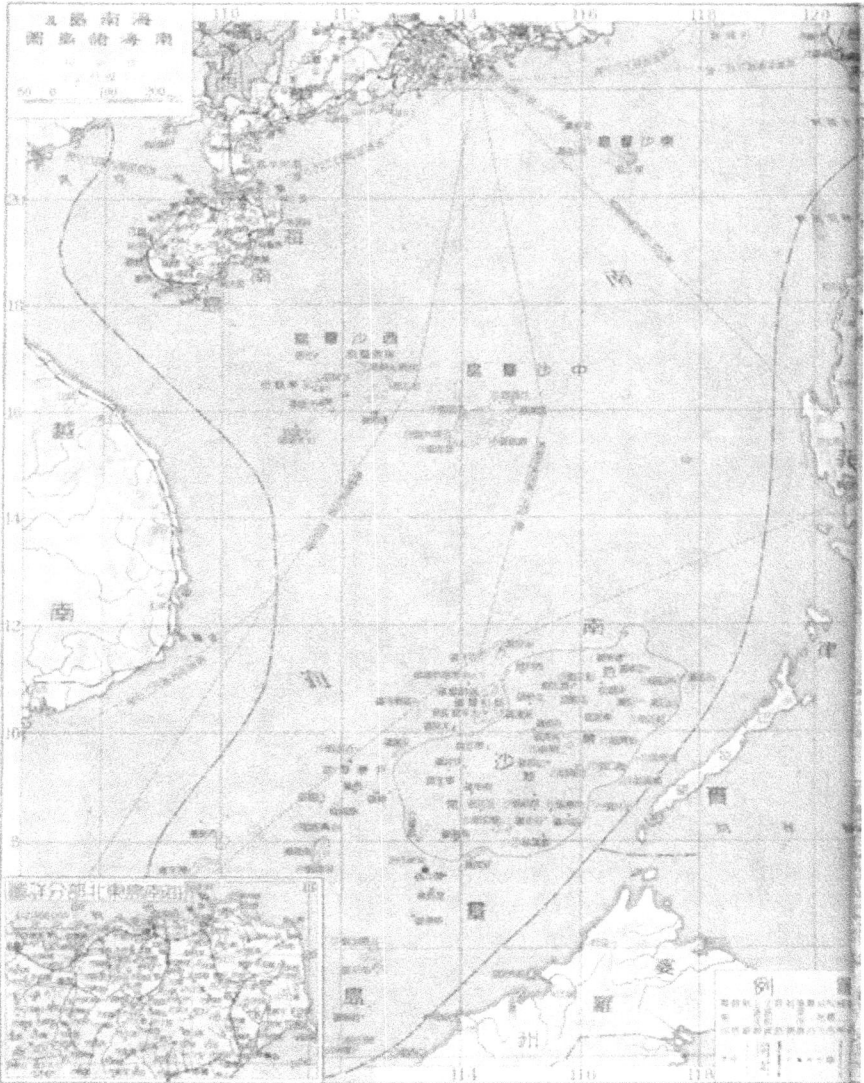

Source: Ministry of Interior, ROC <http://www.land.moi.gov.tw/filelink/uploadlink-1045.pdf>.

Figure 11.3
The ROC's First Amendment to the Baseline, 1988

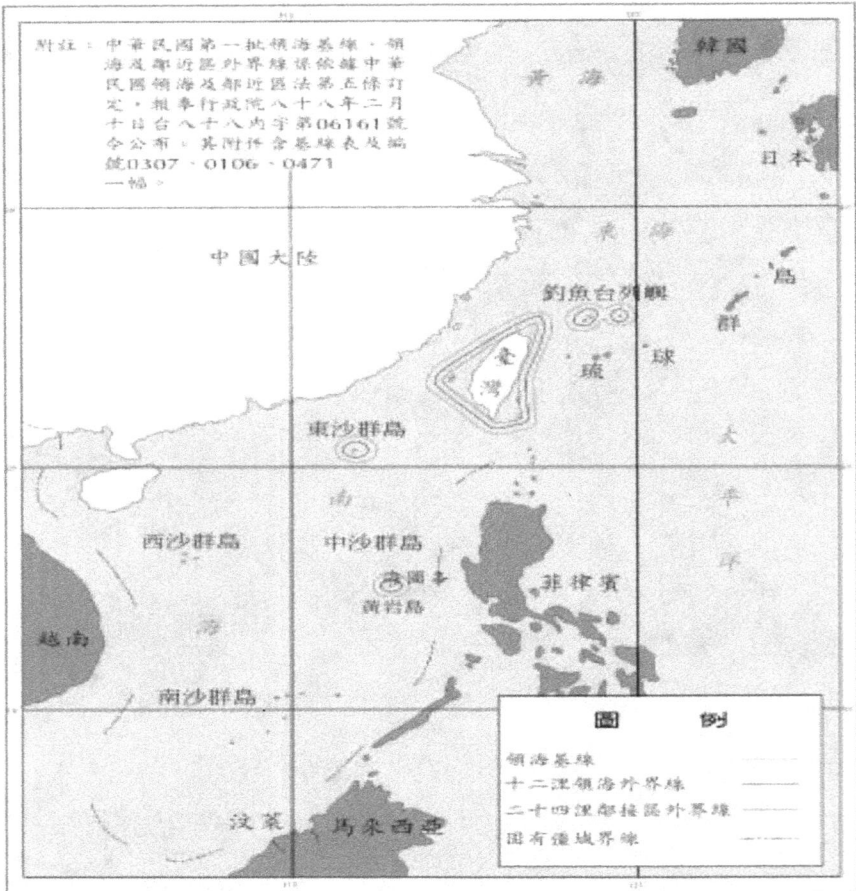

process. Legally, Taiwan claims sovereignty over the entire area within the U-shaped line, but it has been denied political involvement in any territorial discussions. It was plausible for the government to launch stern protests at the negotiation process, though it also respects the principles of peaceful settlement of all territorial disputes. Despite lacking momentum in the domestic political context to review the SCS policy, the government went ahead to dissolve the "policy guideline" and reassemble the SCS policy decision-making body at the National Security Council (NSC) in 2005. At the recommendation of the NSC, Taiwan began to build an airstrip on Taiping Island in 2006. President Chen visited the island on 2 February 2008 to inaugurate the completion of the airstrip and to reiterate sovereignty over the large part of the SCS. In order to take political advantage of his highly publicised trip, he announced the "Nansha Initiative". But due to his negative image both at home and abroad, the initiative did not catch much attention either in Taiwan or the region. It did however carry the real policy intention of Taiwan in working peacefully with all partners in the region. The main points of the initiatives are:[2]

1. Taiwan would accept the spirit and principles of the DOC and emphasize that all parties concerned should resort to peaceful means to resolve disputes.
2. The exploration of the SCS should consider environmental and ecological protection a top priority. Taiwan appeals to all parties to prioritize policy agenda for the establishment of an oceanic ecological protection zone.
3. Taiwan would invite international ecological experts and environmental groups to research in the Dongsha Islands, Taipin Islands, and Zhong Zhou Reef (or in Vietnamese, Ban Than Reef).
4. The government of Taiwan supports establishing Centres of the South China Sea Studies and encourages regular dialogues among all parties to reduce tension in the region.

Following President Ma Ying-jeou taking office in May 2008, the situation in the SCS has become more complicated than ever before, as several changing factors have intensified tensions in the region. China has continued to build its military strength in the region and has quickly become a strong and assertive power. President Ma's belief in maintaining the sovereignty claim in the SCS is much stronger than that of his predecessor. Warmer cross-strait relations since 2008 have fundamentally changed the limits of Taiwan's manoeuvrability in regional politics and have increased the opportunity for Taiwan to pursue a better position in the SCS. As China is now facing more challenges and a greater backlash to its assertive diplomacy in the region, mounting pressure has made China desperate to strengthen its position and legal claims. Now, in the new political climate, Taiwan and China's similar claims for sovereignty in the SCS have served as a catalyst to facilitate ideas for bilateral cooperation. President Ma is now facing a daunting challenge at home, as any fine tuning of policy would have to be in line with his domestic political agenda, especially since he is preparing to run for the next presidential election scheduled for early 2012. It would be a political risk for the Ma administration to present itself as too close to China in pushing bilateral cooperation on SCS issues. The opposition is checking the government on every issue related to the mainland. Unless the Ma administration finds a convincing strategy for policy discourse and can reach sufficient political mutual trust with China, it is not going to take any proactive step in SCS policy.

LEGAL CLAIMS AND POLICY APPROACHES

For Taiwan and China, legal claims of sovereignty in the South China Sea have been based on the U-shaped line (previously eleven-dotted line or currently nine-dotted line in China) drawn in 1947. When it was published the line was not based on a clear baseline and was not drawn according to latitudes. It refers more to islands and reefs of the Xisha and Nansha, than directly referring to the surrounding sea. It could be understood that during that time international regulation was not so clear-cut. As the People's Republic of China (PRC or China) has concurrently joined (or inherited) the claim of the ROC since 1949, both claims of sovereignty in the SCS — covering entire areas including islands, reefs, shoals, atolls and sea — within the U-shaped line are overlapping. After all, the legal basis for both claims is exactly the same. But what is the U-shaped line? How did it come about? And what does it mean in the legal sense?

At least four different positions have developed regarding this over the years. First, that the U-shaped line is the national boundary of China and that the entire area indicated is China's legitimate territory.[3] The argument was later refuted by experts because the PRC government had not clearly indicated whether the waters within the nine-dotted line were internal waters or territorial sea.[4] The second position is that the line indicates China's historic waters.[5] The third position it is the theory of historic right over the entire area within the line, emphasizing China's sovereignty over the whole islands, reefs, shoals, surrounding water and natural resources. The fourth is that the line defines the theory of islands ownership. China has claimed jurisdiction over the indicated islands and surrounding waters encompassed by the line.

Due to political antagonism across the Taiwan Strait for the past six decades or so, there has not been much direct discussion on the matter, let alone a chance of consensus. Now that both sides are able to sit down together to discuss the matter, the critical part is what their legal definition will be based on. It remains difficult to prove that either Taiwan or China have ever exercised continuous administration over entire areas within the line. However, following the ratification of the 1983 United Nations Convention on the Law of the Sea (UNCLOS), more and more studies have challenged the Chinese theory of historic waters in the SCS. The real legal battle would be on the Chinese/Taiwanese claims of historic waters, which was announced long before the UNCLOS was approved.

Taiwan's claims in the South China Sea have been defined according to the argument of the historic waters. For many years Taiwan has not built on its position to offer what the historic waters within the U-shaped line may refer to. Due to the long mistrust between Beijing and Taipei, there has so far been no collaboration on how to deal with criticism on the legal claims in the SCS. Since Taiwan is not a member of the United Nations and has not been part of the UNCLOS regime, Taiwan's policy approach on SCS legal issues has tended to be rather ambiguous.[6] Up to the end of 2010, many attendees of international conferences have still questioned China/Taiwan's position on how to clearly define the historic waters in the SCS. Currently there is no consensus among Taiwan experts on how to respond to or approach this question. The conventional wisdom in Taiwan suggests that Taiwan's claims predate the signing of UNCLOS by a considerable period. Taiwan has continually exercised its effective occupation. A pressing need now is for joint research by China and Taiwan on how to define the U-shaped line and the historic waters according to existing international law.

Taiwan's sovereign claims in the SCS are likely to remain as they are for some time before the government will be able to find a convincing definition that will be broadly acceptable to the domestic population. And beyond this complicated internal situation, Taiwan further needs to reach cross-strait understanding on the issue.

TAIWAN'S SOUTH CHINA SEA POLICY AND DOMESTIC RESPONSE

In 1993 Taiwan issued the "Policy Guidelines for the South China Sea" that stipulating that "[o]n the basis of history, geography, international law and the facts, Nansha (Spratly Islands), Shisha (Paracel Islands), Chongsha

(Macclesfield Bank), and Dongsha (Pratas Islands) have always been a part of the inherent territory of the Republic of China". The Guidelines expressed "Taiwan's desire to resolve all disputes peacefully, step up the exploration and management of resources in the South China Sea, promote cooperation with the other claimant states, and protect the ecology of the region."[7] Since then, the government has pursed a peaceful policy by gradually implementing unilateral confidence-building measures.

In 1999 the government decided to shift the responsibility for defending the Dongsha and Taiping Islands from the Ministry of National Defense (Marine Corps) to the Coast Guard Administration of the Executive Yuan. Both Dongsha and Taiping Islands were officially administrated by the Kaohsiung City Government. The decision aroused tremendous debate at home as to whether the shift in the policy would be in accordance with Taiwan's best national interest in the SCS, as it may mean showing weakness to the other claimants. Obviously there have been great doubts in Taiwanese society. A decade later a general review of the policy suggested that it was not an appropriate policy to shift responsibility to the coast guards amid the expansion activities of the other claimants.

Less than a year later, in May 2000, Taiwan saw its first ever transformation of political power. The long-time ruling party, the Kuomintang (Nationalist), lost power to the Democratic Progressive Party (DPP). The immediate impact on the SCS issue was that the KMT government's policy outline was completely neglected. The DPP government (2000–2008) was more eager to challenge Beijing for independent political status than to strengthen its position in the SCS. As a result, the relationship between China and Taiwan deteriorated. There was no possibility for the two sides to work together, although their claims on the South China Sea were similar. From a political perspective, the DPP was trying hard to differentiate its policy approach from the Chinese one. Another factor was that the DPP had come into power for the first time and lacked experience in handling the complicated SCS issue. The result was a neglect of much of the earlier planning that had been made and inconsistency on the part of Taiwan.

Even the Cabinet-level "South China Sea Task Force" under the Ministry of Interior was inactive during the DPP era. There was a perception among Taiwan's policy making circle that Taiwan may need to distance itself from the SCS disputes in order that the linkages between Taiwan and China may be more easily cut. In so doing Taiwan may be able to win friendship with regional countries. The government of the day was working hard on transforming authorities from military to coast guards for Tongsha Islands and Taping Island. The task force did not become the core of the SCS policy making body and ended its mission in December 2005. Its portfolio was then moved to the National Security Council.

Today the DPP's perspective on the SCS is not really known to the outside world. Because the DPP had long been in opposition, the traditional SCS sovereign claims of Taiwan had been regarded as emphasizing the historic links with Mainland China, links that the DPP hoped to sever. Many DPP politicians are focused only on pursuing independence for Taiwan, and do not give much consideration to a rational mainland policy or foreign policy, let alone an SCS policy. Attempts to break through diplomatic isolation with regional countries have been considered of greater importance than protecting sovereignty in the SCS. For the DPP, even if there is no integrated SCS approach as yet, likely policy based on DPP's political tendency would focus on developing diplomatic contacts with neighbouring countries and pursuing a peaceful settlement in the SCS. Today the DPP is once again in opposition. Although its view is not decisive at this moment, it may have a degree of influence over general public opinion in Taiwan. In short, the SCS issue has not been the focus of the domestic political agenda in Taipei now. Once Taiwan starts the process in cooperation with China it may become a political issue for discussion.[8] This is the reason the KMT government, with low domestic approval ratings, is so cautious about the idea of cooperation with China.

In June 2010 Taiwan and China signed the Economic Cooperation Framework agreement (ECFA), which will in effect lead to institutional economic integration along the lines of follow-up negotiation. Once economic cooperation has been formally recognized and moved to an institutional level of cooperation, many would expect it to be an appropriate time to move quickly into cooperation on political issues. So far the SCS issue is at the top of perceived agendas for both sides. The question is when and how to proceed.

The progress of the government implementing policy is obviously too slow to cope with the changing strategic environment in the region, but the majority of Taiwanese would be much in favour of strengthening Taiwan's position in the SCS. Steps could include establishing a national oceanic park surrounding Taipin Island, protecting bio-resources and exploiting energy resources, and establishing emergence centres. If such efforts could be made, Taiwan should try to push for project cooperation with China, engage more with other claimants, and demand for participation in the process of peaceful settlement in the SCS.

TAIWAN'S DILEMMA AND POLITICAL CHALLENGES

In the regional context of increasing security reassurance in the SCS, Taiwan is unfortunately positioned on the fault lines of potential regional tension. However, due to China's political weight in the region, Taiwan is either completely absent or not considered to be part of the formal regional security architecture. Although Taiwan does occasionally appear in some track-two dialogue mechanisms, even in those forums the issue of the Taiwan Strait is without exception removed from all agendas of discussion, e.g., in the case of the Council for Security Cooperation in the Asia Pacific (CSCAP). Therefore, although Taiwan has time and again shown its willingness to abide by international norms and practices, its security is not and will not be guaranteed through international security regimes in the foreseeable future. Today, the cross-strait relations have improved dramatically. Frequent contacts between the two societies have closely tied their relations and future development together.

While China is continuously building tremendous military strength and projecting political pressure on Taiwan, Taiwan seems to be gradually losing its political and economic advantages. It is natural to think that Taiwan would be absorbed into the big market soon, unless more drastic measures can be taken to cope with the challenge. Strategically, Taiwan is facing multiple challenges. Internally, the opposition's strong challenge to the government's mainland policy may have further crippled Taiwan's manoeuvrability. It has become a hard policy choice for the KMT government whether it should continue to purchase weapons from the United States and whether it should consider pushing forward cooperation on the SCS issue. Externally, U.S. suspicion on cross-strait development is increasing, due to uncertainty and ambiguity about the progress made between Taiwan and China. Both these factors serve to constrain the course of Taiwan's mainland policy.

Today regional strategic development poses a great challenge to Taiwan. Taiwan is now meeting a critical juncture and its SCS policy dilemma is highlighted in stark relief. If the region becomes divided over the SCS position, where does Taiwan lie? Taiwan should start thinking of working closely with China and try to manage from within the bilateral cooperation framework. Hopefully, a new cooperation on the SCS would spill over into other cross-strait policy issues and generate a better atmosphere of mutual trust. Nevertheless, Taiwan would have to review its strategy regarding what it could obtain from cross-strait cooperation on the SCS issue while trying to achieve its national interests. In reality, the change of Taiwan's policy does not imply a complete shift in the external strategic environment, but rather the opening of a new opportunity for the government on the SCS issue.

EXTENT OF FUTURE CROSS-STRAIT COOPERATION

Since Taiwan and China so far have not come to touching on political issues, the feeling of mistrust remains very high among the decision-making courts of both capitals. The two sides need to find ways to enhance mutual predictability in bilateral security relations and expand the scope of mutual reassurance before addressing the political agenda for the future. Taiwan has for years proposed several approaches to confidence-building measures in the hope of building mutual trust with China, including issues related to the SCS. But so far these have met with little success because China insists that confidence-building measures can only be arranged between states. Beijing will not allow cross-strait relations to be categorized as relations between equal states. However, the progress made in cross-strait relations has given rise to hope of initiating cooperation in the SCS. Under recent trends it might be possible to work out some appropriate flexible options. Beijing has already set the tone for cooperation with Taiwan in the international community, as long as an approach would not be interpreted as practicing "two Chinas" or "one China, one Taiwan".[9] Taipei may worry that any further consultation with China would be tightly fitted into the framework of "one China". Greater opportunities in the international community may only come with a stricter political line drawn by Beijing. This would then leave Taipei little room to manoeuvre and in the long run it would find itself naturally treading the course of "unification".

Moreover, Taiwan's security structure has for years been dominated by the China-centred approach. Whenever ways of increasing policy predictability and mutual trust with neighbouring countries are raised among Taiwan's security officials, China-oriented thinking inevitably prevails. Even with warming cross-strait relations, Taiwan's national security focus remains largely on China. The reason is obvious: China has not made any strategic adjustment in the light of improvements in cross-strait relations and remains a hostile power. The be all and end all of Taiwan's security focus is what approach will be taken towards China. Under such a strategic calculation, it is obvious that Taiwan will continue to align with the United States. Any move towards substantial cooperation with China in the SCS will cause security concerns in Taiwan and in the United States. Taiwan needs to define its strategic goal clearly before it can launch any attempt to work with China in the SCS.

For China, cooperation with Taiwan on the SCS will bring about multiple policy rewards: (1) further enhancing cross-strait relations; (2) integrating the strength that Taiwan and China have in the SCS; (3) leading a peaceful process in the region; (4) breaking through cross-strait economic barriers and moving into political and military areas; and (5) strengthening China's common legal claim in the SCS.

Taiwan has greater constraints on cooperation than China has on account of security reasons. Apart from security cooperation, the extent of bilateral cooperation remains to be seen. Possible areas to begin include synchronizing common legal claims, protecting the environment and biological resources, maritime security and joint exploration of natural resources.

A LEGITIMATE SCS PARTY: TAIWAN

It has been nine years since the DOC was signed. Many observers agree that not much that was agreed upon has been implemented. Taiwan is one of the key players in the SCS; its absence means that the peaceful settlement mechanism is incomplete. China and ASEAN now need to work out how to bring all parties concerned into the peaceful process. Claimants should approach Taiwan either on the basis of multilateral or bilateral talks. Claims of ownership in the SCS over islands, reefs, shoals, and waters are mostly overlapping. But for Taiwan to raise this issue is always a big challenge. It may once again lead this issue back to the court of Beijing to determine how much ground China will give away.

After the diplomatic heat in the summer of 2010, China has been eager to push talks with ASEAN on the possible code of conduct.[10] This unprecedented eagerness has a strategic implication for regional security. China may perceive it as a way to keep the United States out of SCS negotiations. As long as the existing China-ASEAN forum takes central stage, the United States does not have an excuse to form another regional institution to resolve the SCS disputes. The trust-building process may prove to be critical to the future course of SCS cooperation. At least big power competition on SCS issues may tentatively quiet down.

No matter what political reasons exists, Taiwan would have to be brought into the confidence-building process. If a code of conduct in the South China Sea should be considered, it would have to be respected and implemented by all claimants, including Taiwan. Otherwise the ASEAN-China cooperation mechanism would leave a gaping omission of Taiwan, with Taiwan occupying the largest of the Nansha Islands. There is a serious question that ASEAN and China have not thought about: If a conflict with Taiwan's interests occurs in the SCS, would any informal diplomatic effort count? ASEAN may now need to consider how Taiwan would be included in the SCS peace process. It would also be in the interest of ASEAN to see "ASEAN–China plus Taiwan" develop as opposed to two competing series of "ASEAN-China" and "China-Taiwan" mechanisms.

IMPLICATIONS OF CROSS-STRAIT COOPERATION ON THE SCS

Confidence-building measures have been introduced to SCS issues for over two decades. A number of measures have achieved the credible result of facilitating dialogue to reduce tension and enhance cooperation among claimants. The Informal Workshop on Managing the Conflict in the South China Sea (South China Sea Workshop) has been the leading example. Since 2009 even the old rivals of China and Taiwan have begun cooperation in joint research projects and a training programme for ocean scientific research. Although the current impact of the cooperation has been quite limited, policy circles in Taiwan and China have often quoted this unprecedented experience to argue for further cross-strait cooperation. The cooperation itself already carries significant implications for confidence-building measures for the two.

Regional experts observe that it is common to note that China and Taiwan have similar competing claims on the SCS. Hasjim Djalal stated that Taiwan's claim in the South China Sea is basically the same as China's. In fact the positions of the participants from China and Taiwan in the South China Sea Workshops were sometimes very similar.[11] The peace process in the SCS has always had implications for Taiwan's security and the development of cross-strait relations. Taiwan's major difficulty in regard to SCS claims is that it is yet to develop a clear strategy or make any statement as to where its policy stands in relation to that of China.

STRATEGIC PREFERENCE: THE UNITED STATES AND CHINA

Since May 2008, cross-strait relations have improved. This has given rise to hopes in Taiwan and China that both sides would soon work out a favourable integrated framework. However, progress has only so far been made in economic and functional areas.

The SCS happens to be the strategic focal point of the United States, China and Taiwan. As China and Taiwan would be preparing to move on SCS cooperation in the near future, some believe that the U.S.-Taiwan security ties may be affected as a result. Taiwan has long-established security ties with the United States. In facing up to the massive Chinese military build-up, Taiwan's security will have to rely more, not less, on the support of the United States. On security, Taiwan alone will not be able to guarantee its security from a Chinese military attack. The military balance in the Taiwan Strait has already been tilting towards China for some time. Taiwan today must depend more on politics for security rather than its military. But the real problem is that Taiwan does not have diplomatic links with any neighbouring countries, which leaves it isolated and vulnerable. So if the cross-strait cooperation does go ahead in the near future, would the structure of Taiwan's security be forced to change? And where would the threshold be?

The current government in Taipei has calculated that the political costs in cooperating with China would be high, both in terms of the relationship with the United States and the domestic political arena. If cooperation with China becomes inevitable, Taipei would at least try to limit the scope covering non-traditional security factors, such as humanitarian relief, search and rescue, joint scientific research and logistics. The best strategy for Taiwan would be to convince China that it has a common interest in the SCS and to strengthen its international efforts to gain access to regional multilateral diplomacy.

REDEFINING TAIWAN'S SOUTH CHINA SEA POLICY

Recent momentum in the South China Sea could lead to new trends. Five factors that should be watched closely for their effects on Taiwan's policy shakeup are:

1. Energy hunting: Exploitation of natural resources in the South China Sea is still on the agenda. Competition to control energy and exploitation rights continues to be a substantial issue, especially following the events of 2007 when the global oil market met with a dramatic increase in demand and oil prices reached a record high. It immediately alerted many countries to search for secured energy supplies. Claimants in the SCS also responded by inviting Western oil industry partners to jointly exploit oil reserves in the region. Energy hunting serves as the first factor of this momentum.

2. Military build-up/arms race: As China is undergoing a military modernization process, its effort to increase its naval capability in the South China Sea has enhanced its strategic stand. China has caused shockwaves in the region as it advances further to fulfil its long-term goal of establishing a blue-water navy. Recently, ASEAN countries have been in the process of upgrading their military capabilities, especially with regard to naval forces. China's military expansion has created the incentive for a regional arms race.

3. Competing and expanding existing occupation: After ASEAN and China agreed to the terms of the DOC in 2002, tension in the SCC, at least on the surface, appears to have quietened down. Individual claimants, however, continue to push their claims by all possible means.

4. Attempting to legalize occupation: In 2007 China first attempted to strengthen its claim for sovereignty in the South China Sea by establishing a prefecture — Sansha — to administer the Xisha, Zhongsha, and Nansha Islands. Vietnam and other claimants immediately launched protest campaigns. In March 2009 the Philippines Congress passed a "Baseline Act", later endorsed by President Arroyo as Republic Act 9522 or the Philippine Archipelagic Baseline Law. In April 2009 Vietnam followed suit and appointed a chairman (equal to city mayor) of Hoang Sa (Paracel) People's Committee. Although such measures do not involve military operations, they can result in increased confrontation. These events show that most claimants are skilfully utilizing any opportunity to expand their interests. This trend will continue in the short run. The most worrisome development in the region is that claimants are pushing for general public support and are trying to mobilize nationalist backing. Two points are worth noting in regard to this. First, any government advocating a firm policy for sovereignty will be fully supported by their people. And second, mobilization will be considered legitimate to domestic politics.

5. Since 2010 the big powers have become increasingly involved in SCS issues. For strategic reasons the SCS is regarded by China as its "core interest" and it has become a key point of national interest to the United States, Japan and India.

The above factors demonstrate trends that will have an impact on future developments. It is anticipated that further cooperative mechanisms would follow the momentum of ASEAN-China discussions on the code of conduct. Taiwan knows that if it maintains its past policy it will soon be completely left out of the regional game of competing claims. Whilst the situation has not been in Taiwan's favour for several decades, a new situation is now emerging. Today there are favourable cross-strait relations that may in due course lead to fair discussions on SCS issues in regular platforms (Strait Exchange Foundation, Association for the Relations across the Taiwan Strait, SEF-ARATS Talks) between Taiwan and China. Recently, in the policy communities of Taipei and Beijing, there have even been calls to set up an "SCS task force" under the SEF-ARATS mechanism so that SCS issues would be brought into the negotiation platform from time to time.[12]

The current government has reckoned with various new factors and strategic interests, and would gradually come to redefine its new interest in the SCS. Clearly, the SCS would be redefined as a significant strategic interest for Taiwan. The national security strategy would include the SCS as part of the national goal to be emphasized. The critical point for Taiwan now is to abandon its hands-off attitude on SCS issues. Foreign policy, defence policy, and the mainland policy would gradually be integrated under the umbrella of the national security policy. As one would perceive the results of the new efforts, Taiwan would be back on the core of the SCS and in line with the developing regional trend. It will also help further integrate internal policy coordination and step up Taiwan's confidence in cooperating with China. Practical dimensions on the SCS policy would be flexible and open for cooperation:

1. Finding ways to strengthen its sovereign claims: encouraging more research on the legal argument, planning practical efforts to highlight effective measures, and reinforcing awareness of the general public.
2. Pushing the possibilities of regional cooperation: focusing on joint exploration of energy, conducting joint scientific research and

environmental monitoring, and securing maritime security and sea-lanes of communication.

3. Leading ecological and environmental protection: establishing an ocean ecological park in the Nansha Islands.

4. Seeking participation in all related dialogue mechanisms. Taiwan needs to launch active diplomatic efforts in both bilateral and multilateral contexts and more actively engage with Beijing.

CONCLUSION

In November 1999, without any direct consultation with other claimants, Taiwan decided to put forward the idea of implementing unilateral confidence-building measures of demilitarization by replacing marines with coastguards in the Dongsha and Taiping Islands. It has been more than ten years, but Taiwan's basic position on the SCS has not really changed. Instead, with its hands-off attitude and mistaken policy orientation, Taiwan has been completely isolated from the current progress made between China and ASEAN on the SCS. In a complicated situation, national interests remain a dominant factor of Taiwan's SCS policy. Taiwan's unilateral confidence-building measures may prove to be too naïve and wishful thinking, though the original exercise was very much in accordance with international norms of peaceful processes. The practical steps of seeking dialogue should have been taken first before any mechanisms had been implemented.

Taiwan's construction of an airstrip on Taipin Island gave it a new strategic posture in the region. From a traditional security point of view, the new airstrip effectively extends Taiwan's strategic outreach into the SCS, depending on how much Taipei wants to push it. It could also serve as an interim logistics and rescue station regarding challenges of non-traditional security in the SCS. Taiwan needs to take advantage of this new development and articulate its policy flexibility. By making a direct contribution to regional security in the SCS, Taiwan should start a new round of diplomatic re-engagement with countries of the region. It may be time for Taiwan to start working on bilateral efforts with other claimants, as Taiwan has been left out of the regional process for so long.

As Taiwan has come to the point of needing to redefine its SCS policy stance, it will need extra effort to work with regional countries. It will need, obviously, to find answers to the legal nature of the U-shaped line, the legal status of the geographical features located in the Nansha Islands, the claim to historic waters in the South China Sea and, most importantly, strengthening its presence in the region. Taiwan will need to be more proactive in drafting proposals to explore oil and gas resources in the South China Sea together with China and perhaps the other claimants. The need to revive the SCS policy has become all the more critical to Taiwan's security. The policy needs to address more than just sovereignty and jurisdiction, but also the essence of national security.

Notes

1. "Spratlys Cruise Stirs Policy Debate", *Taiwan Today*, 14 April 1995 <http://www.taiwantoday.tw/ct.asp?xItem=13117&CtNode=122>.
2. "Chen Urges Cooperation with 'Spratly Initiative'", Government Information Office, 15 February 2008 <http://info.gio.gov.tw/ct.asp?xItem=36002&ctNode=2499&mp=4>.
3. Hsu Xen An, *Nana Hai Duan Xu Guo Jie Xien De Nei Han* [The meaning of dotted national boundary in the South China Sea]", paper presented at the Issues and Outlook of the South China Sea in the 21st Century conference, Haikuo, Hainan, 2000.
4. Wu Shicun, *Nansha Jen Duen De Qi Yuan Yu Fa Zang* [The origin and development of the Spratly disputes] (Beijing: China Economic Publishing House, 2009), pp. 37–39.
5. Argued by Professor K.T. Chao of Taiwan's National Chengchi University.
6. Yann-huei Song and Peter Kien-hong Yu, "China's 'Historic Waters' in the South China Sea: An Analysis from Taiwan", *American Asian Review* 7, no. 4 (1994): 83–101.
7. "Policy Guidelines for the South China Sea", Ministry of Interior, 13 April 1993 <http://www.land.moi.gov.tw/law/chhtml/historylaw1.asp?Lclassid=224>.
8. Cheng-yi Lin, "Taiwan's South China Sea Policy", *Asian Survey* 37, no. 4 (1997): 338.
9. Hu Jintao, "Let Us Join Hands to Promote the Peaceful Development of Cross-Straits Relations and Strive with a United Resolve for the Great Rejuvenation of the Chinese Nation (Hu's Six Points)", Speech at the Forum Marking the 30th Anniversary of the Issuance of the Message to Compatriots in Taiwan, 31 December 2008 <http://www.gwytb.gov.cn/en/Special/Hu/201103/t20110322_1794707.htm>.
10. Ho Ai Li, "China Wants to Resolve South China Sea Issue", *Strait Times*, 26 January 2011 <http://www.viet-studies.info/kinhte/China_wants_to_resolve.htm>.

11. Hasjim Djalal, "South China Sea Island Disputes", *Raffles Bulletin of Zoology*, Supplement No. 8 (The Biodiversity of the South China Sea, 2000), p. 12 <http://community.middlebury.edu/~scs/DOCs/Djalal,%20South%20Chin a%20Sea%20Island%20Disputes.htm>.

12. The annual cross-strait SCS conference organized by the China Institute of South China Sea Studies (Haikuo) and Institute of International Relations (Taipei) has continued the momentum of cooperation for more than a decade. Since 2009 the idea of establishing an SCS Task Force has been reinforced during the conference.

Part Five
The Interests of Others

12

THE U.S. POSITION IN
THE SOUTH CHINA SEA

Barry Wain

The South China Sea is clearly of concern to many countries and parties apart from China and the Southeast Asian states that have rival claims there. In terms of larger questions of peace, regional stability and global commerce, those with deep and legitimate interests heavily outnumber claimants. Indeed, it can be safely asserted that the entire international community — multinational corporations, private traders and energy companies, as well as governments of all political persuasions — has a huge stake in the maintenance of the South China Sea as a peaceful and open waterway.

The multiple sea-lines of communications traversing the South China Sea, which carry significant amounts of international maritime trade, are of crucial importance to the countries within the broader region and beyond. Economic powerhouses China, Japan, South Korea and Taiwan all depend on uninterrupted energy supplies, largely in the form of oil, natural gas and coal from the Middle East, Australia and Africa, much of which flows through the South China Sea.[1]

This chapter examines American interests in the South China Sea. Although other non-claimant countries could be expected to offer comments, engage in diplomacy and make representations in the event of looming instability in the South China Sea, only the United States possesses the power to intervene decisively. Other parties might not agree with specific American actions in the event of intervention, but the United States broadly would represent their desire for an outcome that preserves peace and permits freedom of navigation and overflight in the South China Sea.

SUMMARY

The United States has maintained a consistent policy on the South China Sea, even as the attention it gives the area has been, at best, intermittent.[2] America is not only a non-claimant and does not back anyone else's claims in the South China Sea, but it adopts no position whatsoever on the legal merits of the six sets of overlapping and competing sovereignty claims. As the world's pre-eminent power, the United States is overwhelmingly concerned with freedom of navigation, ensuring no disruption to the flow of maritime trade that is vital to its own prosperity and that of its friends and allies in Northeast and Southeast Asia. At the strategic level, the U.S. Navy depends on unimpeded passage through South China Sea transit corridors to deploy vessels rapidly between the Western Pacific and Indian oceans, greatly facilitating America's global military posture.[3]

Until relatively recently, the United States took a hands-off approach to the South China Sea. While the area was regarded as a potential flashpoint in East Asia, it was usually overshadowed by the more immediate and dangerous situation at two other strategic locations: in the Taiwan Strait and on the Korean Peninsula. Even when ASEAN became alarmed about China's more assertive policies in the South China Sea in the 1990s, the United States was content to register routine concern over growing tensions and call for calm and the observation of international law.

However, China's evolving stance caught American attention — dramatically, if fleetingly — in 2001, when a U.S. EP-3 surveillance aircraft and a Chinese air force fighter collided near Hainan Island. After the crisis subsided, one critical point of difference between the two nations came into sharper relief: They differed in their interpretation of international maritime law. Washington added its interpretation to U.S. policy in the South China Sea: No state may legally restrict military survey operations within — or above — its 200-nautical mile exclusive economic zone (EEZ).[4]

With the United States preoccupied with terrorism after the 9/11 attacks in 2001, Washington was pleased to see the apparent easing of tensions between China and ASEAN the following year, when they signed the Declaration on the Conduct of Parties in the South China Sea (DOC). It was not until 2008 that the United States began to sit up and take note of not only the failure of the DOC, but a seriously deteriorating situation in the South China Sea, caused principally by China's more aggressive posture in consolidating its jurisdictional claims, expanding its military reach and seeking to undermine the claims of other states through coercive diplomacy. The Americans gradually ratcheted up their response, voicing concern at developments, increasing naval operations in the area and strengthening defence contacts with Southeast Asian countries. A number of United States–China confrontations took place at sea in 2009, the standoff involving the U.S. hydrographic survey vessel *Impeccable* and five Chinese-flagged vessels drawing most attention.

The build-up reached something of a climax at a meeting of the ASEAN Regional Forum (ARF) in Vietnam in mid-2010. U.S. Secretary of State Hillary Clinton, encouraged by some ASEAN members who had grown uneasy over Chinese intentions in the South China Sea, weighed in heavily by declaring the sea "pivotal" to regional stability. Her forthright intervention, which was supported by eleven other countries, upset and angered the Chinese, and was another indication that the contentious territorial dispute had worked its way back to the top of Southeast Asia's security agenda.[5] Although she did not alter U.S. policy on the South China Sea, Clinton gave the policy its most expansive, robust and clearest exposition to date.

Renewed U.S. focus on the South China Sea has been animated not only by increased Chinese naval activity in support of Beijing's extravagant claims, as indicated by the notorious nine broken lines on official maps. As China has poured vast resources into its navy and given priority to developing an anti-access area denial defence system designed to make it difficult for the United States to send help to key Asian allies being attacked, Washington has concluded that a much larger prize is ultimately at stake: United States supremacy in the Asia-Pacific region. So while the familiar contests among coastal states continue over fisheries, energy resources and ownership of rocky outcrops, they are being overshadowed by competition between the world's only superpower, in relative decline, and the only serious contender that might match or replace it in the foreseeable future.[6]

In short, United States–China great power rivalry is being projected into the maritime domain in the western Pacific and directly transmitted into Southeast Asia via the South China Sea.[7]

BACKGROUND

During the Cold War, the United States was able to largely ignore the South China Sea because it was not the subject of active dispute and Washington had a long list of other geopolitical priorities. Besides, with the United States devoting vast resources to the Vietnam War, there was no question of a challenge to American military superiority in the waters of Southeast Asia. When the Chinese evicted U.S.-backed South Vietnamese troops from the Paracel Islands in 1974, it appeared to be a minor event in the closing stages of the conflict and not a new development with wider repercussions. Even when China waged war to obtain a permanent foothold in the Spratly Islands in 1988, sinking three Vietnamese naval vessels and killing seventy-two personnel, it evoked little international response. Vietnam at the time was isolated in the West and in non-communist Southeast Asia over its occupation of Cambodia, and a declining Soviet Union showed no inclination to go to Hanoi's assistance.[8]

Although the United States welcomed the 1992 ASEAN Declaration on the South China Sea, Washington's support for the Southeast Asian group appeared to be perfunctory, with little understanding of festering trends, or willingness to get involved in efforts to contain them. ASEAN was disturbed by China's adoption of legislation five months earlier explicitly asserting Beijing's claim to the Spratlys and Paracels, and by the still-fresh memory of China's use of force in the Spratlys. The Declaration called for the peaceful resolution of sovereignty and jurisdictional issues without resort to force, the exercise of restraint, possible cooperation in maritime safety, environmental protection, search and rescue, and action against piracy, robbery at sea and drug-trafficking, and the application of the principles of ASEAN'S Treaty of Amity and Cooperation as the basis for a code of conduct for the South China Sea.[9]

The United States seemed reluctant to abandon its aloof attitude even when, in early 1995, the Philippines discovered Chinese structures on Mischief Reef, well within the country's EEZ and just a little over 100 nautical miles west of Palawan island. Manila made it clear it regarded the structures, complete with living quarters, satellite dishes and Chinese flags, as an outright occupation of its territory.[10] ASEAN recognized the intrusion as a test of its 1992 Declaration and, acting with unprecedented cohesion, called "specifically" for the "early resolution of the problems caused by recent developments in Mischief Reef". ASEAN's remarkable success in forcing Chinese officials to discuss the South China Sea — despite their insistence that it should be dealt with bilaterally and not between China and ASEAN as a group — left the Americans largely unmoved.

Despite public promises to go to Manila's aid in times of crisis after relinquishing the Clark air force and Subic Bay naval bases in the Philippines in the early 1990s, the United States offered cold comfort to its treaty ally over the occupation of Mischief Reef. Washington made it clear that the provisions of their 1951 Mutual Defence Treaty did not apply, leaving a disappointed Philippines, which lacked a credible defence force, to fend for itself.[11] The failure of U.S. surveillance satellites and sea or air patrols to detect six months or more of Chinese construction on Mischief Reef aggravated bilateral relations. In fact, word circulated in the Philippine defence establishment that the Americans had known about the structures for some time before they informed the Philippine coastguard. One senior official went so far as to suggest that the United States had deliberately withheld the information as a way of reminding the Philippines that since the Americans had been expelled from Subic, Manila could no longer automatically expect Washington to share intelligence.[12]

It was only after intensive diplomatic lobbying by Southeast Asia that the United States finally issued a statement intended to placate the Philippines and its ASEAN partners. Privately, the statement was considered barely adequate by the group: While expressing concern about increased tensions in the South China Sea due to "a pattern of unilateral actions and reactions", it did not mention Mischief Reef or China.[13]

The episode undermined U.S. credibility in several ways. It called into question Washington's commitment to the security of Southeast Asia, at a time when the public perception was of a United States in retreat after its defeat in Vietnam and eviction from the Philippine bases.[14] Although China's policy of "creeping assertiveness" in the South China Sea had alarmed ASEAN into solidarity in order to rebuke a rather startled Beijing, the United States did not share Southeast Asia's concern. Washington apparently was not prepared to risk damaging its relations with China by involving itself in the South China Sea dispute, unless and until freedom of navigation was at stake. The United States favoured ASEAN taking its security concerns with China to the ARF and other multilateral forums, where prospects of a serious discussion were, in reality, exceedingly dim.[15]

However, the American statement, issued by the State Department on 10 May 1995, served an important purpose. It spelled out U.S. policy in the South China Sea, the core of which has remained unchanged since then. The United States:

- Regards maintaining freedom of navigation as a "fundamental interest".
- Takes no position on the legal merits of sovereignty claims over islands, reefs, atolls and cays in the South China Sea. It would, however, "view with serious concern any maritime claim or restriction on maritime activity" not consistent with international law, including the 1982 UNCLOS.
- Strongly opposes the use or threat of force to resolve competing claims and urges all claimants to exercise restraint and avoid destabilizing actions, while intensifying diplomatic efforts that "address issues related to the competing claims".
- Offers "to assist in any way that the claimants deem helpful".

RESPONSE FROM 2008

The United States began responding on the South China Sea in 2008 after Beijing hardened its attitude towards ASEAN and Southeast Asian claimants while continuing its military build-up in the area, most notably the construction of a naval base on Hainan. One provocative move by Beijing was to warn Western oil companies privately that they would jeopardize their commercial operations in China if they proceeded with exploration ventures authorized by Hanoi off the coast of Vietnam. U.S. Secretary of Defence Robert Gates alluded to the Chinese action when he addressed the Shangri-La Dialogue in 2008. Gates underscored the security implications of rising demands for resources and the inherent dangers of "coercive diplomacy ... even when they coexist beside outward displays of cooperation". Although Gates did not name China, his reference was clearly to the controversy over British Petroleum's commercial activities in Vietnam, which had been the subject of media reports. Within months of his oblique comment, it became known that ExxonMobil had come under similar pressure from China.[16]

In September 2008, then–Deputy Secretary of State John Negroponte travelled to Hanoi to confirm U.S. support for the rights of U.S. corporations to conduct business in the South China Sea. The visit was undertaken quietly, unnoticed by the media.

However, the United States became more open and forthright in its criticism of China in mid-2009, when two senior administration officials testified before the Senate Foreign Relations Committee on maritime disputes in East Asia. Scot Marciel, deputy assistant secretary in the Bureau of East Asian and Pacific Affairs, confirmed that China had put foreign energy companies under pressure to suspend work offshore Vietnam, that Washington objected to "any effort to intimidate U.S. companies" and that it had made known its concerns directly with Beijing. Marciel also raised questions about the extent of China's jurisdictional claims in the South China Sea. He said their ambiguous nature had become of greater concern to Washington because the areas in which Beijing had warned U.S. companies not to operate seemed to lie outside China's claimed maritime boundaries. He joined the chorus in calling on the Chinese government to provide greater clarity on the substance of its claims.[17]

In his testimony, Deputy Assistant Secretary of Defence Robert Scher said that while the United States supported a negotiated settlement to the dispute, rising tensions over the past two years had prompted the Pentagon to reinforce measures designed to enhance stability in the area. This strategy consists of a continued U.S. military presence in the region, U.S. Navy operations in the South China Sea to assert freedom of navigation rights, and the expansion and deepening of defence diplomacy and capacity building programmes with regional states such as Malaysia, Vietnam, the Philippines and Indonesia "to prevent tensions in the South China Sea from developing into a threat to U.S. interests". U.S.-led security cooperation activities, such as regular exercises, helped these countries "overcome longstanding historical and cultural barriers that inhibit multilateral cooperation", he said. "In short", two eminent analysts summed up, "America's military presence in Southeast Asia helps provide a stable environment for the claimants to pursue a political solution and encourage the ASEAN states to increase defence cooperation among themselves at the same time".[18]

In January 2010, the top U.S. military officer in the Pacific, Admiral Robert Willard, declared that China's "aggressive" programme of military modernization appeared designed to "challenge U.S. freedom of action in the region and, if necessary, enforce China's influence over its neighbours".[19] Speaking at the Shangri-La Dialogue at mid-year, Defence Secretary Gates expressed the United States' "growing concern" over the South China Sea, and extended his warning against the attempted intimidation of U.S. corporations to "those of any nation engaged in legitimate economic activity".[20] The tension in U.S.-China relations was obvious in comments at the Shangri-La Dialogue by a Chinese general, who put the blame on Washington for, among other things, surveillance activities in China's exclusive economic zone.[21]

A tipping point for the United States, or perhaps a convenient opportunity, arose with reports that the Chinese had elevated the South China Sea to a "core interest". If true, the implication is that it would be on a par with Taiwan, Tibet and Xinjiang, and that Beijing would be willing to use force or the threat of force to defend its sovereignty. Chinese officials reportedly first used the term in talks with two senior American officials, Deputy Secretary of State James Steinberg and Jeffrey Bader, senior director for Asian affairs on the National Security Council, when they were visiting Beijing in March 2010. Significantly, the Chinese are reported to have talked tough in that exchange, declaring that Beijing would not tolerate any interference in the South China Sea.[22]

Since then, an ever-widening controversy has surrounded the issue, with both American and Chinese sources offering a host of explanations, mostly off the record, ranging from a claim that the Chinese use of "core interest" was inadvertent, to the likelihood that it did not apply to the entire South China Sea and the preposterous suggestion that the term was never uttered at all. It was voiced for sure and more than once. Clinton has disclosed that it was spoken in her presence, at the United States–China Strategic and Economic Dialogue in Beijing in May. She identified the source — Chinese State Councillor Dai Bingguo.[23]

Since the first reports appeared, Chinese officials have been equivocal when questioned as to whether the South China Sea has been raised officially to a "core interest" or a "core national interest".[24] Now that the matter is in the open, no doubt the government is reluctant to clarify it: A public affirmation would be seen as unnecessarily provocative and harmful to relations between China and not just the United States but also large sections of the international community; a denial would tend to weaken China's proprietary stance on the South China Sea and invite a domestic backlash from nationalists.

Prominent analyst Carlyle A. Thayer devoted nearly five pages in a recent paper to unravelling the mystery, without reaching a definitive conclusion. He detected signs of an internal debate in China over the term "core interest" and picked up suggestions that the matter is being "walked back" quietly by the government. But, significantly, he also found frequent use of "core interest" by the Chinese media.[25]

True or false, authorized or not, these reports generated a new level of anxiety about Beijing's strategic ambitions in the South China Sea. It became a public relations disaster for China. According to Secretary of State Clinton, she "immediately responded" to Dai Bingguo's view of the South China Sea as a Chinese core interest and said, "We don't agree with that." Clinton added:

> So they were on notice that if they were ... in the process of extending their efforts to claim and control to the detriment of international law, freedom of navigation, maritime security, the claims of their neighbours, that was a concerning matter. And therefore, we worked with a lot of the ASEAN countries who are directly impacted.[26]

Directly impacted, of course, were the four Southeast Asian claimants, but concern about China's truculent behaviour had widened in the region beyond them. In 2010, when Vietnam was chairing ASEAN, China thwarted Hanoi's diplomatic attempts to get the South China Sea back on the agenda. Indeed, all the evidence suggested that China had reverted to its uncompromising position of the 1990s, insisting that the territorial dispute was a bilateral issue to be discussed separately by China with each of the other claimants.[27] Beijing successfully relegated the issue to the ASEAN-China Joint Working Group on the Implementation of the DOC.[28]

And China ensured that these discussions among officials went nowhere. The working group has met five times and is due to meet again in March, in Indonesia. It has made next to zero progress in more than eight years on what is the only regional framework to keep the peace in the South China Sea. Originally, both sides agreed on six projects to implement the DOC, which was to be upgraded to a legally binding code of conduct. Beijing objected to the standard ASEAN practice of the ten members conferring as a group, and even to the four ASEAN claimants holding discussions before meeting the Chinese. Southeast Asian countries regarded China's stand as obstructionist, since there is no practical way to prevent ASEAN members from meeting and discussing whatever they like.[29] To be fair, at the Joint Working Group's last meeting — in Kunming, China, in December — China proposed a compromise that might have broken the impasse. But host Vietnam, approaching a five-year congress of the ruling Communist Party in January, blocked progress.[30]

China's unwillingness to go ahead with the DOC's implementation provisions for many years — and refusal to give a credible public reason for its stand — frustrated ASEAN. One senior Southeast Asian official, with access to the discussions in the working group, said of the Chinese in 2010, "This contradicts all of their protestations of peaceful intentions in the South China Sea. But ultimately they do not care."[31]

Vietnam was one of several ASEAN countries that urged the United States to intervene. In reality, the United States needed little encouragement, as some American specialists, inside and outside the government, felt that Beijing was deliberately testing the Obama administration across a range of issues in East Asia and that Washington must respond, or lose serious ground to China. The administration was also keen to show there was substance in Clinton's well-publicised comment earlier in the year that "the United States is back in Asia to stay".

The Americans alerted selected participants that Clinton would make a statement of U.S. interest on the South China Sea at the ARF ministerial meeting in Hanoi in July 2010. While not revealing the details of Clinton's proposed speech, the Americans lobbied other ARF members to make supporting statements. The Americans even "tried to calibrate the order of ASEAN speakers", only to be told by some Southeast Asians "that the ARF could not be stage managed to that extent and ASEAN did not want to be used by any great power".[32] Beijing caught wind of U.S. plans and joined the lobbying, reiterating its objection to the South China Sea issue being "internationalised".[33]

When Clinton spoke at the meeting and urged a multilateral approach to resolving the South China Sea dispute, she received a "sharp rebuke" from Chinese Foreign Minister Yang Jiechi. According to Singapore Foreign Minister George Yeo, "There was quite an interesting and sharp exchange between the Americans and the Chinese. At some points, the atmosphere was just a little tense."[34]

Clinton immediately repeated her key points to reporters outside the meeting, which was closed to the public. She said the United States, like every other nation, has a "national interest" in freedom of navigation, open access to Asia's maritime commons, and respect for international law in the South China Sea. Resolving the disputes was "pivotal to regional stability". Washington supports a "collaborative, diplomatic process for all claimants for resolving the various territorial disputes without coercion". Throwing her weight behind the DOC, she said, "We encourage the parties to reach agreement on a full code of conduct."[35]

While adhering to existing U.S. policy, Clinton made several remarks that were bound to needle the Chinese.[36] She said that consistent with customary international law, "claims to maritime space in the South China Sea should be derived solely from legitimate claims to land features". While factually correct, her comment was undoubtedly a swipe at China's nine-broken lines, which can be seen as a claim to the waters of the South China Sea. For the representative of a country that has yet to ratify UNCLOS — it is stalled in Congress with little chance of early passage — Clinton rather audaciously cited UNCLOS in her arguments. She also said the United States was prepared to facilitate talks on the DOC, an offer that was never likely to be accepted by either ASEAN or China, but one that indicated a more proactive U.S. role in a dispute in which Beijing says the United States has no business.[37]

Despite the Chinese warnings that the issue was a bilateral one and inappropriate for ARF, eleven of the twenty-seven members joined the United States in raising maritime security and South China Sea concerns. They included six ASEAN countries — Brunei, Malaysia, the Philippines, Vietnam, Indonesia and Singapore, whose comments were consciously nuanced to avoid a fight with China[38] — as well as India, Australia, Japan, South Korea and the European Union.

Although Chinese Foreign Minister Yang later ticked off seven points in a considered rebuttal, which was posted on the ministry's Web page, it was his immediate reaction at the ARF meeting that made the headlines. According to press reports, he accused the United States of orchestrating an anti-China plot and threatened economic punishment for Southeast Asian nations that sought to stand up to Beijing.[39] "China is a big country and other countries are small countries, and that is just a fact", he reportedly said, staring directly at his Singaporean counterpart, George Yeo.[40]

ASEAN was taken aback by the ongoing ferocity of China's counterattack, which included strong commentary by the media, think tanks and analysts, who warned Asia about "divide and rule" tactics by outside powers and accused Vietnam of "playing with fire". Initially buoyed by the willingness of the only counterweight to China to buy in on their behalf, some ASEAN governments soon began to rue asking the United States to play a role. They worried that they would be caught in the middle if the crucial Washington-Beijing relationship deteriorated. As Singapore's ambassador to Indonesia Ashok Mirpuri put it, "Nobody in Southeast Asia wants to choose between the United States and China." In the opinion of one Southeast Asian insider, the Americans miscalculated both before — in deciding on the tone and content of Clinton's intervention — and after, in their assessment of its ultimate impact on ASEAN.[41] In the fallout, strategic reality began to weigh heavily on the region, summed up succinctly by the same official: "China is a geographic fact that ASEAN has to live with, whereas the United States is both far away and fickle."[42]

Certainly ASEAN was in a more conciliatory mood towards China when the Southeast Asian group and the United States held their second Leaders Meeting in New York in September 2010. A draft joint statement prepared in advance by the Americans, which was leaked, included the wording that the leaders "oppose the use or threat of force by any claimant attempting to enforce disputed claims in the South China Sea".[43] China applied intense pressure on Vietnam particularly, and reinforced its view with a public statement. Three days before the summit, Chinese foreign ministry spokesman Jiang Yu said Beijing was concerned about "any kind of statement that might be issued by the United States and ASEAN over the South China Sea". He said, "Words or acts that play up tensions in the region and concoct conflicts and provocations in relations between countries in the region are against the common wish of the countries in the region to seek peace and development."[44] The record shows that the ASEAN side accepted the Chinese view that the proposed U.S. language was not appropriate. Singapore and the Philippines were the only two ASEAN members to explicitly mention the South China Sea in their interventions,[45] and the official United States–ASEAN joint statement contained no reference to the threat or use of force, and did not mention the South China Sea by name.

CONCLUSION

All three parties — the United States and China as well as Vietnam — seemed to have been somewhat chastened by the ARF clash and prepared to make adjustments at the margins in the hope of improving the atmosphere at least.

While sticking to their position on the South China Sea, the Americans have toned down the rhetoric. For instance, Kurt Campbell, Assistant Secretary of State for East Asian and Pacific Affairs, backed away from

Clinton's offer to arrange multilateral talks on the dispute. "There's not a desire for a facilitator, to be perfectly honest", he said. "So I don't think it would be appropriate for the United States to play a direct role". The United States would support ongoing ASEAN-China efforts to upgrade the DOC into a code of conduct.[46]

In the same way that ASEAN was shaken by the prospect of a United States–China confrontation, the Chinese seem to recognize that their intransigence might have contributed to the situation. They have taken steps to see that what happened at ARF is not repeated. Instead of twisting ASEAN arms generally, they have found it more productive to pressure their next-door neighbour, Vietnam. Not only did the United States–ASEAN summit communiqué omit any mention of the South China Sea, but two other key regional gatherings — the ASEAN Defence Ministers Meeting Plus (eight partners) and the East Asia Summit, both held in October 2010 — discussed the issue indirectly as "maritime security", which is acceptable to Beijing. Now a mollified China has offered to compromise in the Joint Working Group on the DOC, a sign that a process long on "life support" may be activated at last.

However, while it is possible to be cautiously optimistic about the DOC, the larger game for strategic advantage in the Asia-Pacific between the United States and China will only intensify. Much of this rivalry will be played out in and around the South China Sea as the United States insists on the right to monitor developments in China and the Chinese seek to keep the Americans out. Given the proximity of their two navies, and their differences over what military activity is permitted in and above exclusive economic zones under UNCLOS, more incidents like those involving the EP-3 spy plane and *Impeccable* can be expected.

Notes

1. Clive Schofield and Ian Storey, "The South China Sea Dispute: Increasing Stakes and Rising Tensions", *The Jamestown Foundation*, November 2009, pp. 7–8.
2. Bronson Percival, "The South China Sea: An American Perspective", paper presented at "The South China Sea: Cooperation for Regional Security and Development" conference, Diplomatic Academy of Vietnam, Ho Chi Minh City, Vietnam, 11–12 November 2010, p. 1.
3. Clive Schofield and Ian Storey, "The South China Sea Dispute: Increasing Stakes and Rising Tensions", pp. 38–39.
4. Percival, "The South China Sea: An American Perspective", p. 2.

5. Ian Storey, "Implementing CBMs in the 2002 DOC: A Roadmap to Managing the South China Sea Dispute", paper presented at "The South China Sea: Cooperation for Regional Security and Development" conference, Diplomatic Academy of Vietnam, Ho Chi Minh City, Vietnam, 11–12 November 2010, p. 1.

6. Aileen S.P. Baviera, "Territorial Disputes in East Asia: Proxies for China-U.S. Strategic Competition?", *East Asia Forum*, 27 November 2010 <http://www.eastasiaforum.org/2010/11/27/territorial-disputes-in-east-asia-proxies-for-china-us-strategic-competition> (accessed 29 November 2010).

7. Carlyle A. Thayer, "Recent Developments in the South China Sea: Grounds for Cautious Optimism?", *RSIS Working Paper*, No. 220 (14 December 2010), p. 9.

8. Rodolfo C. Severino, *Southeast Asia in Search of an ASEAN Community: Insights from the former ASEAN Secretary-General* (Singapore: Institute of Southeast Asian Studies, 2006), p. 182.

9. Ibid., p. 184.

10. "Asia 1996 Yearbook", *Far Eastern Economic Review*, p. 195.

11. Ian James Storey, "Creeping Assertiveness: China, the Philippines and the South China Sea Dispute", *Contemporary Southeast Asia* 21, no. 1 (1999): 96, 109–10.

12. Ibid., p. 110.

13. "U.S. Policy in the South China Sea", U.S. Department of State, Statement by Acting Spokesperson, 10 May 1995, cited in Bronson Percival, p. 3.

14. Barry Wain, "The Yankees Go Home", *Asian Wall Street Journal*, 14 April 1995.

15. Storey, "Creeping Assertiveness: China, the Philippines and the South China Sea Dispute", p. 114.

16. Schofield and Storey, "The South China Sea Dispute: Increasing Stakes and Rising Tensions", p. 39.

17. Ibid., pp. 39–40.

18. Ibid., p. 40.

19. Ian Storey, "Power Play in S. China Sea stirs up tension", *Straits Times*, 27 July 2010.

20. Thayer, "Recent Developments in the South China Sea", p. 10.

21. Ian Storey, "Shangri-La Dialogue Highlights Tensions in Sino-U.S. Relations, *China Brief* 10, no. 13 (24 June 2010) 10–12.

22. Edward Wong, "Chinese Military Seeks to Extend its Naval Power", *New York Times*, 23 April 2010.

23. "Interview with Greg Sheridan of *The Australian*", Hillary Rodham Clinton, Secretary of State, Melbourne, Australia, 8 November 2010.

24. Thayer, "Recent Developments in the South China Sea", p. 4.

25. Ibid., pp. 2–6.

26. "Interview with Greg Sheridan of *The Australian*".

27. Schofield and Storey, "The South China Sea Dispute: Increasing stakes and Rising Tensions", p. 1.
28. Thayer, "Recent Developments in the South China Sea", p. 12.
29. Barry Wain, "ASEAN Caught in a Tight Spot", *Straits Times*, 16 September 2010.
30. Anonymous ASEAN source.
31. Wain, "ASEAN Caught in a Tight Spot".
32. Interview with senior Southeast Asian official who wishes to remain anonymous, 25 August 2010.
33. Wain, "ASEAN Caught in a Tight Spot".
34. Sarah Stewart, "Asia Wary as China Asserts Territorial Ambitions", Agence France-Presse, 23 September 2010.
35. Hillary Rodham Clinton, Secretary of State, Remarks at Press Availability, National Convention Centre, Hanoi, 23 July 2010.
36. Ibid.
37. Jeremy Page, Patrick Barta and Jay Solomon, "U.S., ASEAN to Push Back against China", *Wall Street Journal*, 22 September 2010.
38. Interview with senior Southeast Asian official.
39. Greg Torode, "Vietnam Revives Guerrilla Tactics", *South China Morning Post*, 13 October 2010.
40. John Pomfret, "U.S. Takes a Tougher Line with China", *Washington Post*, 30 July 2010.
41. Interview with senior Southeast Asian official.
42. Ibid.
43. Teresa Cerojano, "Obama, ASEAN to Call for Peaceful End to Sea Spats", Associated Press, 19 September 2010.
44. Thayer, "Recent Developments in the South China Sea", p. 17.
45. Second interview with senior Southeast Asian official who wishes to remain anonymous, 24 September 2010.
46. Kurt M. Campbell, Assistant Secretary, Bureau of East Asian and Pacific Affairs, Media Roundtable at the U.S. Embassy in Tokyo, 6 October 2010.

Part Six
Conclusion

13

CONCLUSION

Pavin Chachavalpongpun

A conference on "Entering Unchartered Waters? The ASEAN and South China Sea Dispute" was held at the Institute of Southeast Asian Studies (ISEAS) on 18 February 2011. It was organized by the ASEAN Studies Centre (ASC). Conference speakers were former journalists, legal professionals, academics, government representatives, and other analysts. The aim of the conference was not to provide an instant solution to the disputes but to highlight the claims of the states involved, understand these claims in the context of the legal framework, such as the 1982 United Nations Convention on the Law of the Sea (UNCLOS), and illuminate how external parties to the disputes, such as the non-claimant member-states of ASEAN, can help to resolve these disagreements by peaceful means.

The day began with an overview of the current state of affairs in the South China Sea, provided by a former ASEAN Secretary-General, Rodolfo C. Severino, and Professor Robert Beckman, Director of the Centre for International Law, National University of Singapore. Severino, now head of the ASC at ISEAS, explained that everyone's objective regarding the SCS was essentially to "prevent conflict". It was extremely unlikely, he said, that there would be a "grand solution" to what was a matter, for the individual states concerned, of "strategic national interest". In this light, none of the countries involved were prepared to compromise on territorial issues. It was important, Severino declared, for the claimants to align their claims with the provisions and requirements of UNCLOS and come to agreement on what is and what is not allowed in an individual country's exclusive economic zone (EEZ). To prevent the disputes from escalating, the ASEAN states, China and the United States should play their parts. This was, of course, easier said than done.

Beckman's international law perspective provided participants with an understanding of how the law could be applied and utilized. However, Beckman echoed Severino's sentiment that the law was "not determinative" when it came to resolving the dispute. It was more a tool to "influence the conduct of the parties" involved and to make possible a "frank and fair debate". The legal instruments that were available and applicable to the SCS dispute included the 1982 UNCLOS, which clearly defined the maritime zones to include the twelve-mile territorial sea, the 200-mile EEZ and the continental shelf. China's claims to "historic waters" within the nine bars on a Chinese map issued in 1947 were deemed to be inconsistent with UNCLOS.

ASEAN and China had attempted to deal with the SCS dispute through the 2002 Declaration on the Conduct of Parties in the South China Sea (DOC), which called for "dialogue, confidence building and cooperative measures". One of the key components of the declaration was the clause stipulating that countries should refrain from taking action "that would complicate or escalate disputes and affect peace and stability including ... refraining from action of inhabiting on the presently uninhabited islands, reefs, shoals, cays, and other features". However, the DOC had proved extremely difficult to implement. Beckman suggested that one solution to the disputes would be to enter into "provisional arrangements of a practical nature", which UNCLOS called for in Articles 74 and 83, principally concerning "joint development".

Severino emphasized that ASEAN could not become legally involved in the disputes. However, it could provide the framework and platform for dialogue and consultations. A common policy could not be arrived at within ASEAN because of the differences among the claimant countries and the overlapping claims of the four ASEAN countries and China (including Taiwan).

Session Two explored ASEAN's "View on the South China Sea", with papers presented by Dr Hasjim Djalal, member of the Indonesian National

Maritime Council and Vice Chairman of the Indonesian delegation to the Third U.N. Law of the Sea Conference, and Professor Aileen S.P. Baviera from the Asian Centre, University of the Philippines.

In presenting his paper, entitled "South China Sea: Contribution of 2nd Track Diplomacy/Workshop Process to Regional Peace and Cooperation", Djalal explained the history of armed conflicts that had taken place between China and Vietnam. One of the causes of the disputes, according to him, was the rush to secure resources (living and non-living). Although such resources could be obtained from as far afield as Africa, they still needed to be transported to China through the Strait of Malacca. There had been confrontations and conflicts between China and other Southeast Asian countries. Relations between Indonesia and China, for instance, were frozen for twenty-three years. Countries outside Southeast Asia had also become more interested in the SCS, particularly in terms of freedom of navigation and overflight, such as the United States and Australia. More recently, India, with her "look east" policy, had also taken an interest.

Indonesia's position in the 1980s was that the disputes in the SCS could have effects on peace and stability in Southeast Asia. Because of this, Djalal personally undertook a tour of the then five other ASEAN countries to see what could be done and established the following:

1. Practically everybody thought that something should be done to address the SCS dispute;
2. There was apprehension that territorial disputes could pose major difficulties in developing cooperative efforts;
3. It would be better if the approach was informal (2nd track), at least at the initial stage;
4. There are important bases for cooperation under UNCLOS 1982, regarding "enclosed and semi-enclosed seas" like the SCS, particularly in Articles 122 and 123;
5. Article 122 defines "enclosed and semi-enclosed sea" as a "gulf, basin or sea surrounded by two or more states and connected to another sea or the ocean by a narrow outlet or consisting entirely or primarily of the territorial seas and exclusive economic zones of two or more coastal states".
6. Article 123 recommends that "States bordering an enclosed or semi-enclosed sea should co-operate with each other in the exercise of their

rights and in the performance of their duties under this Convention. To this end they shall endeavour, directly or through an appropriate regional organisation".

The first meeting of the then six ASEAN member countries to address the SCS issue took place in Bali in 1990. Three objectives were set:

1. Devise "cooperation programs" in which everyone could participate regardless of size or scope of the issue;
2. Promote "confidence building";
3. "Encourage dialogue" between the parties to aid the solution-making process.

Over the past twenty years, the number of countries participating has grown, with the addition of more ASEAN members, China, and Chinese Taipei (Taiwan). Technical Working Groups (TWGs) have been set up for the following areas:

1. Marine scientific research
2. Resource assessment
3. Marine environmental protection
4. Safety of navigation, shipping and communication
5. Legal matters

All of these measures are meant to promote a spirit of cooperation among the claimant countries. It is in part because of them that no violent conflict has taken place since 1988. However, this is not so say that this goodwill can last indefinitely; this process has to be carefully managed so as to ensure that the momentum is sustained and good relations continue. Efforts have to be made to maintain a combination of formal and informal (2nd track) channels of communication and to nurture "the habit of cooperation rather than the habit of confrontation".

Baviera's paper, "The South China Sea Disputes Writ Large: Intra Asian Contest or U.S.-China Hegemonic Competition?" argues that with the rise of China both economically and militarily and potential U.S.-China strategic competition, the "environment for addressing SCS disputes has changed". Baviera suggests that only a U.S. "supportive of China-ASEAN dialogue and a peaceful dispute settlement can have a positive impact". Baviera pointed out that tensions had increased over the last two years, as assertions of sovereignty rose, with incidents ranging from Chinese intimidation of oil and gas companies operating in the SCS and disagreements over fisheries territories to military activities in general. Included in these was China's declaration that the SCS was part of its "core interest", implying that it was not ruling out the use of force in the area. In turn, the United States proclaimed the SCS as being in its "national interest" with respect to freedom of navigation and respect for international law. Both of these stances have brought about mixed reactions from ASEAN member states that are seemingly caught in the crossfire while trying to maintain peace and stability in their immediate surroundings. Baviera pointed out that the United States benefited from ASEAN countries' perceived "mistrust" of China; however, ASEAN needed to combine "tactical hedging" and "strategic balancing/containment".

Baviera concluded that the state of play had changed; thus, all parties needed to "take stock" of the "new challenges (and opportunities)" arising from the growth of China and the dynamics of China-U.S. relations. According to Baviera and Djalal, one way in which to address this was to foster closer cooperation in areas such as fisheries, oil and gas, and marine life. Baviera contended that there was a danger that the "SCS disputes ... could deteriorate into a proxy for great power conflict" and that this should be avoided at all costs; however, "time is not on ASEAN's side".

Session Three concerned China's position, with two papers from Dr Wang Hanling of the Chinese Academy of Social Sciences and Dr Li Mingjiang, Assistant Professor at the S. Rajaratnam School of International Studies. Explaining that he had been asked to provide a paper on "China's Stance on Some Major Issues of the South China Sea", Wang provided a definition of the SCS issue from the Chinese perspective:

1. Chinese territories are illegally occupied and resources exploited by foreign countries (continually and escalating);
2. Some parties have denied their recognition before the mid-1970s of Chinese sovereignty over islands and archipelagos and adjacent waters;
3. Outsiders inappropriately interfere in SCS affairs.

According to Wang, China "has always stood for the peaceful settlement of the SCS disputes, particularly through bilateral negotiation and consultation between the parties concerned, and opposes outsider interference". China believes that:

1. The best and long-term solution is the recognition of Chinese territory and sovereignty and sharing SCS resources;
2. The best short-term solution is shelving disputes and going in for joint development;
3. Possible confidence-building measures are environmental protection, conservation of resources, anti-piracy, marine scientific research (MSR) and search and rescue (SAR).

Wang defined what he called the "changeable" and the "unchangeable". Essentially, these meant that while the "fundamental principles such as territory, sovereignty and peaceful settlement" could not be changed, the ways to achieve the latter were "flexible". He declared that "outsiders" intervention is unlikely to change China's position on the SCS.

Li examined "The Changing Contexts of China's Policy on the South China Sea Dispute", which covered China's policy in the first decade of the twenty-first century, China's move towards "non-confrontational assertiveness", and the "implications for ASEAN". In the latter part of the previous century, according to Li, China's three key conflicts were the 1974 battle over the Paracels, a result of the perceived threat from the Soviet Union; the 1988 Sino-Vietnamese conflict, which was largely fuelled by the completion of China's defence budget; and the 1995 Mischief Reef skirmishes. However, since the late-1990s, the policy had shifted to one in which "strategic interests became more important", and so a policy of "calculated moderation" ensued, leading to China's "Golden Decade" of participation in maritime cooperation. The final policy change was linked not only to the SCS but to joint naval exercises and maritime control.

Li provided some possible explanations for the "paradigm shift" that took place in what he described as "an unfortunate year" for Chinese security policy. Possible factors included an "inflated self-confidence" and "bureaucratic politics" as manifested in the J20 test flight, which had been undertaken apparently without communication between the military and the government. As Li argued, this newfound "non-confrontational assertiveness" can be attributed to:

1. Growing capabilities, which have allowed for more options and the boldness to try to do things differently;

2. China's frustrations and concerns with outside intervention and the perception of others ganging up on China;
3. Higher expectations of interests;
4. Leadership transition in the Chinese Communist Party, with top-level changes taking place in 2012;
5. Rising nationalism; for example, scholars who refuted the statement on the SCS as an area of "core interest" were silenced;
6. Bureaucratic politics, which continues with no coordinated policymaking process.

Such a change in policy is meant to avoid strategic confrontation and maintain the status quo.

Session Four centred on ASEAN claimants' positions and that of Taiwan, with Dr Nguyen Thi Lan Anh from the Diplomatic Academy of Vietnam, former Visiting Fellow, Centre for International Law of the National University of Singapore; Mr Henry Bensurto, Secretary-General, Centre for Maritime and Ocean Affairs, Department of Foreign Affairs, Philippines; Dr Dzirhan Mahadzir, independent defence and security analyst based in Kuala Lumpur; and Dr Liu Fu-Kuo, Executive Director, Centre for Security Studies, Institute of International Relations, National Chengchi University, Taipei, Taiwan, making up the panel.

Lan Anh provided "A Vietnamese Perspective" on the SCS, from the legal angle, encompassing the role of law and the role of transparency. She declared that it was essential that all parties act in good faith in the application and interpretation of the law, implementing existing commitments, such as in the DOC, and "avoiding inconsistency between words and actions". Providing examples of recent "good practice", Lan Anh cited the new archipelagic baselines law of the Philippines and the joint and partial submissions on the expanded continental shelves of Vietnam and Malaysia. Lan Anh highlighted three "needs" — the "need for resources", "the need for peace", and "the need for cooperation".

Bensurto's paper, "Filipino Archipelagic Agenda for the Twentieth Century and the South China Sea: Unlocking the Gridlock", which had not been sanctioned by the Philippine government, aimed to address the dangers of overlapping claims, the imperatives for delimitation, and the Philippines' template for the South China Sea. It offered a framework for how the "convoluted lines of overlapping claims and territorial disputes could be smoothed and simplified to provide a much more stable base". Bensurto pointed out that the Philippines is an archipelagic state comprising more than 7,100 islands, with 62 out of 71 provinces categorized as coastal. Its central location at the "heart of Southeast Asia" makes it a "crossroads" for major international routes. It is also a "hotbed" of geological resources and activity with a high potential to yield oil and gas. Finally, the Philippines hosts the "greater part of the Coral Triangle", making it a "centre for biodiversity".

Dzirhan Mahadzir gave an overview of the Malaysian position, explaining that Malaysia's stance on the Spratly Islands had been "fairly consistent". The Malaysian military had always been preparing for the "worst case", with all military exercises carried out in public. Dzirhan argued that the "step-up" in military operations was in response to the actions of others in the region.

Liu Fu-Kuo highlighted "Taiwan's South China Sea Policy Revival", focusing on Taiwan's claim from a historical perspective and on the legal claims and policy approaches that the Taiwanese government had adopted to address the SCS disputes. The SCS issue had to be "redefined as a strategic interest for Taiwan", said Liu, so that Taiwan could become "more proactive".

"The Interests of Others" was the title of Session Five, the "others" being mainly the United States. In presenting his paper, Barry Wain, Writer-in-Residence at ISEAS, Singapore, and a former editor of the *Asian Wall Street Journal*, acknowledged that many points had already been covered. According to him, the overriding theme of the others' interests was that the "international community [had] a stake in the peace and security of the SCS". The U.S. position arises mainly from its insistence on "freedom of navigation". The United States had "no position" on the territorial or sovereignty claims, but it strongly opposed the use or threat of force and offered to "assist in any way that the claimants deem helpful". However, there was always a suspicion that China was hoping to challenge the United States for "supremacy" in the Asia-Pacific region. The danger was that the "U.S.-China rivalry ... will play out with the SCS as a battleground".

Lastly, I would like to express my sincere thanks to Dr Mikael Weissmann for allowing us to publish his informative paper in this volume. His chapter makes a good summary of the conflict in the SCS, particularly on the suggested solution through a series of dialogues between China and ASEAN. I shall end this chapter with Weissmann's statement (Chapter Three) highlighting the Sino-ASEAN connection in the SCS dispute:

The stability of the peace is dependent on how much faith one puts into China's commitment to peaceful settlements of the South China Sea disputes and the continuing progression of East Asian regionalization and community-building processes. The assessment here is that Sino-ASEAN relations have transformed to the extent that in the current climate, war is increasingly unthinkable. Some issues remain unresolved, but the positive relations have built solid conditions conducive for peace. Central to this assessment is the trust gradually built up at length between China and ASEAN, the institutionalized regionalization through the APT process, and the acceptance of the ASEAN way.

Index

www.ingramcontent.com/pod-product-compliance
Lightning Source LLC
Chambersburg PA
CBHW050703280326
41926CB00088B/2441